HOW THEY RULE THE WORLD

Lisbon
Aug 2019

HOW THEY RULE THE WORLD

The 22 Secret Strategies of Global Power

PEDRO BAÑOS

TRANSLATED BY JETHRO SOUTAR

EBURY
PRESS

1 3 5 7 9 10 8 6 4 2

Ebury Press, an imprint of Ebury Publishing
20 Vauxhall Bridge Road
London SW1V 2SA

Ebury Press is part of the Penguin Random House Group of companies
whose addresses can be found at global.penguinrandomhouse.com

First published by Ebury Press in 2019
First published with the title *Así se domina el mundo* in Spain in 2017
by Editorial Planeta, S. A., Barcelona

Maps and graphics © 2017, El Orden Mundial, Abel Gil Lobo (director),
Joaquín Domniguez y Daniel Aparicio

Image on page 193: © Randy mexrevolution – Wikipedia Commons

www.penguin.co.uk

A CIP catalogue record for this book is available from the British Library

Hardback ISBN 9781529102864
Trade paperback ISBN 978152910871

Typeset in 11/14.35 pt ITC New Baskerville
by Integra Software Services Pvt. Ltd, Pondicherry

Printed and bound in Great Britain by Clays Ltd, Elcograf S.p.A.

This book is dedicated to those who strive every day to make our world more just, free and secure.

Contents

Author's Note

This book represents a fair summary of my work and research of the last twenty-five years. Some of the content is drawn from articles I've had published in newspapers and magazines, some of it from chapters and prologues I've contributed to books. I have also made good use of the reams of personal notes I made in teaching hundreds of classes and speaking at conferences at military institutions, universities, research centres and foundations, on the topics of geopolitics, strategy, intelligence, defence, security, terrorism and international relations. The experience I acquired through my many years of teaching Strategy and International Relations at the General Staff Higher College of the Armed Forces, and as head of the Geopolitical Analysis Unit of the Ministry of Defence in Spain, has also been invaluable.

I have sought to complement my own findings with reference to an extensive bibliography. It should be noted that not all the quotes in the book have been reproduced verbatim: some have been abridged – without changing the original meaning, of course – to better serve the narrative flow. My intention has been to produce a work that is accessible to a wide reading public, appealing to seasoned enthusiasts without alienating those drawn to the book out of mere curiosity or for simple entertainment. That said, whenever I have employed an idea or specific concept from a third party, I have endeavoured to cite the author. Otherwise, and so as not to try the reader's patience, the source is assumed to be implicit through the bibliography.

The reader will notice that a number of the twenty-two strategies that I present overlap with each other, and certain historic examples often serve to illustrate more than one strategy. If I refer to some countries more than others, that is simply because they have more power and, therefore, more capacity to influence the world by implementing these strategies. I do not mean to come across as being for or against any specific country, ideology or religion; I have no particular hostility towards anyone, other than those who clearly take advantage of the less fortunate and less educated, often by deliberately hindering such people's development so that they can be more easily controlled.

In seeking to produce as rigorous a work as possible, I have consulted and cross-referenced all the cited data, making use of sources ranging from the highly specialised to the more generic. I have included in the endnotes those references that I consider to be of most interest to anyone seeking further information.

Nevertheless, there is always room for improvement. If any reader comes across an anomaly or discrepancy, their feedback would be most welcome. To this end, I can be contacted via the following email address: director@geoestratego.com.

PEDRO BAÑOS

Introduction: Geopolitics and Geostrategy

The powerful have always tried to seize control wherever their tentacles can reach. Different groups may have been dominant over the years and technologies have changed, as have the ways human aspirations are met, but the ambition to rule is timeless.

Major powers have always tried to subjugate lesser ones, all the while attempting to block others from exerting a rival military, economic or religious influence. Up until the sixteenth century, empires were fairly geographically limited, but in the globalised world of today, dominance is far less restricted, and in the years to come it will become interplanetary – the great powers are already jockeying for position to control the Moon's resources.

But if powerful nations are now able to exert their will over much larger areas, the methods they use to do so are essentially the same as they always have been. This book presents twenty-two fundamental geopolitical strategies: some have not changed for centuries, while others have been adapted to suit modern times. These universal rules are used by countries to protect themselves and to pursue their interests; the strongest use them to impose their will on the weak, while the weak use them to escape the influence of others.

It's important that we are aware of these strategies that allow the powerful to rule the world. We like to think of ourselves as free individuals who make autonomous choices about our lives: what we wear, what we eat, what we strive for and how we entertain ourselves. However, we are in fact constantly being induced to make certain choices, and the same thing is happening at the geopolitical level – countries are manipulated into making particular decisions and alliances, and their populations have no say in the matter.

The term 'post-truth' has recently become popular when referring to the global scale of disinformation, but it's not really a matter of true or false – the level of deceit is much more constant and complex than that. Every geopolitical decision, from the forging of alliances to the declaration of war and the introduction of economic sanctions, has an ulterior motive. Concepts such as 'human rights' may be referred to, but countries will always act out of self-interest.

Being aware of these geopolitical strategies and being able to recognise them will enable us to be more questioning of our leaders and less easily led; only by being more informed and engaged can we help forge a world where human security is prioritised over national security. But to understand how 'geopolitics' works in the modern world, we need to move beyond traditional definitions and examine the term in the current global context.

According to the traditional view, political events can be understood by considering geographical factors and historical precedents; this approach assumes the existence of geopolitical constants that create patterns that cause history to repeat itself. It's an approach that has its merits, but technology has rendered many of these constants redundant. One that remains fundamental is geography. Whether a country has a mountain range or a coastline, natural resources or a cohesive local population may be the product of chance, but such things nevertheless define its place in the world. However, globalisation means that countries no longer trade and compete solely with their neighbours – geopolitics is no longer restricted in this way.

By reframing 'geopolitics' in a global context we can look for patterns, in order to re-examine the past with a new perspective and also to try to anticipate the future. Technology has made for a fast-changing world, but we still need to plan ahead, and even the smallest country nowadays needs a geopolitical plan – very little happens in any country that is totally independent from developments elsewhere.

Geostrategy is an aspect of geopolitics and is concerned with how a country pursues its aims and interests, which are based on its geographical position and standing in the world. Different geostrategies will be appropriate to different countries, but all rely on an astute understanding of the nature of the world they will be applied in. This book will, I hope, offer the reader some insight into a realm of great rivalry and subterfuge, examining the geopolitical strategies currently at play, as well as those that could be applied by competing nations in the future, and that will, ultimately, define our world.

PART ONE

The Nature of the World

In every school in the world, there are children who are the dominant members of their class or year group, and are respected and feared by everybody. This power hierarchy is especially evident at break time, when children let their guard down. Watching them in the playground, it is easy to see the influence that some wield over others. It can have a number of roots: physical strength, a born facility for leadership, sporting ability, belonging to a powerful family, being favoured by the teachers or simply being malicious and cunning.

The children who rise above the others, for whatever reason, may act in ways that benefit the group, but they more often cause trouble, scheming behind the teachers' backs, undermining school rules and psychologically or physically bullying their more vulnerable and less popular classmates. Children who behave like this become accustomed to being surrounded by others who seek protection and recognition from them. These followers will laugh at the leader's jokes, applaud their teasing of the weak and hail their feats of skill or displays of strength. They are prepared to sacrifice part of their own personality in order to belong to the leader's court of admirers, for this confers upon them a certain status.

In order to be able to act like this, the leader and their entourage need others around them to provide a constant source of affirmation. They will simply ignore some children, perhaps because they are not in the same social group or don't play whatever sport is most popular in the school to the same standard. However, others become the unfortunate targets of the group's poison arrows, which the members must keep throwing in order to keep feeling superior. There is all the more reason to target these unfortunate children if they happen to be outstanding students: they must be prevented from threatening the group's superiority or becoming rivals. Some of these targets, if they lack mental strength or family support, may end up irreparably damaged by such childhood experiences, while others will wish to join the dominant group in order to stop being a daily target – these converts often become the group's cruellest members.

Other children manage to resist the influence of the leader and the pressure of the group and are content to lead their own lives – to command respect but not to bully others. In certain situations, alliance with whichever group wields the most power might interest them, but in general they enjoy independence. Lastly, there are those who decide to isolate themselves from the main pack and not participate in any school activity.

The same dynamics exist in any group of people whose members spend a considerable number of hours together, whether in a barracks, a prison or a workplace. And something similar happens on the international stage, where different countries have distinct capacities for influencing global decisions.

THE GAME OF INFLUENCE

On the global stage, there are essentially two types of country: the dominant and the dominated. The former exerts control on a regional or global scale, while the latter is controlled, more or less directly, and in various ways – militarily, economically, culturally or technologically. The dominated countries accept their condition, to a greater or lesser degree, often with resigned passivity. They may also subordinate themselves to a bigger power in order to become respected, and even feared, by others who are also dominated by that power.

The countries that do not feel powerful, for whatever reason, seek shelter under the umbrella of a superior power that can offer them security and immunity, at least theoretically. This is what the nuclear powers provide, and what the permanent members of the United Nations Security Council (UNSC) are able to offer, through the threat of international sanctions. It is how China has protected Sudan and its President, Omar al-Bashir, who has remained in office despite an international arrest warrant issued against him by the International Criminal Court (ICC) in March 2009 for war crimes and crimes against humanity. Al-Bashir knows he is untouchable as long as he remains in China's shadow. Beijing offers this 'service' to countries as part of its famous 'win–win' negotiating policy, a deal from which both parties benefit; in this case, China gains access to oil and arable land. Syria is another recent example of a weak state under attack that has sought support from a third-party 'tough guy'. Syria's President, Bashar al-Assad, accepted help from Russia – which was, of course, pursuing its own geopolitical interests – in order to avoid being toppled by pressure exerted by rebel forces, which were supported by the United States and its allies.

When a country doesn't have sufficient regional influence or global standing, it forms alliances with others to increase its geopolitical weight. Some seek simply to shield themselves, aware, as Otto von Bismarck, Prime Minister of Prussia (1862–73 and 1873–90) and Chancellor of the German Empire (1871–90), put it, that 'any people that totally isolates itself, believing itself capable of defending its homeland and interests, will eventually disappear, overwhelmed by other nations'. Subordination can become so complete that certain countries, even those considered to be medium-sized powers, are sometimes dragged by the superpowers of the day into wars that are completely irrelevant to their own aims. Governments of these subordinated countries send their troops to remote places where they have no real strategic interest of their own – though there will always be people in the news media keen to please the government of the day, offering theories of proactive defence and talking about global perils requiring unilateral solutions, the defence of human rights or the promotion of democratic values. However, in many cases, the only things these 'backing singer' countries manage to gain are new enemies, which can lead to attacks on their own territory, especially if groups that are active in whatever distant theatre of war they have entered are willing to use terrorism tactics abroad. Such regrettable military operations can bring about social upheaval at home due to lack of support among the general public for ill-defined military ventures, and can even cause the downfall of the government responsible.

A small number of states don't fit into the above categories – they don't have sufficient capacity to be dominant, but refuse to be dominated. Isolated from the international system, these countries become 'rebels' or, as a statement of the United States National

Security Strategy of 9 February 2015 termed them, 'irresponsible'. Any state that refuses to play global power games runs an undoubted risk, for it must rely only on itself for survival. Certain countries, including Saudi Arabia, Turkey, Egypt and Iran, are part of a small group that, having established themselves as regional leaders, wish to grow and gain in influence, but restrain themselves in global terms so as not to offend the superpowers with whom they maintain ambiguous relationships.

The Polish-American political scientist Zbigniew Brzezinski made the distinction between 'geopolitical players' and 'geostrategic pivots'. The former are the states with the capacity and national will to exert power or influence beyond their borders and alter the prevailing geopolitical situation – they will always be important and powerful countries, though not all important and powerful countries are 'geopolitical players', for it depends on whether they choose to engage in power games. 'Geostrategic pivots', on the other hand, are states such as Ukraine, Azerbaijan, South Korea, Turkey and Iran, which owe their relevance to a geographical location that enables them to allow other countries access to key areas or natural resources.

RIVALRY, AMBITION, VIOLENCE

Conflict, inherent in human nature, is an inevitable by-product of diverse interests, perceptions and cultures, and armed conflict is inherent to any international system for the same reasons. In recalling the Peloponnesian War (431–404 BC), the Athenian historian Thucydides stated that the conflict's true cause was the fact that Athens had become so powerful and inspired such fear in the Spartans that they felt an obligation to fight. The same scenario can be applied to almost every conflict in history: the dominant power will use any means necessary to prevent another from rising and threatening its supremacy; the conflict that results will take different forms, will be more or less bloody and brutal, and will range from the direct to the subtle, but nothing will ever end the cycle of conflict. This is undoubtedly a pessimistic view, but it seems to tally with the global picture and likely future developments.

In 1929, the League of Nations commissioned two academics Moritz Bonn and André Siegfried to draft a report entitled 'Economic Tendencies Affecting the Peace of the World'. They concluded that much of world history could be explained in the context of once-powerful states seeking to maintain their privileged position, while other states sought either riches that would give them more power or power that would give them more riches. In other words, 'He who has nothing wants something, he who has something wants more, and he who has plenty wants to keep it.' Such patterns of behaviour can be seen in people as well as in countries. History is also filled with examples of people who claim, while underprivileged, that they will forever stand for equality for all, but then change their perspective as soon as they reach a privileged position, and end up suffering from the vices they previously condemned in others.

According to the analysis of Peng Guangqian and Yao Youzhi, Chinese generals and current members of the country's Academy of Military Science, *Wuzi*, the classic work on military strategy attributed to Wu Qi, established five motivations during the period of the Warring States (475–221 BC) for a state to go to war: fame, reward, animosity, internal disorder and hunger. Count Alexandre de Marenches, Director General of the French Service de Documentation Extérieure et de Contre-Espionnage between 1970 and 1981, asserted that all international conflicts result from the struggle to control raw materials and gain a psychological hold on populations, whether through the media, church, education or disinformation. He said this in 1986, before the Internet and social media exponentially increased the psychological manipulation of the masses.

Conflicts have always been about power, status and the control of people and resources, as lust for material gain develops into the desire to rule. And whenever violence has been the most effective means to triumph in conflict, there has been no hesitation in using it.

HAMMER OR ANVIL?

Bismarck had no doubt that force, whether employed or threatened, was a determining factor in human relations – he argued that 'gratitude and confidence will not bring a single man to your side; only fear, used skilfully and cunningly, will do'. Almost four centuries earlier, the Italian thinker Niccolò Machiavelli had gone further still, stating that it was better to be feared than loved. However, being feared, while effective in the short term, can also foster hatred that is liable to explode in the long run, with unpredictable consequences.

There's an old saying that some people act out of love, others out of fear, and the rest out of conviction. In truth, people are motivated by a combination of all three. In international relations, it is vitally important to know how to get others on your side at the critical moment, while understanding that the same tactic might not be successful in a different scenario. The fear of force, even if it is only ever used as a last resort, is a basic ingredient of any international relationship. It is only possible to negotiate with those who are prepared to listen, understand and reason. There is no avoiding the fact that manners and courtesy can do nothing against violence and savagery; no matter how regrettable it may be, some people will only react when threatened with force.

As long as there are groups determined to impose their ideas on others, war will exist as a violent means for a state to enforce its will. At some point, even the most peaceful societies have to decide between fighting back or yielding. The German philosopher Immanuel Kant considered that 'the natural state of man is not peace, but war', and believed that 'war itself needs no special motive, it would seem to be grafted on to human nature'. This was nothing new: long before him Plato had said 'it is a law of nature that war between cities will be continual and eternal'. Despite this, we have long been aware of the total dehumanisation that war represents, the spiral of violence it unleashes and the base instincts it brings to the fore – for the classical humanist Erasmus, it was 'so fierce and cruel as to be more suitable to wild beasts than to men'. War has always brought the worst human traits to the surface and magnified them. Once set in train, plentiful reasons, motivations and justifications can be found for conflict, and from then on there is a single goal: to win, at any cost. How war is won seems not to matter. Anything goes, including behaviour that would previously have been dismissed as unthinkable.

On 9 May 2007, Vladimir Putin gave a speech to mark the sixty-second anniversary of the Soviet victory in the Second World War:

> We have the responsibility to remember that the causes of any war lie in the errors and mistakes of calculations made in times of peace, and that these causes have their roots in the ideology of confrontation and extremism. It's extremely important to remember this today, because these threats are not diminishing, they are merely transforming and changing their appearance. These new threats show the same disregard for human life and the same aspiration to exclusively impose themselves on the rest of the world that were seen under the Third Reich.

It is possible that the threats he referred to came from the United States as much as jihadism but, either way, there can be no doubt that his words show an awareness of the inherent human ambition to assert authority over others. According to the French general and geopolitician Pierre M. Gallois, it is not always the strong who start wars and, as the British military historian J.F.C. Fuller argued, 'there is nothing illogical in the desire of the "have-nots" to appropriate the wealth of the "haves"'. There are 900 million people in the so-called 'Western world',[1] but there are a further 6.8 billion human beings on the planet, many of whom consider themselves to have lost out as a result of development and globalisation in the West or carried out by the West in their own countries, and yearn to be among the privileged.

IS IT POSSIBLE TO EFFICIENTLY CONTROL VIOLENCE?

Henry Kissinger, US National Security Advisor (1969–75) and Secretary of State (1973–77), said that, in a world where violence is endemic, superpowers have a tendency to act like two heavily armed blind men trying to escape a room, each convinced that the other, whom they assume has perfect vision, represents a mortal threat. They can cause tremendous damage to each other, to say nothing of the room. Given the immense destructive power global superpowers hold today, the consequences of this dynamic could be dire. The only solution to this situation is regular dialogue between the major powers, but given the ambition of some for complete domination, this seems like a utopian dream.

The journalist and political analyst Robert D. Kaplan highlighted the main problem with the situation when he said, 'the world continues in a natural state, with no Hobbesian Leviathan to punish the unjust'. What he was saying is that, although there is an international legal framework established with precisely the aim of 'punishing the unjust', the powerful always find ways around it, while making sure it is strictly enforced on the weak. As we will explore in greater detail, one of the current geopolitical maxims is that smaller powers aspire to fair and equal relationships between countries, regardless of size and strength, while major powers base their relations on their geopolitical weight and capacity to influence.

One question that always arises relates to the legitimacy of force in international relations, and this tends to be framed in terms of good versus evil. However, the problem is that all parties think they are in the right, that justice is on their side and their opponents are being unreasonable.

On the other hand, the idea that political and military alliances between countries lead to greater collective security must also be questioned; when a group of states unites to attain greater security, it is highly likely that other nations will in turn also form alliances to protect themselves against the first group, thus bringing about the possibility of a more destructive war between larger entities. Alliances do not necessarily bring greater stability or make the world less violent.

How to survive in the geopolitical jungle?

Nothing is more hypocritical and cut-throat than international politics, because all decisions are based entirely on fleeting and ever-changing interests. Domestic politics can also be merciless and fratricidal, devoid of all consideration for adversaries, to the point that any measure aimed at weakening one's opponent, or expelling them from power in order to take their place, is deemed valid. However, it can still be assumed that all political groups seek the best for the nation and its citizens, though this may, of course, be interpreted in many different ways and pursued according to different ideologies.

In the international arena, on the other hand, there is no such common goal, nor is there anything to discourage the basest instincts from coming to the fore. Even things that might be considered of mutual concern, such as climate change, don't exert any real influence because every country is too busy acting in its own interests. It may sound trite, but the only situation in which nations might make decisions for the benefit of the whole of humanity would be in the unlikely event of an alien invasion.

In a world in which violence prevails, the British military historian Michael Howard has recommended that 'to preserve peace you have to be aware of those for whom the present order does not constitute "peace"; and whether they're prepared to use force to change an order that seems acceptable to us'. In other words, it is essential to know who your enemies are, both current and potential, and to understand their intentions. Just because you are adverse to starting a war, doesn't mean they are too.

In the complex world of international relations, the less powerful nations end up assessing whether what the major powers are doing will help or hinder them, and either seek to extract the maximum benefit or minimise the damage. They can remain neutral in conflicts between the major powers as long as being isolated doesn't disadvantage them, or they can make alliances according to the circumstances. Idealistic stands tend to be no more than window dressing. In geopolitics there are no moral rights or wrongs, but there are a number of key principles.

PART TWO

Geopolitical Principles

THE STATE IS A LIVING ORGANISM

According to classic geopolitical theory, conceived during the nineteenth century, the state is a living organism and, as such, needs to feed itself in order to survive and grow. Friedrich Ratzel, the father of human geography, first made the analogy in *The Laws of the Spatial Growth of States*, listing seven universal laws:

1. The growth of a state is related to the development of its culture.
2. The expansion of a state runs parallel to its economic, commercial and ideological power.
3. A state expands by incorporating and assimilating political entities of lesser importance.
4. The border of a state is a living organism in a constant state of flux.
5. The principal logic for state expansion is to absorb richer territories.
6. A state is able to extend itself due to the presence on its periphery of a civilisation that is inferior to its own.
7. The process of assimilating and absorbing weaker civilisations becomes self-sustaining and self-fulfilling.

All of these principles are underpinned by the idea that not all people are equal. There will always be those who are more culturally, militarily or economically developed and feel compelled to take over those they deem to be inferior. In Ratzel's view, nations are in a state of constant competition to control and expand their *Lebensraum*, or 'living space'. At the beginning of the twentieth century this notion was extremely relevant to Germany, which was quickly industrialising but lacked the almost limitless resources of France

15

and Great Britain with their considerable colonial territories, or Russia with its vast land of rich soil.

The ideas of the Swedish geographer and politician Rudolf Kjellén – the first person to employ the term 'geopolitics', in 1899 – were similar to those of Ratzel. He believed that states were living things; a state was born, fought for its survival, developed, exerted influence, became decadent and then died. As a living being, it could also be considered to be in control of its own destiny.

The German geographer Karl Haushofer, founder of the Munich School and the magazine *Geopolitik*, was highly influential in shaping the political thinking behind the idea of 'living space' that would eventually lead to the Second World War. Haushofer, who was a general as well as an academic, believed that German expansion was justified because it represented the only way to satisfy the needs of a growing state. He was influenced by Japan's military strategy, having spent time there as a military advisor. Haushofer visited Hitler in Landsberg Prison in 1924 after the failed Munich Putsch, and gave him the work of Ratzel to read; the idea of 'living space' became a major influence on Hitler's geopolitical thinking. From a military perspective, Haushofer believed that Germany was disadvantaged both geographically and in terms of raw materials and natural resources; his thinking, together with the works of Ratzel, enabled Hitler to furnish his ideas with almost scientific justifications, which he would set out in *Mein Kampf* and bring forward in his expansionist plans. These theories would eventually materialise as Operation Barbarossa, the invasion of the Soviet Union, through which he hoped to acquire the *Lebensraum* that Germany needed.

Years later, Pierre Gallois wrote that the story of the 'war for space' – which started as a pursuit of provisions before becoming a pursuit of security and ultimately of supremacy – is actually the history of humanity. Gallois follows Kjellén and Ratzel's thinking in asserting that humans have always pursued expansionary objectives, though what the objectives are has varied throughout history according to particular needs and capacities.

This assumption remains true today. As a living organism, a state must attend to its vital needs, from the preservation of the status quo to those relating to its development and evolution. To satisfy these 'physiological' requirements it must meet the basic needs of both its population, essentially maintaining food supplies, and industry, principally raw materials and energy.

MONEY SHAPES GEOPOLITICS

It was Vladimir Lenin, the Bolshevik leader of the 1917 Russian Revolution, who said that 'politics is a concentrated expression of economics'. Even today, economic considerations have always been the driver of interstate relations. The Prussian strategist Carl von Clausewitz said that 'war is a continuation of politics by other means'; by the same logic, war is therefore a continuation of economics. For example, most navies were first established specifically to protect merchant fleets. International political relations today can likewise be described as a product of economics: despite political ideals expressed largely for the benefit of their own citizens, world leaders have no qualms about doing business with dictators, tyrants, absolutists and other governments that are in no way democratic.

The German historian Walter Görlitz believed that the financial patronage of Anglo-Dutch oil magnate Henri Deterding was instrumental in Hitler's rise to power. The Director General of the Royal Dutch Shell group, he backed Hitler because he was a staunch enemy of Russia's Bolshevik regime, which had appropriated Shell's lucrative oil exploration sites in Baku in Azerbaijan. Görlitz also pointed out that, during the Spanish Civil War (1936–39), the US company Texaco similarly supplied Franco with all the oil he needed – in return, Texaco not only made Franco pay back the debt, but also obtained a monopoly on selling petrol in Spain that would last for years. The then-Chairman of Texaco, oil magnate Torkild Rieber, justified these actions by arguing that it was imperative that they stopped Russian oil from flooding into Spain, as would have happened had the Republicans won the Civil War.

States often impose economic measures in wartime, in preparation for the arrival of peace. The Belgian diplomat Jacques de Launay recounted that, on 10 August 1944, representatives of German industrial interests, led by Krupp, Röchling, Rheinmetall and Volkswagen, met in Strasbourg to discuss measures that might safeguard their industrial assets if Germany was defeated in the Second

World War. At a second meeting, a special envoy from the German Ministry of Armaments urged the industrialists to establish commercial bases abroad, in secret and without delay, in order to ensure continued operation after the war.

The strength of an economy is so fundamental to a country's stability and security that, according to Richard A. Clarke, who was Chairman of the United States Counter-terrorism Security Group in 2001, President George W. Bush's immediate concern following the 9/11 terrorist attacks was the material economic damage they might cause. His first instructions were designed to keep the economy going: businesses, banks, the stock exchange, flights. Despite the physical damage to Wall Street, the White House ordered that everything should reopen as soon as possible.

In a joint study, Alexandre de Marenches and the American journalist David A. Andelman have suggested that Italy developed close relations with Libya because Gaddafi had large investments in Italy – he was a major shareholder in Fiat and other companies. The same could be said about the close economic relationships other European countries enjoy with the Egyptian government of General Abdel Fattah el-Sisi, who took power following a *coup d'état* in 2013. Germany has since sold four Type 209/1400 submarines to Egypt, while France supplied two Rafale fighter planes, in an order that both countries agreed might be increased to a dozen.

Another clear example relates to opium production in Afghanistan. The poppy, from which opium is extracted, has long been a traditional crop in Afghanistan, but the Taliban practically eradicated its cultivation because they deemed it to be against Islam. However, since the 2001 invasion by America, production has recovered and reached record figures. When the US Army produced a detailed investigation into what might be grown in Afghanistan instead of poppies, it reached the conclusion that the most profitable crop would be cotton, which would have had high yields in areas where the climate was well suited to growing it. However, when US cotton producers heard of the plan, they put every possible barrier in its way: the cheap, high-quality cotton Afghanistan could have produced would have meant fierce competition for them.

The conquering of markets and the control of leading technologies are increasingly important in geopolitics. It can be argued that economic weapons have replaced military ones when it comes to the power that states exert on the international stage. The same might be said of domestic politics, in which economics can have just as significant an influence on policy. The French writer François Thual defines separatism as the process by which a country's rich regions seek to rid themselves of poorer ones – such movements can be viewed as a manifestation of their selfish attempts to expel the dispossessed.

THE THREE OBSESSIONS: NATURAL RESOURCES, ENERGY AND TECHNOLOGY

In its desperate search for profit – the be all and end all of capitalism and economic liberalism – globalisation has established a number of rules from which no nation can escape. Following the disappearance of the Soviet Union and the communist bloc, under which production followed Marxist–Leninist principles and was determined by need, almost all countries now base their economies on free trade. Even countries that are still officially socialist, such as China and Vietnam, employ systems that are closer to capitalism than the old Soviet-style economic principles.

In the modern world, commercial liberalism and capitalism reign supreme, and economies are geared exclusively towards profit. To manage this, countries need to maintain solvent and stable markets, consistently expanding into new ones while also protecting existing ones – a constant struggle in an increasingly competitive field. They also require a number of the elements that are essential to maximise efficient and profitable industrial production, in order to dispose of 'saleable' goods: natural resources (such as minerals and wood), energy (primarily fossil fuels and electricity) and technology. This is where the battle begins, because such goods are scarce.

'Natural resources' is a broad category that ranges from those that are essential to industry to those that generate energy or are required in the manufacture of high-tech goods, such as copper, nickel, uranium, diamond, gold, bauxite and coltan. Until the second half of the eighteenth century, when mechanisation began, energy came primarily from human beings and animals. Capturing

19

Principal natural resources

Copper ● Lithium ○ Hydrocarbons ■ Uranium □ Coltan ◀ Rare earths ◁ Gold ◆ Phosphates ◇

prisoners for slave labour was therefore as important an objective in war as seizing resources. However, following the Industrial Revolution, it became increasingly common for conflicts to focus on the growing need to secure vast quantities of raw materials (such as rubber and minerals) and energy (principally coal, which was used for steam power).

The accelerated industrial development that is currently taking place all over the world, including in countries such as China and India that have until recently lagged behind, is consuming ever more natural resources. According to Thual, the United States began a push into Africa during the Reagan administration, with the aim of controlling the continent's mineral and energy resources, as well as its agriculture. Thual believes that economic warfare conducted by the world's superpowers wrestling to control Africa's resources is a primary cause of the continent's conflicts. He views Ukraine in the same light; a stage upon which the United States and its allies play out their rivalry with Russia. Their principal motivation lies in trying to block Moscow's access to the Black Sea – hence the struggle for Crimea – and in gaining control of the significant natural resources held within Ukrainian soil. By the same token, Thual and his colleague Richard Labévière are in no doubt about the importance of oil and mineral riches in the Arctic; according to them, the United States is working hard to ensure that any future exploration, industrialisation and trade in natural resources there will be carried out by American companies. Greenland's largest employer is Alcoa; the American company is one of the biggest global producers of raw aluminium, which is widely used in the armaments, aerospace, transport and construction industries.

In the case of mineral resources, a number of issues can generate tension: many natural resources are scarce and even when there are generous deposits, their extraction can be costly, due to complicated terrain, transportation difficulties or environmental issues; access is usually controlled by a single country or a small group of countries; deposits are often located in unstable regions that are subject to outbreaks of violence; and health risks for workers are high. For all these reasons, securing a regular supply of a strategic mineral is a major priority for states and multinational corporations.

Which minerals are deemed strategically important has changed throughout history, according to the requirements of the time. Iron and coal were needed to fuel the Industrial Revolution, before the focus changed to uranium, copper, coltan, manganese, chromite and the rare earth metals – germanium, beryllium, bauxite, lithium and the platinum group – which are all considered essential today. The major powers stockpile sufficient supplies of these to enable them to keep up a good rate of industrial production for between two and five years, in the event of a high-intensity conflict that cuts off their supply entirely. The term 'strategic mineral' is therefore usually considered from a perspective that involves war, though in the modern-day context it seems more fitting to see mineral resources in the context of a permanent international economic struggle.

As long as the final outcome is profitable, nations and businesses are prepared to make huge sacrifices and test the limits of international law. Acquiring reliable data regarding the production and commercialisation of certain minerals is a near-impossible task because such information is wilfully concealed to prevent detailed analysis. In official United States documents, such as the *Minerals Yearbook*, published annually by the Geological Institute, it is acknowledged that some minerals – including coltan, which is used in the microelectronics, telecommunications and aerospace industries – are not traded openly. The importance of these minerals was spelled out in a US diplomatic message from 2009, obtained by WikiLeaks, that cited which natural resources the US deems critical to its needs, along with the countries in which they can found: bauxite in Guinea, coltan in the Congo, chromite in South Africa, Kazakhstan and India, manganese in Gabon, Brazil and Ukraine, germanium, rare earths and graphite in China, tin in Indonesia, iron in Brazil, and uranium, nickel and palladium in Russia.

Another case deserving of special attention is that of Afghanistan. According to various studies, the Afghan subsoil is one giant mineral depository, with many of the minerals found there deemed strategic, including gold, copper, iron, coltan, rare earths, lithium, chromium, lead, zinc, beryllium, fluorite, niobium and uranium, as well as precious and semi-precious stones. This led President Donald Trump (apparently encouraged by Stephen Feinberg, the multimillionaire whose Cerberus Capital Management owns the military security contractor DynCorp, and Michael Silver, CEO of American Elements, a company that specialises in the extraction of rare earths) to say, between late July and early August 2017: 'The extraction of minerals could be a reason for the United States to remain involved in Afghanistan', 'The United States is not doing enough to exploit the mineral riches of Afghanistan' and 'China is making money in Afghanistan with rare minerals, while the United States is making war'.

The geopolitics that surround energy are best defined as the struggle to control energy sources (whether reserves, extraction-production, transport, transformation, storage or distribution). As the political scientist and diplomat John G. Stoessinger explained, the First Gulf War was shaped by the importance of oil. Had Saddam Hussein seized control of Saudi Arabia's oil, he would have controlled half the world's known reserves, which would have had huge implications for the United States and the West – as a result, the defence of Saudi territory became a strategic objective. We should also be aware of the importance of transport routes for energy and natural resources, particularly the maritime routes through which over 80 per cent of all world trade passes. It is no exaggeration to say that whoever controls the oceans controls the world markets, and thus secures a pre-eminent position in the world. This explains the specific strategic importance of parts of the world such as the Horn of Africa, the Suez and Panama canals and the Hormuz and Malacca straits.

For now, oil and gas still keep the world ticking over, from individual transport and heating needs to mass industrial consumption. In a not-too-distant future, however, electricity may become the most important resource, meaning that whoever controls the production, storage and transport of electrical energy will have the potential to rule the world. As far as technology is concerned, the key focus is currently the economic struggle to control scientific and technological innovation. Any state that does not invest sufficiently in these areas is at risk of being overtaken by more developed countries.

To get a sense of where future battle lines for securing natural resources are likely to be drawn, one need look no further than the ambitions of major powers, including China, the USA, Russia and India, to conquer other planets. A new age of space exploration will seek to establish human settlements, but also to gain access to key resources that are scarce on Earth. Planets, satellites and asteroids may well become sources of strategic minerals, energy and even water, with countries competing to gain control of outer space.

Setting foot on other planets brings prestige and is a demonstration of technological prowess, but for some countries it has become important to their survival. If China is to maintain its pace of development and ensure continued economic and social advances, it will require vast quantities of energy and natural resources, as well as food and water to satisfy the needs of its huge population. Beijing, in fierce competition with other major powers, is looking to space for alternative sources of supplies, beginning with the Moon. Less than 400,000 kilometres and three days' travel away, the Moon is rich in aluminium, titanium, neon, iron, silicon, magnesium, carbon and nitrogen. It is also possible that water might be extracted from the Moon's elements. Perhaps its most valuable commodity is helium-3, a non-radioactive isotope that, while extremely rare on Earth, has been found in vast and easily extractable quantities on the Moon. It is expected to be a major source of energy in the future through nuclear fusion, and according to some estimates around five tonnes of the isotope is immediately accessible; while this might not sound like much, it would be enough to produce 50,000 times the electric energy that is currently consumed annually by our whole planet.

Outer space will only have been truly conquered when a human being lands on Mars. At least three million cubic metres of pure ice has been confirmed to exist on the red planet's surface, with liquid water thought to be underneath it. With characteristics that are similar to Earth, Mars is an ideal place for the establishment of a sizeable permanent settlement, whether to alleviate the pressure of a growing population or as a possible refuge in the event of disaster – and as a base to launch the further colonisation of space.

ECONOMICS AND CONFLICT

Economic factors have been either a principal or secondary objective of most wars, or a major influence on the outcome. The French sociologist Gaston Bouthoul argues that Germany resorted to war in 1914 because the economic battle in which it had been engaged with other major industrial powers had become too costly. The French-Lebanese writer and journalist Amin Maalouf and the Chinese colonels Qiao Liang and Wang Xiangsui argue that the infamous Opium Wars (1839–42 and 1856–60) were fought in the name of free trade. China had refused to open itself up to the lucrative business of drug trafficking that Great Britain planned to control, which led to the largest organised drug-smuggling operation ever undertaken by a state. J.F.C. Fuller is a particularly perceptive analyst on the relationship between wars and economies. He believes that the American Civil War (1861–65) was, for the most part, an economic dispute between the industrialised north and agrarian, slave-owning south, and also focuses on Anglo–German economic rivalry as giving rise to both world wars.

There is a long history of confrontation between London and continental Europe over economic interests. In the late eighteenth century, Britain needed to export its manufactured goods to remain prosperous and powerful, while France needed to protect its growing industry to attain prosperity and preserve its political power. To this end, Napoleon tried to strangle British commerce, preventing Britain from supplying goods to other European nations. For its part, London couldn't allow a federal Europe to threaten Britain's maritime dominance, so forbade third parties from trading with France and its allies. In this manner, the two sides began an economic war that would lead to the battlefields.

The Industrial Revolution compelled the most powerful nations, as well as those in the process of industrialising, to capture the raw materials and energy sources they needed. Significant trade was developing from the US west coast towards China and Japan, turning the Philippines into a key springboard. Furthermore, the USA needed to transport raw materials from Latin America and its own southern states to serve the burgeoning American textile industry. The problem was that transporting supplies from the south involved sea travel through the Straits of Florida, while materials coming from South and Central America had to pass through the Yucatán Channel. Washington was worried that having to use maritime routes that passed through the Windward

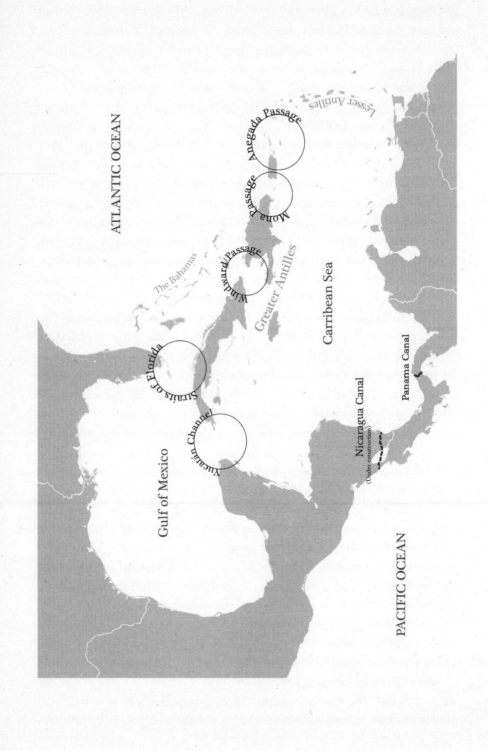

Passage, the Mona Passage and the Anegada Passage, all of which were controlled by Cuba and Puerto Rico, was a risk to its commercial security. The fear that Spain could exert strategic pressure on the United States by blocking off these routes grew with the construction of the Panama Canal, access to which would also come via these straits.

The fates of Cuba and Puerto Rico had been sealed almost a century earlier, when Spain and the United States first confronted one another. John Quincy Adams, the sixth president of the United States (1825–9), implemented the Monroe Doctrine, which stated that any European country interfering in the Americas risked confrontation with the United States – this threatened the colonial interests that had existed in the region for centuries.

Spain's American possessions were located in areas of particular strategic interest for a USA that was consumed with expansionary vigour. Washington tried several times to buy Cuba from Madrid, threatening simply to seize the island if a sale wasn't agreed. The situation intensified as the US began to establish powerful naval fleets on each of its seaboards, to patrol the Pacific and Atlantic. The two units were to be connected by the artery that would become the Panama Canal, which allowed the transport of goods between oceans without having to go around Cape Horn, thus making great savings in time and cost. For the strategy to work, Washington needed complete control of Central America and its outlying waters; Spain's presence in Cuba constituted a major threat to the project; moreover, American investors had been pressurising the White House to take control of Cuba in order to appropriate its prosperous sugar sector, the production of which was destined almost entirely for US consumption.

A worldwide financial crisis in 1873 ushered in a new era of protectionism – free trade was abandoned and tariffs introduced, and the consequence was open economic warfare between the leading industrialised powers. This economic instability was further aggravated by the emergence of new developing powers, such as Germany, Japan and the United States.

On the European stage, Britain viewed Germany's rapid rise with increasing concern. In a short space of time, Germany had managed to dominate in sectors such as steel and chemicals. It benefited from a large population, with a well-trained and organised labour force. London was also aware that Berlin lacked colonies from which to extract natural resources at low cost – it seemed only a matter of time before Germany sought to conquer new territories. Such suspicions were confirmed when the Germans started building a powerful naval fleet. With British maritime dominance threatened, London began to contemplate war with Germany. The strengthening of the German fleet also threatened to nullify French naval superiority. Britain and France both favoured destroying their new commercial competitor; all that was missing was a pretext for doing so.

For Lenin, the outbreak of war in 1914 was about carving up the world and redistributing colonies, areas of influence and financial capital. Indeed, by the end of the war, over half the world's people were under the thumb of the major industrial powers. The defeated German and Ottoman empires were largely divided up between Britain and France. According to the French historian Pierre Renouvin, the United States ultimately entered the European conflict in 1917 to defend its economic interests.

In the 1930s, the United States and Britain were the two major world powers in terms of financial wealth, a hegemonic situation that was threatened by Hitler's plans to refuse foreign loans with interest attached and instead base the German currency on industrial production rather than on gold reserves. Alongside importing goods through a system of barter and subsidising exports as necessary, he pledged to end free monetary exchange – the flow of debt and the transfers of private fortunes between countries, which supported international capitalism. Furthermore, if Hitler was successful, there was a risk that other nations might follow his example, which would lessen the importance of gold and cause it to lose value. The United States held 70 per cent of the world's gold reserves at that time; destroying Hitler's financial system became an imperative of money-lending capitalism.[1] At the same time, Germany's burgeoning industry needed markets to sell its products to. By September 1937, a sudden and devastating economic depression had left millions of Americans out of work, while Germany – where only seven years earlier 17.5 million people had been maintained by the state – had hugely reduced unemployment and re-established prosperity.

Germany also felt obliged to pursue a course set for war. According to the British military historian Basil Liddell Hart, during the Second World War the leaders of the German economy put considerable pressure on Hitler to seize oil in the Caucasus and wheat in Ukraine, both items vital to the war effort. The same thing happened with manganese and iron ore deposits in Norway that were essential to the German steel industry.

Walter Görlitz states that as early as 1937, during the Spanish Civil War, Germany had drawn up plans, known as Project Mountain, that earmarked a series of Spanish mines containing iron, copper, lead, tungsten, tin, nickel and other vital minerals. Tungsten in particular was strategically vital to Germany, as it was used to reinforce armour-plating on combat vehicles. The region's mines had been paralysed due to lack of manpower, and Hermann Göring was interested in getting the thousands of tonnes of minerals stored in warehouses in the port of Bilbao to Germany.

By the start of the 1940s the situation had become urgent, for the supply line from Korea and China, previously the principal global providers of tungsten, had stopped. Germany was forced to turn to Portugal and Spain – a country sympathetically aligned and furthermore in debt to Berlin, after Germany assisted Franco in the Spanish Civil War.

Wars in the Middle East, though they are usually dressed up with ethnic, religious and political components, have always also had deep economic roots. The US diplomat William C. Bullitt asserted that, towards the end of the 1940s and throughout the 1950s, Iran became a battleground as the Soviet Union, the United States and Britain fought for control of Iranian oil wells and the Persian Gulf. Washington's interest in Saudi Arabia at the time was entirely limited to acquiring its oil reserves, while the only political consideration was to ensure that peace and security reigned so that the oil fields could be explored.

Returning to Iran, it is worth recalling that in 1953 the UK and the US instigated a *coup d'état* in the country because Iran's democratically elected prime minister, Mohammad Mosaddegh, wanted to nationalise the oil industry, which would have meant Britain losing control of the Persian oil fields. According to Amin Maalouf, when Mosaddegh encouraged the nationalisation of the Anglo-Iranian Oil Company – a company controlled in London, which paid the Iranian state a negligible sum – Britain immediately imposed a world trade embargo on Iranian oil. When Iran began to run out of resources, its economy strangled, conditions were then ripe for a *coup d'état*, which the CIA codenamed Operation Ajax. To speed up the process, the CIA and MI6 employed the Fedayeen of Islam terrorist group to organise street disturbances.

A decade later it was Iraq's turn. In 1963, the Kennedy administration instigated a coup against the government of Abd al-Karim Qasim, who five years earlier had brought about the end of the rein of King Faisal II. Seeking to recover Western influence in the country to the benefit of US and UK oil concerns, the CIA collaborated with the new Ba'ath Party government under the guise of fighting communism, sponsoring the assassination of large numbers of people who belonged to the more learned sections of Iraqi society and sometimes even supplying lists of suspects.

In another example of the hypocrisy in evidence whenever geopolitics and economic interests combine in the Middle East, Marenches says that during the Iran–Iraq War (1980–8) many oil-producing countries favoured a deadlock between the two parties, for this way neither Baghdad nor Tehran could increase its oil production, which might have triggered a collapse in the oil price and a global financial crisis. Marenches also points to the fact that several foreign powers were supplying armaments to both sides – for example, France sold fighter planes, advanced weapons and munitions to the Iraqis, while furnishing Iran with replacement parts. The latter was done secretly in collaboration with Israel and through a complex network, whereby fake companies were set up in Spain and Portugal to supply the spare parts and repair planes and boats. The ultimate objective was for Iran and Iraq to exhaust their military potential so that neither could constitute a threat to the region. There was an underlying fear that Tehran could tip the balance of power in the Middle East by taking control of Baghdad and establishing a Shia empire that would stretch from

Pakistan to the Mediterranean. Such a scenario would have been a dangerous development for the countries of NATO, particularly Turkey.[2]

Richard A. Clarke offers a credible theory that when Saddam Hussein decided to invade Iran in 1980, the United States approved his plan, thinking that his control of the oil-rich Khuzestan Province would allow the Americans continued access to Iranian crude oil.

An article by the marine-turned-reporter Brad Hoff states that, although the French-proposed United Nations Security Council Resolution 1973 imposed a Libyan no-fly zone under the UN's mantra of 'the responsibility to protect' civilians, in reality French President Nicolas Sarkozy wanted to gain access to Libyan oil, increase French influence in the region, boost his own standing in the eyes of the French electorate, show off the country's military might and prevent Gaddafi from gaining influence in francophone Africa.[3] Speaking about the intervention on 19 March 2011, a solemn Sarkozy said, 'We are doing this to protect the civil population from the murderous madness of a regime that, in killing its own people, has lost all legitimacy. Our intervention will enable the Libyan people to decide their future for themselves.' A few months later, the French newspaper *Libération* announced that the National Transition Council of Libya had signed an agreement with the French government allowing French companies 35 per cent of Libya's oil deposits in exchange for its support. According to the report, Amr Moussa – Secretary-General of the Arab League – received a copy of the accord, drafted just seventeen days after the United Nations Security Council had adopted Resolution 1973.[4]

The most persuasive motivation for attacking the country and expelling Gaddafi from power would appear to have been the danger that Gaddafi's gold and silver reserves – estimated to be around 143 tonnes of each metal, with a total value of approximately seven billion dollars – represented to the CFA franc,[5] the French-backed currency used in much of Africa. The Libyan leader apparently hoped to create a pan-African currency based on the Libyan gold dinar, which, backed by his vast precious metal reserves, would serve as an alternative to the CFA. To truly understand the significance of this, it must be appreciated that if any country using the CFA fails to fulfil French demands, Paris deems it a 'rebel' country, blocks off its currency reserves and shuts down its banks. This happened, for example, in Ivory Coast at the end of President Laurent Gbagbo's reign in 2011. It's a far from trivial factor, for according to the former French President, Jacques Chirac, 'the French government collects 440 billion euros in levies annually from its former colonies'.[6]

Some sources suggest that prior to the resolution Gaddafi was planning to sell oil in a currency other than the US dollar. Washington could not allow this to happen because its economic prosperity relies on the vast majority of international transactions being conducted in dollars. Any leader who suggested using another currency immediately became a target.

Prominent geopolitical commentators believe that, while North Korea is undoubtedly keen to preserve its political regime, there is also a strong economic component to its stand-off with the rest of the world. The Korean peninsula controls all maritime traffic to the north-east of China and encloses the Bohai Sea, which contains China's largest offshore oil reserve. According to Robert D. Kaplan, if North and South Korea were to unite, it would be a powerful economic entity, for each has what the other lacks: the south has technology and urban development, while the north has natural resources and disciplined manpower. A united Korea would have 75 million inhabitants, compared to Japan's 127 million – so Tokyo would be opposed to such a union because a new Korea would be a powerful competitor, one with historical reasons to be wary of Japan and well within the orbit of China, which is already South Korea's principal commercial partner. Such a situation would raise tensions between Tokyo and Beijing, and would likely encourage Japan to increase the pace of its rearmament.

It would likewise be foolish to ignore the possibility that the USA's interest in North Korea is shaped by considerations of regime change; a friendlier government in Pyongyang would allow American companies to enter the highly promising North Korean mining industry, and a number of studies suggests there are vast quantities of hugely valuable and unexplored mineral reserves in North Korea. Carbon deposits are known to be abundant, but many other substances are also thought to be plentiful. It is believed that North Korea may possess two-thirds of the world's reserves of rare earths, six times more than China. Magnesite deposits could be the second largest in the world, while the subsoil could contain huge amounts of tungsten. The prospect of such a treasure trove is dazzling to America, and inevitably informs its geopolitical strategy.

The economy as a weapon

Although it goes largely unnoticed, we live in a permanent state of war. The intelligence services, the diplomatic corps and the media are the main combatants, with cyberspace the latest battleground. Economic considerations trump military ones in importance, although armed force is still important in supporting other actions. The French analysts Pascal Lorot and François Thual argue that the defining characteristic of modern geopolitics is the diminished importance of the military relative to economic factors, and argue that the quest for economic might is the primary strategy of all developed governments. While disputes over territory, religious conflicts and the struggle to control areas of influence remain principal motivations for going to war, conflicts are increasingly economic in nature, with the appropriation of resources, the capture of markets, the control of capital and the introduction of trade embargoes among the tactics.

Alongside these methods of contemporary warfare are other financial weapons that can be used with devastating efficiency to weaken and, in extreme cases, destroy an enemy: the concession of loans,[7] the implementation of sanctions, the release of reports assessing countries' credit ratings, investment by foreign wealth and venture capital funds, the dominance of markets, stock exchange manipulation and debt management. As the economy has increasingly become an instrument of war, in such confrontations economic tools are used to pursue primarily economic aims. Economic warfare may be bloodless in theory, but its consequences often cause blood to be spilled.

The American analyst Fareed Zakaria highlights a prime example of how countries can be controlled through their economies. In the 1990s, Russia was totally dependent on aid and loans from the United States, which undoubtedly drove Vladimir Putin to prioritise the establishment of an empire based on the expansion of the rouble, with the aim of being able to compete with the world's major economic powers.

The strategists Liang and Xiangsui have no doubt that in the future financial hostilities will escalate without blood being shed, recalling the conditions the United States imposed on South Korea in the late 1990s to allow it to access a 55-billion-dollar loan from the International Monetary Fund (IMF). South Korea was required to completely liberalise its market, enabling American capital to buy up Korean companies at low prices and exercise a form of economic occupation. Financial warfare, they assert, has become a 'hyper-strategic' weapon with devastating destructive power. Foundations, whether set up by companies or individuals, are nowadays able to rival states in terms of wealth – the financial magnate George Soros, for example, forced the Bank of England to devalue the pound in 1992 – and are able to control the media, finance political organisations, bring about radical change to the social order and bring down governments.

The public are usually kept in the dark regarding this sort of economic warfare, especially when significant economic and geopolitical interests are at stake. Richard A. Clarke is of the opinion that, although Washington had announced economic sanctions against Iran at the outbreak of the Iran–Iraq war, as well as the freezing of Iranian funds and shares registered in US territory, Iran nonetheless continued to export oil to the United States. We see a similar pattern even in situations of heightened tension between countries; according to Amin Maalouf, Israel received oil from Iran for much of the 1960s, through a secret deal struck with the Shah. Although Israel and Syria never signed a permanent peace accord following the Yom Kippur War of 1973, a cease-fire overseen since 1974 by the United Nations Disengagement Observer Force has held, and commercial relations between the two countries have been productive. The fact that the Syrian government still claims sovereignty over the Golan Heights, occupied by Israel, does not prevent Israeli goods produced there being exported to Syria. Similarly, despite the tense political relationship between the two countries, Venezuela still sells significant quantities of oil to the United States.

NEOGLOBALISATION

Globalisation is currently experiencing a moment of profound transformation, the results of which remain unpredictable. China, though still officially communist, has become a champion of capitalism – it is currently the second largest economy in the world (after the USA), and is aiming to become the world leader in globalised free trade. China's President, Xi Jinping, placed great emphasis on boosting liberalised commerce and investment at the Davos Forum in January 2017, while also declaring himself to be firmly opposed to any type of protectionism, a clear response to the threats of the newly installed President Trump, who had repeatedly expressed a desire to impose heavy tariffs on Chinese goods that he said were harming the US economy. Xi Jinping felt that nobody would gain from a trade war; with ambitious objectives geared towards dominating the global economy, Beijing wants innovation to be the motor of its next 'leap forward', backed by a network of free trade and open market agreements.

In reality, the Asian giant is seeking to create and lead a 'neoglobalisation' process in which China would be the dominant player. The country has the capacity to flood markets with a variety of products, from the mass-produced to the high-tech, at much lower prices than its competitors, generating profits that in turn lead to advances in fields such as military, technology and space. All of this is of grave concern to the countries that have until now pulled the global strings.

To achieve such ambitious development, China is moving forward with concrete plans to increase connectivity. The New Silk Road and the Maritime Silk Road, also known as the Belt and Road initiative, aims to connect China to Europe by land, and to Africa and perhaps even South America by sea.

The paradox of watching a country that is officially communist become the standard-bearer of capitalism is the perfect indication of how much influence economics has on a country's geopolitics. It remains to be seen how the United States will react to China's globalisation, but it is hard to imagine Washington remaining indifferent to Beijing's push for economic world domination. A tariff-led trade war is already developing and it's hard not to see it as a fight to the death, though we must hope it will not transform into a conventional war.

THE IMPORTANCE OF ECONOMIC INTELLIGENCE

Given how vital the economy is to the stability of any state, any investment in economic security is money well spent. To gain an understanding of a country's real needs – where its interests lie, what threats are on the horizon, who may seek to harm it and what measures might be applied to defend it, economic intelligence is essential.

An example of just how important economic considerations are to a country's sustainability was provided by François Fillon, the Prime Minister in Nicolas Sarkozy's French government. In a document entitled 'The action of the state with regards to economic intelligence',[8] Fillon defines the latter as the 'gathering, analysing, evaluating, disseminating and protecting of strategical economic information, with the aim of bolstering the state's competitivity'. He goes on to state that 'France's economic intelligence is a key component of its global economic policy. It contributes to growth and the support the economy is afforded on home soil, by ensuring competitivity and security for French companies.' The paper suggests that there are three pillars for French economic intelligence aims:

1. Ensure a strategic vigilance that enables public figures to make economic decisions.
2. Support company competitivity and the technology transfer capabilities of research entities, to the benefit of French and European companies.
3. Guarantee the economic security of companies and research bodies.

The document ends with instructions for ministries on the role each is expected to play within the national economic intelligence framework. Perhaps the most noteworthy is the specified mission of the diplomatic corps, spelled out as being to 'support major contracts as a matter of priority, by being alert to potential projects and their requirements, the political context, the decision-making circuits and the competition, and by providing necessary accompaniment to the French bid'.

Nothing should surprise us about what Fillon sets out, for France has been a pioneer not only in the field of economic intelligence,[9] but also in the coordination of the public and private sectors (such as sales contracts or commissions for public works) to ensure a competitive advantage abroad. Fully aware that this synergy is essential if it is to triumph over other countries, the French state sees this initiative as being of clear benefit to its citizens.

THE WEIGHT OF HISTORY

In 1992, the American political scientist Francis Fukuyama declared 'the end of history'. The Berlin Wall had fallen, the Soviet Union had collapsed and the Cold War was over; it seemed likely that democracy would spread to the rest of the world in the same way it had reached Eastern Europe. Economic and political liberalism had been established as the only viable ideology, which implied that we had reached the end point of humanity's sociocultural evolution and that globalisation would enable international security. However, despite Fukuyama's optimism, the reality has proven very different. The 9/11 terrorist attacks in 2001 began a new era that changed the international panorama. Revised and revamped ideologies clashed with the Western thinking that Fukuyama assumed had won out. History hadn't ended after all.

Marx believed that human beings moved from one developmental stage to the next, leaving more primitive society behind and moving ever closer to full civilisation and reason, in such a way that the struggle between classes and beliefs would eventually cease to exist. When the Soviet Union fell, several thinkers including Fukuyama believed that the final stage in human evolution had arrived. They were unable to conceive of the possibility that new confrontations over different ways of understanding the world would surface. Others understood that the collapse of the Cold War system that had divided the world in two would cause a readjustment that would lead to a new reality. *The Clash of Civilizations and the Remaking of World Order* by American political scientist Samuel P. Huntington (1996) argued that Western and non-Western societies would be in perpetual conflict, but one needn't subscribe to this pessimistic view to believe that there is a clash between different ways of thinking. However, to properly understand international relations and put them in a historical context, we must examine the ways in which the different tribes interact and the mechanisms that connect them – in many cases, confrontation appears to be based not on ideology, but rather on the age-old struggle for space and resources.

Humans today tend to obsess over everyday incidents but take a rather blinkered view of the overall picture – we are immersed in the information age but show a lack of interest in what's really going on. The information we're fed offers only partial accounts of events but never fully explains the causes of confrontations, conflicts and wars. History is, therefore, the best tool for deciphering the whole chain of events – ultimately, as Mark Twain is reputed to have said, 'History doesn't repeat itself, but it often rhymes.' In Greek, *historia* means 'learning through research'. To learn what happened previously and to suggest what might happen in the future is important because, as Cicero said, 'To know nothing of what happened before you were born is to forever remain a child.' However, because history is always open to interpretation, it can be controversial and is highly susceptible to manipulation.

During the Second World War, the Nazis destroyed or confiscated thousands of works of art and books that didn't correspond to their ideology and in recent years Islamist groups have destroyed ancient ruins such as the Buddhas of Bamiyan in Afghanistan and the city of Palmyra in Syria. These actions are not the consequence of a lust for violence, but of a yearning to remove all signs of a previous way of life with which the current rulers do not agree. The rewriting of the past has been a weapon employed by rulers throughout history, in order to push society in a particular direction.

Authoritarian leaders and oppressive regimes have systematically sought to invent parallel realities through historical revision. Even today, political leaders who are neither oppressive nor authoritarian misuse and distort historical facts. Informing ourselves about the reality of events – or at least the most balanced account of these events we can find – helps us to determine who we are and where we're heading.

Historical events have an undeniable influence on geopolitics. For example, it is impossible to understand the tense relationship between Armenia and Turkey without understanding the genocide committed by Turkey a century ago,[10] and nor would it be possible to understand the close ties that exist between the United States and Britain, or the connections between certain African countries and European ones, without being aware of their imperial relationships.

The political world map is not the same as it was fifty years ago, and nor will it be the same in fifty years' time. Geographical spaces don't change, but within those spaces states are born, grow and disappear. Different nationalities have long tried to gather into a single state, while at other times multinational states have exploded as a result of their diverse ethnicities, leaving behind historical achievements and making way for new nations to form. History is therefore fundamental to geopolitics because it shows how states came into being, the interests and conflicts that have persisted and how they have been satisfied or resolved. History helps us learn from our errors, though often they are repeated and we trip over the same stone time and again.

Over the centuries, almost identical events have occurred in the same place under similar circumstances. Some scholars see this as a consequence of certain peoples being belligerent, or of culture or geography, but in fact conflicts have recurred in the same places primarily because they are strategically sensitive.

If we analyse a historical world map, we notice that certain areas have always been flashpoints of tension. In some cases, confrontation has occurred as a result of inconsistencies between geography

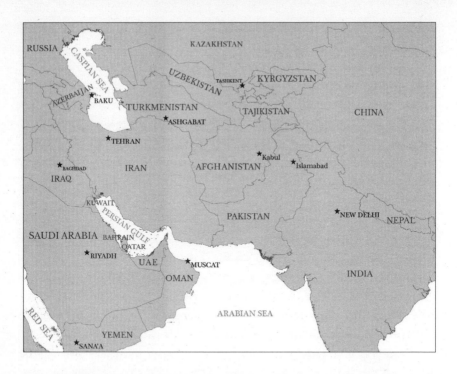

and identity – the borders between some countries were marked out according to the lie of the land, but without taking into account the ethnic, cultural or religious differences among the people living there. Such is the case with much of Africa and in the Middle East. In other places, the natural resources necessary for survival were confined to a 'no-man's-land', prompting fights for control and rule of a neutral space. Demographic pressures can also force people to expand into new territories. More often than not, areas of conflict are areas of transit, places which are key to accessing and controlling resources or other geopolitical spaces.

Afghanistan is one such country – in the mid-nineteenth century, Britain tried to seize control of this mountainous country in order to halt the Russian advance towards the colonial borders of India. It was an unsuccessful campaign; the Afghans resisted the occupation and expelled them, but the British would not be the last country to make such an error of judgement. A century later the Soviets sought to take control of the country and expand their international sphere of interest, but they too were defeated. Following the attacks on the World Trade Center in 2001, the war on terror resulted in further failure, as Afghanistan again showed itself to be an 'unconquerable' country.

Russia is another good example; in 1812, Napoleon embarked on a campaign against Tsar Alexander I and failed spectacularly. Over a century later, in 1941, Hitler sought to conquer Soviet territory and was defeated. Both leaders had underestimated the strength and capability of the enemy and failed to factor in the threat of winter. Both made fundamental errors of judgement – in Hitler's case they might have been avoided had he studied history and been prepared to learn from it.[11]

UNDERSTANDING THE HISTORY OF A PEOPLE

An awareness of culture, religion and language is indispensable in understanding the evolution of a people, but the geographic space they occupy also determines their social conditioning. Cultures, traditions and beliefs, nowadays more diffuse than ever as a result of globalisation, were traditionally products of a society's environment – clothing, food and buildings were all determined by their surroundings. The physical geography of a place has major repercussions on the evolution of a nation, its tensions and its conflicts, which makes for a complicated picture that is impossible to interpret without studying the past.

At the same time, one of the most common errors when assessing other peoples is the failure to consider the importance that they place on historic events. For some groups, their ancestors have left a defining mark on their way of seeing the world, not least in terms of who are friends and foes. In certain cases, history is decisive in understanding why a group acts in a particular way, which may be totally different from even their closest neighbour. A society's past – its victories and defeats, conquests and submissions, triumphs and failures, strengths and weaknesses, hardships and moments of splendour – shapes its vision of itself. In other words, it is important to understand the history of a people, but also to know how it perceives its history – otherwise, interaction with that people will be doomed to failure. For example, it is not possible to understand what is happening in Ukraine at the moment without understanding the history of the Russian people. And if you want to know what Kosovo means to the Serbian people, you have to appreciate that there was a decisive battle in Kosovo Polje in 1389, in which the Ottoman Empire defeated the Serbian army.

The image typically presented of North Koreans in the Western media is of a uniform mass of people with no capacity for personal awareness, blindly following a leader who has brainwashed and subjugated them. Whether or not the regime does impose a way of thinking on its subjects, it is a major and misleading simplification to present North Koreans in this light – they may be considered the most homogeneous people in the world ethnically, linguistically, historically, culturally and religiously, but they are also as idiosyncratic as they are unknown. If we want to understand them we have to learn about North Korea's recent history – only then can we hope to understand the animosity North Koreans feel towards the USA and its allies, in particular Japan, which feeds into a general distrust of the capitalist world most immediately represented by South Korea.

During the nineteenth century Korea was a 'hermit kingdom', averse to establishing diplomatic and commercial relations with the West and preferring to maintain an alliance with China. The First Sino-Japanese War (1894–5) was primarily concerned with taking control of Korea, which Tokyo did upon victory. In 1897, Emperor Gojong proclaimed the foundation of the Korean Empire, which principally meant it would no longer be a client state of China, as it had been since the seventeenth century.

Having become an industrial power, Japan annexed the Korean Empire in 1910, in order to exploit it economically. The Japanese government encouraged their farmers and fisherman to settle there, giving them land for free or selling it for a token sum. The Japanese considered the Koreans to be ethnically inferior and treated them with great cruelty; while the Koreans went hungry, the Japanese helped themselves to the rice harvest. Among the many atrocities committed, the employment of 'comfort women' stands out, a practice in which Korean women were forced to provide sexual services to Japanese soldiers during the Asia-Pacific War (1931–45), a huge number of whom died.

The Japanese occupiers employed a policy of assimilation from 1919, which caused some Korean intellectuals to rebel in order to preserve their culture and resulted in the loss of thousands of lives. The initiative failed, and infused the Koreans with a strong sense of patriotism and anti-colonialism. The Koreans were finally freed from Tokyo after Japan's defeat in the Second World War, only to fall into the clutches of the victors of that struggle when the Soviet Union and the United States agreed to divide the Korean peninsula along the thirty-eighth parallel, with the north to be occupied by the Soviet Union and the south by the Americans. A communist government was established in the north and invaded South Korea in June 1950, with the aim of reunifying the peninsula. The justification used by the North Korean leader, Kim Il-sung, was that communist sympathisers in the south had been brutally repressed by Seoul's military regime. Washington, fearing the spread of communism throughout the peninsula, decided to repel the offensive.

American bombing of strategic targets initially seemed to halt the North Korean offensive, but China's entry into the conflict on the side of Pyongyang tipped the balance again. Beijing launched waves of soldiers into battle and, though inadequately equipped, they began to inflict losses on the Americans. Douglas MacArthur, the American Commander-in-Chief, then launched Operation Strangle, subjecting North Korea to a merciless, ruthless and systematic bombing campaign. The exact figures are disputed, but it's thought that in three years of war, around 650,000 tonnes of bombs were dropped on North Korea, including 35,000 tonnes of napalm, which reduced over 600,000 homes, 5,000 schools and 1,000 medical facilities to rubble. When these urban targets had been annihilated, reservoirs and dams were bombed, flooding farms and crops. The United States dropped more tonnes of bombs on North Korea than it had in the Pacific during the Second World War.

Thirty years after the conflict, Army General Curtis E. LeMay, who had been in charge of Strategic Air Command during the war, told the Air Force Historical Research Agency that they had killed about 20 per cent of the North Korean population, around three million people. By comparison, one might consider that during the Second World War just 2 per cent of the British population was killed. North Korean deaths could have been much higher: General

MacArthur admitted just after the war that he had proposed dropping between thirty and fifty atomic bombs on North Korea, which he argued would have ended the war in under ten days.

Kim Il-sung was considered a hero by his people for standing up to the mighty United States and preventing his country from being conquered. This image of heroic resistance, to which the North Korean people still pay homage, was passed on to his son, Kim Jong-il, and to his grandson, the current supreme leader Kim Jong-un. North Korea has for many years featured on America's list of 'rebel' countries and its 'Axis of Evil'; while the Western world may think the North Korean people need rescuing from a communist dictatorship led by an evil and blundering eccentric, the North Koreans see themselves as a people determined to resist foreign interference. They have not forgotten the devastating air raids, which is why they give their support to the regime's efforts to equip the country with anti-air-raid defence systems, as well as underground facilities and shelters. They also support its nuclear ambitions, as a means of deterring would-be aggressors. In summary, the North Korean people have ample reason to fear the United States and Japan – it is a national sentiment, deeply ingrained, and it will not vanish with a regime change.

THERE ARE NO ETERNAL ALLIES, ONLY PERMANENT INTERESTS

In international relations, all sides try to satisfy their own interests. Whether a country has acted honourably or not tends to be judged almost entirely on what effect the actions have on the interests of whoever is doing the judging. Realpolitik consists of every country giving precedence to its own interests, meaning that actions are motivated by gain rather than by morals or ethics.

Given that a nation's interests are constantly changing, international relations are also in a permanent state of flux. Nations sometimes decide to ally with others to achieve specific goals, which might be economic or might relate to matters of security or war. However, their ally of today can potentially be their enemy of tomorrow, which is more true than ever given the accelerated pace at which events unfold in the modern world. Perfect allies, according to American writer Robert Greene, are those that provide you with something you cannot get for yourself and need something you can supply them with. It is the same with countries; there is no alliance that is not based on reciprocal benefits. The secret to good negotiation lies in identifying a strategy for mutual advantage.

Interests and needs occasionally necessitate strange alliances, which might contradict the values to which a country supposedly adheres. There are countless historic examples. In the sixteenth century, despite hostilities between Christian Europe and the all-powerful Ottoman Empire, numerous incongruous alliances arose based on evolving economic and geopolitical interests. Catholic Venice, which relied to a large degree on Ottoman grain, repeatedly used Constantinople to put pressure on neighbouring and rival city-states. Given that Venice was primarily concerned with defending its commercial maritime routes, and the Ottoman Empire was its principal trading partner, there was much more cooperation between the two than there was confrontation. In the early part of the sixteenth century, France and the Ottoman Empire conducted joint naval exercises against the Holy Roman Empire. During the Crimean War (1853–6), France and Great Britain, facing the prospect of a Russian victory over the Ottomans that would disrupt the balance of power in Europe, had no hesitation in backing the Ottoman Empire. Towards the end of the nineteenth century, Great Britain would use the Ottomans to block Russian use of the Turkish Straits that connect the Black Sea to the Mediterranean.

All alliances, including those that seem solid and steady, prove ephemeral and changeable as soon as the causes that prompted them are altered. Many alliances and secret agreements were signed and broken during the two world wars – a prime example is the case of Romania, which had been an ally of the German Kaiser, but entered the First World War against Germany and Austria in 1916. Similarly, Japan fought alongside Great Britain and the United States against Germany in the First World War, but fought alongside Germany against the United States in the Second World War.

According to Richard A. Clarke, during the Iran–Iraq War (1980–8) the United States assisted the Iraqis by passing them information, convoying their oil in Kuwaiti tankers and cutting off military supplies to Iran,[12] but had no qualms in declaring that Saddam Hussein was its worst enemy just two years later. It's worth remembering that during the Iran–Iraq conflict in 1983, the US President Ronald Reagan sent Donald Rumsfeld, who had been Defense Secretary six years earlier, as an envoy to Baghdad to establish diplomatic relations with Saddam Hussein and to offer help in defeating Iran. Twenty years later, Rumsfeld, leading the Department of Defense once more, was the architect of the US invasion of Iraq and overthrow of Saddam Hussein.

For an alliance to be truly effective and long lasting, all parties must share the same perception that a common threat compromises their existence. As soon as one member of the alliance senses a different threat, or considers the original threat to be less grave, the alliance is condemned to unravel. It can still be maintained, but its different component parts will not act in a totally coordinated manner, meaning its initiatives may not have the involvement of all its members. Such is the view of Pierre Célérier, the French former admiral and geopolitical analyst, who argues that groupings of nations are only viable and robust if there is some sense of

overarching agreement between the community in terms of interests and ideas. If this is not the case, the ties will loosen as soon as the military intervention ends or the cause that brought the alliance into being disappears. Too few common interests may be the reason why member states of the European Union have not seen fit to share military power.

Despite Greece belonging to both the European Union and NATO, during the war in Kosovo in 1999 the Greek people sided against Europe in declaring their support for Russia and the Serbs. Were Greece to leave the Eurozone, and perhaps even the European Union, Russia might seek to tap into that popular support and bring the country into its orbit, which would be of significant geopolitical benefit to the Kremlin, allowing it to bolster its Mediterranean presence and gain better control of the gateway to the Black Sea. In such a scenario, Russia might seek to install naval bases at strategic points, such as on the Peloponnese peninsula.

Alliances can also crumble due to imbalances among members. As Cardinal Mazarin, the French chief minister under Louis XIV, said in his *Breviary for Politicians*, 'In a community of interested parties, danger arises the moment one of its members becomes too powerful.' Applying this mantra to today's world, it is possible to see how countries that begin to stand out become a threat to others. For instance, the only alliance that could check China's rise is the United Nations, hardly a model organisation when it comes to promoting collective interests.

In the international arena, betrayals and secret accords, which are typically hidden as adjuncts to public deals, are not the exception but the rule. In October 1898, Great Britain and Germany signed an agreement to share out Portugal's interests in Africa between them. The assumption was that Portugal would have no choice but to sell or pawn its African colonies to the two major powers. Just over a year after signing the agreement with Germany, Britain established the Treaty of Windsor with Portugal, a secret pact in which ancient accords were renewed: Britain and Portugal would mutually guarantee each other's territories, providing defence whenever necessary. As a consequence, the Portuguese signed up with the Allied forces in the First World War and were involved in military actions in Africa.

Against a backdrop of such pragmatism, paradoxes regularly arise, such as Stalin retracting an order to assassinate Hitler in 1944, out of fear that if Germany had a different leader, the Allies would try to agree a peace deal that excluded Russia. In the 1950s, France agreed to join the European Defence Community in return for the United States involving itself in Indochina; Washington wanted France's military might in what it saw as an aid to NATO, and the French government demanded help containing communism in Asia in exchange.[13]

In many other situations, over-eagerness and desperation to achieve short-term aims have caused decisions to be rushed, leading to irreversible errors. In the eighteenth century, the Prussian king Frederick the Great wrote that 'of all Prussia's neighbours, the most dangerous is Russia, due to its strength and location. For this reason, Prussian governors would do well to cultivate friendship with these barbarians.' Nevertheless, towards the end of the following century, Kaiser Wilhelm II, swept along by the advice of his counsellors, renounced a reciprocal security treaty with Russia, which caused Moscow to fall into French hands.

Another case that highlights the changing nature of alliances is that of the children of those Ukrainians who fought on the Soviet side in the war with Afghanistan in the 1980s. In 2001, Ukrainians found themselves fighting against the same Afghan insurgency, but this time on behalf of NATO, the great enemy of the Soviets.

Throughout the eighteenth and the early nineteenth centuries, alliances between different European powers were made according to the interests of the time. Between 1733 and 1789, Spain and France signed three separate accords against Great Britain and its naval hegemony. They were known as the Family Pacts, for the kings involved all belonged to the House of Bourbon. The French Revolution of 1789 spelled the end for such pacts, with the French monarch Louis XVI executed and the Spanish Bourbons anticipating war with France. As a result, in 1793, the alliance mutated and Great Britain and Spain aligned themselves against France. A combined armada took on the French naval fleet and won, a defeat that left France much weaker.

As confrontations between London and Paris became increasingly bitter, Madrid had two options: to side with France, ensuring security at the Pyrenees border and safeguarding Spanish maritime interests by providing a counterbalance to British sea power; or to ally with Britain and against the French. In the end, Madrid chose the former, formalising its alliance with France through the Second Treaty of San Ildefonso, which was signed on 19 August 1796.

When Napoleon was preparing to invade Great Britain in 1805, he knew France would need the support of the Spanish navy in order to defeat the powerful British fleet. One of the best known naval battles in history, the Battle of Trafalgar, was the result. The British naval forces, led by Admiral Horatio Nelson, emerged from behind the Trafalgar Cape off the coast of Cádiz and defeated the Spanish–French fleet commanded by the French admiral Pierre-Charles Villeneuve. When Napoleon's troops entered Spain in 1808, the alliance was recast. Great Britain aligned with Spain to help expel the French from the Iberian peninsula – they eventually destroyed Bonaparte's empire in 1815.

It would take France several decades to recover its status in Europe, while Spain was condemned to a secondary role, a situation that remains to this day. Britain emerged as the strongest power in those tumultuous years, which enabled it to become arbiter of future events in Europe, with London the dominant centre of maritime trade and global finance, until the emergence of the United States towards the end of the nineteenth century.

In the spring of 1939, Stalin sought to improve commercial relations between Russia and Germany and to divide Poland up with Hitler, should the Nazis go to war with Warsaw. Such a scenario came to pass in August that year – Germany and the Soviet Union signed a ten-year friendship treaty and non-aggression pact. The Molotov–Ribbentrop Pact, named after the Russian and German officials who were in charge of negotiations, benefited both sides: the Third Reich would supply machinery in exchange for Soviet cereals, oil and minerals. However, Hitler's alliance with the Soviet Union aroused the suspicions of the United States, who decided to better Germany's offer and proposed the Lend-Lease Act, whereby the US would inundate the Soviet Union with war materials – planes, tanks, munitions and supplies. Stalin happily accepted Washington's unexpected 'generosity', which left the pact with Germany in tatters.[14]

During the Second World War, the United States and Russia collaborated closely. In order to defeat Germany and Japan, the US needed Soviet manpower, while the Soviet war machine benefited from the huge quantities of materials that the powerful US industrial sector could provide. The White House gave dozens of boats to the Soviet Union in exchange for their declaration of war on Japan in September 1945. The declaration of war, as instigated by Washington, broke the pact of neutrality that Moscow and Tokyo had signed four years earlier, which had until then enabled them to focus on their main adversary (Germany for the Soviet Union, the USA for Japan) without having to worry about fighting a war on another front.

To compensate for this rupture, the Kremlin demanded that the White House supply a vast array of war materials, including boats and planes, to make their armed forces potent and modern. The agreement became a programme of huge scope called MILEPOST and, later, Project Hula. The Americans agreed to provide the Soviets with 180 boats, of which 149 were delivered, among them thirty Tacoma-class frigates. The American military also ended up training 12,000 Soviet soldiers, including 750 officers. Curiously, these soldiers went from being allies and training companions to sworn enemies just a few months later, when their respective nations began a period of ideological and geopolitical confrontation that would shape the course of the twentieth century.

These days, Beijing, in its struggle with Washington for control of the waters and islands of the South China Sea, is in the process of making an alliance with the Philippines, a country that has, since winning independence from Spain in 1898, been one of the White House's main allies in the Pacific region. The alliance has given the US a strategic foothold in its bid to encircle China, but the ground shifted when Rodrigo Duterte was elected President of the Philippines in June 2016.

Duterte has been heavily criticised in Western countries for the brutal methods with which he has combated delinquency and drug trafficking. His relationship with President Barack Obama deteriorated to such a degree that Duterte abandoned Washington in favour of Beijing. However, the geopolitical importance of the Philippines is so great that it would be no surprise if Donald Trump were to seek to draw Duterte back into the American fold. The results of this relationship will depend on what benefits the US can offer the Philippines to rival economic advantages offered by China.

THE COMPLEX USA–JAPAN ALLIANCE

US tensions with North Korea could ultimately prove to be no more than a smokescreen for the more serious dilemmas the US has with Japan, which date back to August 1945 and the atomic bombing of Hiroshima and Nagasaki. Analysts who focus on this part of the world believe that Japan, so long as it exists as a nation, will forever exert emotional blackmail on the Americans for the atrocity of their behaviour. At any given moment Tokyo could, in theory, charge the United States with crimes against humanity in international tribunals, which would inflict immeasurable damage on Washington's reputation in Asia and the rest of the world. America needs a smokescreen in the South China Sea, because its principal 'ally' in the region also holds a knife to its throat. Whatever Washington wants or does not want to do in the South China Sea has to be approved by or 'negotiated' with Tokyo.

In addition, the entrenched hatred the Korean people feel for the Japanese military makes any lasting agreement between South Korea and the United States impossible as long as Tokyo is Washington's main ally in the region. These vulnerabilities are well understood in Beijing and Taipei. Their conclusion is categorical: Washington is hostage to Japan in the South China Sea, and the North Korean issue provides cover for an otherwise shameful state of affairs.

TRUST ONLY IN YOUR OWN STRENGTH

Alliances can be highly risky for weaker countries, which can easily be dragged by the group's dominant member into ventures that are of little benefit to them. The influence of the mighty is hard to resist, but rulers of weaker states must be strong and avoid doing everything they're told, while also serving the interests of their own citizens. Leaders would do well to remember that the moment they cease to be useful they will be abandoned by the 'allies' that promised them glory. In the words of Machiavelli in *The Prince*: 'The only defences that are good, sure and lasting are those that depend on you yourself.'

PART THREE

The Rules

Having evaluated the world around you and established your geopolitics – what you want to do and why – the next step is to develop a
geostrategic plan for how you are going to influence, rule or control –
whether directly or indirectly, peacefully or belligerently – territories,
populations and markets, and avoid being unduly influenced or ruled
by others. There are twenty-two different categories of geostrategies
that have been performed throughout the ages.

Rule 1

DETERRENCE

How to win without fighting

'The greatest victory is that which requires no battle'

– SUN TZU

To paraphrase a well-known saying, the best form of defence is the *threat* of attack, which is in keeping with the line of thinking of the Chinese strategists Sun Tzu ('the greatest victory is that which requires no battle') and Lao-Tze ('he who knows how to defeat the enemy need not fight him'). It is based on the principle that well-managed deterrence is an effective strategy.

RAISING THE STAKES

This strategy consists of persuading others to do as you wish them to do through the threat of force or punishment, be it physical or emotional. It is difficult to prove whether people decide whether to obey a law or not after weighing up the pros and cons of their actions, for we only really know about those who disobey the law. In the seventeenth and eighteenth centuries, Thomas Hobbes, Cesare Beccaria and Jeremy Bentham proposed crime be prevented through a system in which the punishment for transgressions outweighed the benefits from committing them.

Intimidation theory can also be applied to international relations: states seek to defend their interests, but in an anarchic system that lacks a central authority, conflicts will inevitably arise; deterrence is therefore an important tool for influencing the behaviour of others. In the geopolitical context, it essentially involves threatening to use so much force that the damage caused will be hard to absorb, warding off attacks through fear of retaliation. Historian Victor Davis Hanson understands it as the creation of a sense of foreboding that war would be a costly, unrewarding and prolonged affair. For Michael Howard, the aim is to persuade one's adversary that a military solution to a political problem is not worth the trouble.

The primary purpose of a country's armed forces in peacetime is to be sufficiently intimidating to discourage anyone from being aggressive against the nation. Understood in these terms, almost every political relationship in history has involved deterrence. After the Second World War, the world divided into two blocs fighting for global supremacy. It was an ideological, strategic and armed struggle marked by confrontation and deterrence in the form of nuclear weapons, the ultimate threat. Throughout the Cold War, the United States and the Soviet Union maintained a 'balance of terror' based on deterrent strategy. The bombings of Hiroshima and Nagasaki had proved what a nuclear bomb was capable of and both superpowers wished to avoid attacks of that magnitude. Strategies therefore focused on how to defeat the enemy, but also on how to defend against a nuclear attack. The theory of assured mutual destruction forced the two superpowers to settle their differences through low-level conflicts that avoided direct confrontation on a self-destructive scale.

The decisive moment of the Cold War was the Cuban Missile Crisis. In the early 1960s, Washington and Havana broke off diplomatic relations as Cuba's leader, Fidel Castro, moved closer to the Soviet Union, eventually becoming part of the communist bloc. In October 1962, US intelligence discovered the existence of nuclear ballistic missiles on the Cuban coast that would be capable of reaching US territory. This strategic advance by Moscow was a clear manifestation of encircling and counter-circling tactics, given that the US had military bases in Turkey and other European countries close to the Soviet border. The White House weighed up whether to launch an attack on Cuba or impose a blockade of the island, and chose the latter option. The week of 22–28 October proved particularly tense, as a number of Soviet boats headed for the island. Washington responded by drawing an imaginary red line: if the USSR's boats went over it, they would launch a nuclear attack. The threat of a nuclear holocaust ultimately curbed the daring of both superpowers: the Soviet boats turned round before they reached the red line; the USSR dismantled the missiles it had stationed in Cuba and the USA did the same in Turkey, while a direct phone line was subsequently established between the White House and the Kremlin.

Although nuclear weapons continue to be a major threat to world peace and international security, there are many other ways to enact the deterrent strategy beyond the use of simple force. Economic threats are very effective; one example is a threat to blockade an important choke point, as Iran is able to do with the Strait of Hormuz, through which 40 per cent of the world's oil travels. Other examples include the fixing of oil prices by the Organization of the Petroleum Exporting Countries (OPEC), the manipulation of foreign exchange rates, or foreign corporations being threatened with nationalisation. The nuclear threat remains the most potent deterrent, but military means are increasingly overlooked in favour of economic, political and social intimidation.

BANGING YOUR FIST ON THE TABLE

The expression *'quítate tú pa' ponerme yo'* ('get out of the way so I can take your place') became famous in the Spanish-speaking world when a stage-show of that title premiered in Cuba in 1933. The revue show depicted a succession of Cuban presidents and satirised the endless, cut-throat battle to occupy the top seat and remain there. The phrase succinctly captures the perennial fight for supremacy; just as there always have been and always will be people who hold the reins of power, there have always been others who, irrespective of their ideology, want to seize the reins for themselves.

In a country's domestic politics, power games often produce new winners, with the people the perennial losers. Populations are routinely manipulated, tricked and exploited, as the scheming that takes place in the upper echelons of political power is kept from the general public. Politicians might reasonably be expected to prioritise the wellbeing of the communities they represent, but if people had any idea of how much horse-trading goes on, they would surely seek a new form of governance.

In *Disordered World*, Amin Maalouf says that whenever a power relaxes its grip, the natural response of its adversaries is not to thank them, but to take the opportunity to attack. This leads powers to occasionally display their might, just in case anyone aspiring to take their place is feeling over-confident. It's a strategy that is crudely known as 'banging a fist on the table' – creating a forceful reminder of who's in charge for the benefit of any pretenders to the throne.

THE DETERRENCE PRINCIPLES

To effectively intimidate your opponent from considering going to war with you, your deterrence strategy must be based on three principles:

1. You should have access to capable and credible force and means, whether your own or shared with allies.
2. You should have the political will to use this force if necessary.
3. You should convey to your adversary that you have credible force and the political will to use it to the benefit of your national security.

The need for the message to reach your adversary is just as important as the existence of the force and the will to use it – your potential capacity is of no use if your potential enemy does not know about it. North Korea employs a strategy of conveyance. Faced with the prospect of being attacked at any moment, it publicises its military capabilities – in particular, its nuclear means – loud and clear, making sure the message reaches its rivals. In this manner, it seeks to avoid the fate of countries such as Iraq and Libya, believing that these countries were not invaded *because* they had weapons of mass destruction – the justification used in 2003 to attack Saddam Hussein – but because they did *not*. North Korea's posturing is hardly surprising, argues Michael Howard, if you consider that the nuclear attacks on Hiroshima and Nagasaki were only possible due to Japan's lack of a potent deterrent.

Perception undoubtedly plays a vital role in this strategy: the real power you have at your disposal is no more important than the image the enemy has of it, and whether they believe you're prepared to use it.

Rule 2

ENCIRCLEMENT

How to outmanoeuvre your adversaries

'If a ruler doesn't understand chess, how
can he rule a kingdom?'

– KING KHOSROW

Geopolitics can be seen as a giant chessboard. In chess, every move is designed to put pressure on the opponent, until checkmate is achieved. Pawns are sacrificed, the adversary is lured into traps and the king is protected through castling or the exchange of pieces. Every manoeuvre builds towards victory; how many pieces you have is important, but guile – how you move them – is just as significant.

There are countless historical examples of encircling strategies. In the early twentieth century, it was British policy to enclose the Saudi centre of power with micro-states, the Emirates. During the same period, France tried to contain a resurgent Syrian nationalism by depriving Syria of its coastline and dividing the country's interior, splintering Lebanon away from Greater Syria. The entire Cold War involved a series of moves aimed at suffocating the enemy, with each side seeking to reduce the other's sphere of influence while expanding its own. The two superpowers used countries in Latin America, Africa or the Middle East as pawns. Lorot and Thual contend that the United States and its allies concentrated their efforts on encircling the Soviet Union, its allies and China, through a series of pacts.

The Cuban Missile Crisis, as we saw earlier, was like a game of chess: the United States placed missiles in Turkey and the Soviet Union sought to place them in Cuba, both seeking to pressurise the other and gain control of the board. And today, the United States provides support to a circle of allies – such as Georgia and Estonia – in order to keep Russia out of certain regions. Israel is another case in point – surrounded by Arab neighbours, it is constantly trying to break the circle. One method it employs is to collaborate on building projects – for instance the Blue Nile Dam in Ethiopia, which will provide a means of putting pressure on Egypt by being able to control the flow of water to its land.

In order to avoid becoming the victim of an encircling geopolitical strategy a country can seek allies beyond its borders or aim to gain control of the seas off its coasts, to prevent superior forces from gathering around a point from where they could attack or impose a blockade.

MARITIME STRAITS AS ENCIRCLING TOOLS

For much of history, whoever ruled the waves has ruled the world, and this remains true today. The key pieces on the maritime chessboard are the 'choke points', narrow stretches through which traders have always had to pass. In modern geopolitics, much maritime traffic is focused on the straits of Malacca and Hormuz and the Suez and Panama canals. For instance, these four passageways, two natural and two artificial, are the arteries through which 63 per cent of the world's oil moves.

When it opened in 1869, the Suez Canal made it no longer necessary to travel around Africa by sea to reach Europe from Asia. Early forms of passage between the Mediterranean and Red Sea date back to the thirteenth century BC, but the current version of the canal was encouraged by Napoleon, who thought that building a canal across the Suez isthmus would give the French a significant advantage over the British, allowing them to control the canal (and charge others to use it). From the beginning, the Suez Canal was as much about one rival country exerting power over another as anything else. In the end, it was built jointly by the Egyptians and the French, but Egypt's debts were such that in 1875 it sold its shares in the canal to Britain. An international convention was signed in 1888 stating that the canal could be used by any nation, but disputes over who could use it flared up throughout the twentieth century. In 1956, France, Israel and Britain clashed with Egypt in a confrontation that became known as the Suez Crisis. Egypt nationalised the canal after the French and British refused to finance the construction of a new Aswan Dam. As war broke out, Egypt sunk 40 boats in the canal, blockading it. The UN, led by the United States, eventually brokered a truce. Cairo obtained Soviet financing for the building of the dam and the canal reopened in 1957.

Strategic maritime passageways

Bosphorus and Dardanelles Straits

Suez Canal

Strait of Hormuz

Strait of Malacca

Bab el-Mandeb Strait

Strait of Gibraltar

Panama Canal

Maritime routes
— Primary routes
— Secondary routes

The Panama Canal joins the Caribbean Sea to the Pacific Ocean and is another key passageway. Some 235 million tonnes of cargo pass through it each year. Before it opened in 1914, vessels were obliged to sail around the American continent in order to travel between the Atlantic and Pacific oceans. The idea of building a canal had been around since the fifteenth century, but it wasn't until the early twentieth century, when Panama, supported by the United States, claimed independence from Colombia, that the project got the green light to proceed with construction. Though owned by Panama, American influence is such that China and Russia constantly fear having their access to it blocked, and since 2014 they have been building a new inter-oceanic canal in Nicaragua.

The Malacca and Hormuz straits are the principal natural passageways for international maritime trade. A fifth of the world's oil, around thirteen million barrels a day, passes through the Strait of Hormuz, making it a vital link in the distribution of Persian Gulf crude oil. The strait is mostly controlled by Iran, though it shares water rights with Oman and the United Arab Emirates. In recent years, Tehran has repeatedly threatened a blockade as tensions mount over the conflict in Yemen, where relations with Saudi Arabia have become increasingly strained. If Saudi Arabia and its allies disadvantage Iran and Yemen, Tehran will respond in kind at Hormuz.

The Strait of Malacca, meanwhile, links the Indian Ocean to the Pacific Ocean and sees 50 per cent of the world's maritime traffic. Agreements such as the Treaty of Amity and Cooperation in Southeast Asia (TAC), made in 1976, have liberalised economic relations between the region's countries and made Malacca a point of common interest, which ensures against political tensions. Unsurprisingly, any move by China in the region is viewed with suspicion by Japan and the Philippines, but also the United States, which has focused its foreign policy on the Asia-Pacific region in recent years. Chinese–American relations and their competing political and economic interests are, in geographical terms, most obvious in the struggles to control the Strait of Malacca and the South China Sea.

Through strategies of encircling and counter-circling, one nation uses choke points to weaken another and strengthen its own position. When several nations are involved, with each looking out for its own interests, the choke point becomes a hotspot, a place where a carefully maintained balance of power is required to avoid conflict.

This encircling strategy can be enacted anywhere. Russia's annexation of the Crimea from Ukraine in 2014 resulted in economic sanctions and a trade embargo from the European Union, while NATO deployed significant numbers of troops near the Russian border, pushing Moscow to perform counter-circling manoeuvres in places such as Syria. If it continues to feel pressured, Russia may well respond with further actions in places such as Transnistria (between Ukraine and the Dniester River in Moldova), Nagorno-Karabakh (in Azerbaijan), Central Asia, Egypt or Libya.

Another area of the planet that is becoming increasingly significant is the Arctic. Whoever controls the maritime passageways and vast reserves of natural resources known to exist there will be well placed in world affairs for the foreseeable future – being able to cross the Arctic would mean avoiding the bottlenecks of the Panama Canal on one side, and Suez and Malacca on the other. This Arctic 'shortcut' would mean significant cost savings, for the Panama and Suez tolls are expensive – to use the Panama Canal

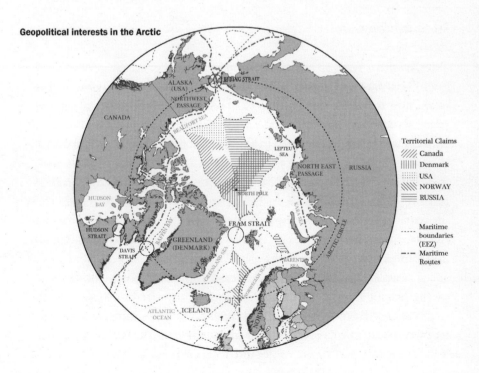

Geopolitical interests in the Arctic

costs an average of 150,000 dollars per ship, plus a further 35,000 dollars for every day the ship is anchored waiting to pass through. Using an Arctic crossing instead would hugely reduce journey times: travel from Europe to Asia would be reduced from the present thirty-one days to twenty-one days. The benefits would be even greater for large ships that cannot use the Panama or Suez canals and have to go around Cape Horn to travel to and from the United States, or those that must go around the Cape of Good Hope to travel between Europe and Asian countries such as China, Japan and South Korea.

The geopolitical importance of the Arctic is so great that the countries that surround it, specifically the United States, Canada and Russia, are making huge efforts to dominate it. Russia, which has long feared being cut off from the Suez and Panama canals, is installing military bases and seeking to build nuclear-propelled ice-breakers. If Russia manages to control the Arctic, fully or partially, and can link it to the new inter-oceanic canal in Nicaragua, it would have a clear strategic advantage.

RUSSIA FEELS ENCIRCLED

The Kremlin feels it has been subjected to a gradual geopolitical encircling by the United States and other NATO countries, and is desperate to break the pattern. As the Spanish geopolitical expert Jorge Verstrynge has noted, the United States has sought to exploit Russia's weakness since the break-up of the Soviet Union; it has established a growing military presence at Russia's borders via its own installations and those of NATO, while at the same time undermining Russian influence in former areas of the USSR, with the ultimate purpose of pushing Russia further away from Europe. According to Verstrynge, the United States also plans to kick Russia and China out of Africa and Latin America.

François Thual agrees with Verstrynge that, since the demise of the Soviet Union, America has sought to encircle Russia, both to prevent it from becoming a great power again and to maintain its own position of regional power. To these ends, Russia's former Soviet empire has been subjected to a process of 'NATOisation', stoking identity conflicts in the Caucasus and Central Asia. Developments in Ukraine show a clear attempt by the US to remove one of Moscow's geopolitical trump cards. Thual describes Moscow's belief that there is a plot to belittle Russia by encouraging separatist movements and imposing a sort of cordon sanitaire[1] between it and the territories it previously controlled.

In the early years of the twenty-first century, the Russian Federation possessed considerable economic power, due to the high prices it could command for its vast energy resources. The United States became concerned and sought to provoke a collapse in oil prices, which would hurt Russia economically and curb its expansionist ambitions.

Feeling increasingly boxed in by the United States, NATO and Japan, and after losing the battle for Kosovo in 1999, Russia turned its attention to the Caucasus, a region deemed vital for its survival. Since the early nineteenth century, Georgian nationalists have dreamed of expelling the Russians from their land, and their resentment has manifested itself in the repression of Armenian, Abkhazian, Adjarian and in particular Ossetian minorities, the majority of whom consider themselves to be Russian. Throughout the twentieth century, Western powers sought to exploit the

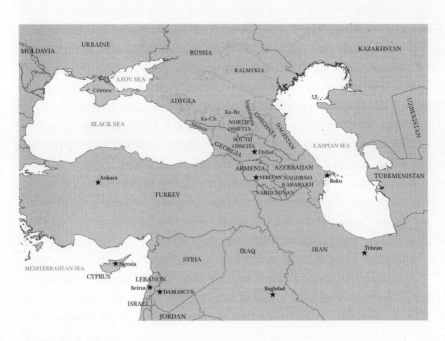

situation by using Georgian nationalism and Georgian hatred of Russia to weaken the Kremlin's grip on the region and, by 2008, Georgia had become one of the focal points of American geopolitical activity in the Caucasus. The country received unconditional American support and, along with the other former Soviet republics of Ukraine and Azerbaijan, joined the list of countries keen to join NATO, which was more than Russia could tolerate. Bolstered by the backing of long-term allies the USA, Germany, Ukraine and Turkey, Tbilisi launched an offensive in South Ossetia, a Georgian region that had long aspired to unite with North Ossetia and become part of the Russian Federation.

Russia could not back down without losing credibility and prestige as a major power. It needed to show it was still a powerful geopolitical force, to recover its former standing and its influence in the world. It decided that a regional alliance with Armenia and Iran would be opportune – allying with Armenia would incite nationalist sentiment among Armenians living in Georgia and threaten Azerbaijan with military actions in Nakhchivan. An alliance with Tehran, meanwhile, would exert considerable pressure from the south. Seizing control of South Ossetia and uniting Ossetia would enable Russia to control the principal passageways of the Greater Caucasus mountain range and the communication routes between the Caspian and Black seas, while further choking Chechnya.

Abkhazia, Georgia's other separatist region, was viewed to be of even greater geopolitical importance – taking control of this Black Sea port would provide Russia with an alternative to Sevastopol on the Crimean peninsula, a port which Russia had rented from Ukraine for 70 million euros a year since 1997. At around the time of the Georgia conflict, Kiev was making noises about rescinding the contract for the lease of Sevastopol from 2017, which was bad news at a time when the Russian navy had tentatively begun sailing the oceans again. With South Ossetia and Abkhazia subsequently recognised as independent states, Moscow had showed the world that Russia was pushing back.

In 2008, as now, Russia viewed the United States as its main geopolitical rival and the principal threat to its superpower status. The then-President of Russia, Dmitry Medvedev, said as much that August, when he presented the fundamentals of his country's

The USA's principal overseas bases

foreign policy. In the Kremlin's vision of a multipolar world order, Russia would develop a web of strategic bases from which to project its future power. With this in mind it courted Yemen, Kyrgyzstan, Tajikistan, Libya and Syria. In Latin America it sought to reinforce ties with Nicaragua and Cuba, but its principal regional partner was Venezuela.

The Caracas government's unabashed anti-Americanism and determination to spread revolution to the rest of the region were key factors in Russia's decision to sell it 3.4 billion euros' worth of arms between 2005 and 2007, to which a further 800 million euros' worth were later added, courtesy of a Russian loan. Despite the fact that the Venezuelan constitution forbids foreign military installations on its territory, the possibility arose of Russia establishing a permanent base for troops there. Cooperation with Caracas would allow Moscow, should the need arise, to threaten the security of the Panama Canal. There was even a fear that Venezuela might decide to revive Japanese and German plans drafted during the Second World War and seek to bomb the canal using the planes Russia had supplied.

As Russia and Venezuela thus upped the ante, the USA restored its Fourth Fleet, which had been decommissioned in 1950, with the express purpose of defending its interests in the Caribbean, Central America and South America, and protecting the Panama Canal. At the same time, it developed plans to establish a base on the Colombian peninsula at La Guajira, practically the only part of the Colombia–Venezuela border where an armoured offensive would be possible. Likewise, and despite a demilitarisation process completed in 1999, the Panamanian President Martín Torrijos offered to make a new mooring dock available to the Americans in exchange for upgrades to Panama's military and intelligence apparatus. The proximity of a Russian military presence was clearly a concern to the US.

According to François Thual, history shows that whenever a country feels encircled it becomes more aggressive. This may prove to be the case with Russia and even with North Korea or Iran. The American strategic analyst Fareed Zakaria estimates that the US has 766 overseas bases, spread over 40 countries, home to 200,000 operatives and occupying 275,000 hectares of foreign land.

Rule 3

KICKING AWAY THE LADDER

How powerful nations stay ahead

'It is a very common clever device that
when anyone has attained the summit
of greatness, he kicks away the ladder
by which he has climbed up, in order to
deprive others of the means of climbing
up after him'

– GEORG FRIEDRICH LIST

This strategy originates in economics, but can be applied to all areas of international relations. In the mid-nineteenth century, the German economist Georg Friedrich List wrote that any nation that attains industrial and maritime capabilities so great that no nation can freely compete with it, is well advised to kick away the ladder that enabled it to reach such heights and from then on advocate the benefits of free trade. List congratulated Britain for having turned itself into a superpower, recognising the part played by its colonies, which supplied the raw materials to manufacture and then trade via its maritime fleet. He felt that the world owed Britain a debt for the progress that had resulted from its industrial revolution, but he also wondered whether it was desirable that London should rule over the ruins of other nations.

APPLYING THE KICKING THE LADDER AWAY STRATEGY

The South Korean economist Ha-Joon Chang has developed List's 'kick away the ladder' theory further. Chang's hypothesis, very popular among countries that feel disadvantaged by globalisation, is based on the premise that less-evolved countries are subjected to tremendous pressure to adopt economic policies that are designed to benefit those who rule the world economy. Furthermore, these countries are at that point prevented from adopting the measures the current champions of free trade used to reach their privileged position – the dominant countries 'kick away the ladder' they used to reach the economic summit, to stop others from following them up.

Chang argues that the countries that are currently the most enthusiastic promoters of free trade, those that argue that it is the path to generalised prosperity, did not follow this doctrine when

77

they were in the early stages of development. On the contrary, they protected their own industrial sector by applying customs duties and tariffs to foreign goods, while offering their own exports support through subsidies, state credit and other such means of promotion. That was how Britain defeated France in the eighteenth century and established itself as the world's factory and principal economic power. By the end of the eighteenth century, with a new world order established, free trade prevailed, until the subsequent period of prosperity was interrupted by the outbreak of the First World War. England had, in fact, been promoting policies to stimulate its wool manufacturing industry since the fourteenth century, and although it is hard to measure the exact impact such policies had on industrial development, they were undoubtedly integral. Indeed, the United Kingdom and the United States were the two most protectionist countries in the world during the eighteenth and nineteenth centuries, imposing tariffs that sometimes topped 50 per cent. Germany, France, Japan and the Netherlands, among others, applied similar policies.

The First World War marked an impasse, with countries everywhere erecting trade barriers to protect their own economies. It wasn't until 1945 and the culmination of the Second World War that conversations about liberalising trade resumed, encouraged primarily by the United States. Nevertheless, protectionism remained in place, albeit hidden in policies such as voluntary restrictions on exports, clothing and textiles quotas, agricultural subsidies and taxes to avoid companies from exporting products at lower prices than they charge in domestic markets. In such a scenario, the 'kick away the ladder' policy that followed the economic crisis of the 1980s was embodied in the Washington Consensus.

The Washington Consensus laid out ten recommendations based on the premise that, in order to create wealth, customs barriers had to be removed and markets opened up to world trade. This plan was orientated towards countries in Latin America that had plunged into a huge debt crisis and were being controlled by the World Bank, the International Monetary Fund and the US Treasury Department. When the plan was applied to Latin American countries, no consideration was given to possible adverse social effects. The initiative failed when a currency crisis in Mexico, provoked by the country's lack of international reserves, had global repercussions. The Washington Consensus was criticised for imposing neoliberal ideas at a time when the countries championing free trade were already in a position of supremacy. Following the 2008 global financial crisis it seemed to be dead, and at the 2010 G20 summit in South Korea – a forum for the world's richest countries – the Seoul Development Consensus was signed, which was designed to reduce inequality and tackle global poverty through sustainable and balanced growth.

While agreements were being sought to curb climate change, a number of countries with expanding economies, such as China and Brazil, noted the 'kick away the ladder' strategy in justifying their own high levels of emissions. Citing the need to develop their own economies, they argued that the countries that were now advocating reduced emissions had achieved their own industrial development with no restrictions whatsoever.

England passed the first of its Navigation Acts in October 1651. The Acts were a series of legal restrictions aimed at keeping the benefits of trade within the English colonial empire. It was decreed that only English boats were allowed to trade with the colonies, while at the same time the colonies were forbidden from developing their own industrial framework. The legislation was born of the desperate situation English commerce had found itself in following the Eighty Years War (1568–1648). The 1647 lifting of the Spanish embargo on trade with the Dutch Republic represented a major boost to Dutch international trade, and the Navigation Acts were an attempt by the English government to curb Dutch maritime ascendancy. The laws' most direct consequence was the First Anglo-Dutch War, in which Admiral Robert Blake's navy ultimately defeated the Dutch fleet, beginning its slow decline as a power.

The establishment of a commercial monopoly proved highly beneficial to England. Merchants became rich buying goods cheaply and selling them at a high price, the profits were invested in the industrialisation of the country and the colonies served as captive markets. The smooth running of this process was guaranteed by the state, which also became the defender of English interests abroad; it doubled the size of its fleet within a year, turning England into the world's principal maritime power.

For almost two centuries this and subsequent Navigation Acts underpinned British trade. Their economic repercussions not only provoked the Anglo-Dutch Wars but were also a cause of the American War of Independence. By the time the Acts were repealed in 1849, it had become much more beneficial to British interests to impose free trade around the globe.

Britain was so opposed to free trade while consolidating its position as a world economic power that towards the end of the eighteenth century, in the midst of war against France and Spain, a significant number of British intellectuals felt that it was preferable to go on fighting than to establish a peace that might mean free trade between Paris and Madrid. Once mechanisation had established Britain as the global supplier of industrial products, the British government became a champion of free trade, knowing it had no competition.

The G8 can be compared to the kind of nightclub bouncers who Spanish journalist Jaime Campmany said are 'your worst enemy when they won't let you in, but once you're inside, they're your greatest ally'. The G8 began as the G6 and was formed in 1973 by the six major global powers of the time: the USA, Japan, Germany, Italy, France and the UK. Canada joined in 1997 and Russia in 2002. In this select club, consensus is negotiated and positions are adopted regarding decisions that will shape the global economy and world politics. The make-up of the G8 has a fair degree of overlap with the permanent members of the United Nations Security Council (China, the USA, France, the UK and Russia), another group of 'bouncers' who, equipped with the right of veto on matters of international peace and security, have little interest in admitting new members.

The 'nightclub bouncer' strategy is also a basic component of the Treaty on the Non-Proliferation of Nuclear Weapons (NPT), signed in 1968, which restricts access to the development and possession of nuclear arms for all countries in the world except the USA, the UK, France, Russia and China. Four members of the United Nations have never signed it: India, Pakistan, Israel and South Sudan. While the latter was only founded in 2011 and has never been truly stable, India and Pakistan have nuclear weapons, and it is rumoured that Israel has them thanks to the USA – if this is indeed the case, it has violated one of the NPT's basic principles. North Korea withdrew from the NPT in 2003 and has since conducted nuclear tests. As for Iran, it began receiving assistance from the USA to develop its military hardware in the 1950s, but development ceased after the country's revolution in 1979. Towards the end of the 1980s, China and Pakistan agreed to help Iran develop nuclear technology for civilian use, but stopped doing so once the US imposed sanctions based on its suspicions that Iran was seeking to develop nuclear weapons.

The 'nightclub bouncer' door policy remains very much in force. The NPT establishes that non-nuclear states must pledge not to develop weapons while nuclear states agree gradually and voluntarily to reduce their arsenals. The vast majority of sovereign states have signed up to the agreement and the United Nations Security Council is committed to ensuring there are no new nuclear weapon-owning states, thus perpetuating the 'Club of Five' (and a few consented others).

The issue of nuclear weapons is arguably the most hypocritical element in the international arena. The United States National

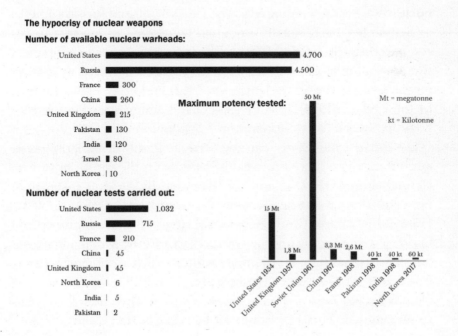

The hypocrisy of nuclear weapons

Number of available nuclear warheads:

United States 4.700
Russia 4.500
France 300
China 260
United Kingdom 215
Pakistan 130
India 120
Israel 80
North Korea 10

Maximum potency tested:

Mt = megatonne

kt = Kilotonne

50 Mt
15 Mt
1,8 Mt
3,3 Mt
2,6 Mt
40 kt 40 kt 60 kt

United States 1954
United Kingdom 1957
Soviet Union 1961
China 1967
France 1968
Pakistan 1998
India 1998
North Korea 2017

Number of nuclear tests carried out:

United States 1.032
Russia 715
France 210
China 45
United Kingdom 45
North Korea 6
India 5
Pakistan 2

Security Strategy has said that 'no threat represents a greater danger to our security and wellbeing than the potential use of nuclear arms and materials by irresponsible or terrorist states'. The United States itself is the only country to have ever used a nuclear weapon on a civilian population, but this does not stop it from labelling as 'rebel' or 'irresponsible' any other country that seeks to develop nuclear weapons.

It is true that the number of operative nuclear warheads globally has been substantially reduced, from 64,500 in 1986 to the 10,315 estimated to exist now;[2] it is also true that Washington and Moscow have for some time been engaged in the questionable and costly process of modernising their arsenals. Russia has until recently dedicated almost a third of a growing defence budget to improving its nuclear weapons. While treaties limit the number of warheads the nuclear countries are allowed, destructive capacity is never mentioned. Furthermore, the restrictions do not cover tactical missiles – small nuclear warheads that can be deployed against limited targets, for which the risk of accidental, unauthorised or undetected use is even higher.

As for the supposed nuclear threat constituted by North Korea and Iran, some perspective is required: North Korea has ten nuclear warheads,[3] compared to the USA's 4,700 and Russia's 4,500; by September 2017, North Korea had completed six nuclear tests, compared to the USA's 1,032 and Russia's 715; in terms of explosive power, the most powerful weapons registered in tests were fifty megatonnes by the Soviet Union (in 1961) and fifteen megatonnes by the USA (in 1954), far in excess of the almost sixty kilotonnes[4] recorded by the North Koreans on 3 September 2017.

Similar conclusions can be drawn about nuclear-powered aircraft carriers: there are currently twelve in the world, of which eleven belong to the USA and one to France. By the same token, just five countries have nuclear-powered submarines: the USA, the UK, France, Russia and China. Obviously, none of these 'bouncers' is interested in allowing another country to join the group, although South Korea has stated the aim of owning a nuclear submarine, and Brazil aimed to have one operational by late 2018.

As Fareed Zakaria points out, when the United States – which, combined with Russia possesses 85 per cent of the world's nuclear arsenal – tells other countries that manufacturing even a single nuclear weapon is a moral and political abomination, while maintaining thousands of nuclear warheads and manufacturing new ones itself, the rebuke rings rather hollow.

Rule 4

BEGGAR THY NEIGHBOUR

How to keep your closest rival weak

'Nothing is great or little otherwise than by comparison'

– Jonathan Swift

Dominant countries are forever engaged in a game of one-upmanship, especially with their nearest competitor; as a result, a number of strategies have been devised to keep neighbours weak and poor. The US's Monroe Doctrine was discussed over a number of years before finally taking shape in 1850 and coming to full fruition in the late nineteenth and early twentieth centuries. Its objective was to extend US influence throughout the Americas while weakening the non-allied European empires, which were already on the wane in the Americas anyway.

German statesman Bernhard von Bülow believed that one of the main reasons London went to war in 1914 was that Germany had built a formidable naval fleet that jeopardised Britain's dominance of maritime trade. According to Bülow, prior to the war, Britain was concerned about Germany being an industrial and colonial rival.

More recently, the opposition Spain met from France when seeking to join the European Economic Community in the 1960s and 1970s was the result of France's attempt to maintain its agricultural primacy – it was worried Spain would undercut it if it was part of the common market and no longer subject to tariffs. France did not prevail (Spain joined in 1986), but it was a clear example of one neighbour wishing to maintain economic dominance over another.

There are parallels in the relationship between the USA and Mexico. It is in Washington's interests for there to be a degree of stability in its southern neighbour, but not for it to evolve enough to become a rival. Mexico, with 125 million inhabitants and a rate of population growth that is 50 per cent higher than that of the USA, and given its large oil reserves and flourishing tourist trade, could in a few years' time become one of the most powerful economies in the world, particularly if it moves from a manufacturing base to high-tech industrial production.

When given the chance to share something, the strong never hesitate to give themselves the largest portion. Sometimes they do it deviously, while at other times it's more obvious. The great powers of the day have done this whenever they could get away with it, in particular by abusing the underprivileged and ignorant, as the history of Africa attests. However, less powerful nations are not beyond such jostling; countries in possession of skilled diplomats or sharp intelligence services know how to take advantage of a situation to gain the lion's share, even in negotiations apparently established for mutual benefit. Avoiding this isn't easy. You may be well aware that you're being short-changed, but the powerful and the cunning have ways to pressurise or indeed bribe those in charge of distribution.

THE PELOPONNESIAN WAR

The Peloponnesian War (431–404 BC) was the forerunner for a recurrent form of conflict: a dominant power (Sparta) felt threatened by the emergence of a rival with similar aspirations (Athens). The development of this confrontation, as related by Thucydides in his *The History of the Peloponnesian War*, has been analysed from a variety of perspectives, ranging from the purely military – strategies, battles, weapons, generals and combatants – to the internal political dimensions of each city and the broader context of regional relations.

Perhaps the least studied aspect of the war is the economic one, despite the fact that it was arguably the determining factor in the outbreak and evolution of the war. This was a geopolitical rivalry in which two opposing systems of government collided – Athenian democracy versus Spartan oligarchy – but the clash was prompted by economic competition.

In 445 BC, Sparta and Athens signed the 'Thirty Years Peace' treaty, whereby Athens accepted that Sparta would remain the dominant power on the Peloponnese peninsula. By way of compensation, Athens was permitted to develop its own maritime capacity, though as the years went by Sparta realised that Athens had gained control of the Mediterranean and was becoming ever more rich and powerful.

Athens also made use of the Delian League, an alliance of city-states created in 478 BC by the Athenian statesman Aristides as a defence against Persian invaders. This gave Athens enormous strength: all the members were committed to providing troops, boats and finance to any campaign that Athens might embark on to defend the rest of the coalition from Persian attack. The success of Athens depended on the founding of this alliance because it allowed the city access to large pools of money in a common fund, which facilitated its social and political development.

To fully understand the situation Athens was in when it went to war with Sparta in 431 BC, we must look further back in time. In the early years of the Delian League, despite some members distrusting the growing power and privilege of Athens, the coalition held because all members benefited from the trade stimulated by Athens. However, this cohesion would weaken over time, not least as a result of Athens abusing its dominant position by raising taxes on other members, with the justification that fighting forces had to be maintained. In 453 BC, several members of the coalition refused to pay the tributes Athens demanded, and Athens responded by imposing penalties for late payment.

From 449 BC, the Peace of Callias, which brought the Greco-Persian Wars to an end, prompted many members of the Delian League to question the league's continued usefulness, given that the reason for its establishment had now passed. Athens wished to preserve the alliance that had given it such power, and sought to convert its former partners into subjects of a new empire. As part of this process of constant development, Athens had to expand its trading markets in order to bring in extra revenues to cover increased social costs.[5] These costs were unavoidable if it wanted to keep its population happy. Sparta did not initially view the increased trade of Athens and the Delian League as a threat to its dominance, though other members of the Peloponnesian League, led by the Spartans, weren't so sure. They considered their economies to be under threat and began to create obstacles to trading with members of the Delian League, which led Athens to consider blockading the cities that were its main competition.

One of the Delian League's major economic and military rivals was Corinth, a rich city with a privileged geographical position that allowed it to control parts of the mainland and certain sea routes. For Athens, Corinth became something of an obsession: it exported a number of highly sought after products throughout the Mediterranean and challenged the monopoly Athens had on the Sicilian market, which furthermore allowed for domination of the Ionian Sea.

As the Peloponnesian War evolved and Athens lost much of its fleet and territories in the Dardanelles strait, it could no longer supply itself with goods from the Black Sea, most importantly the staple cereals. The Spartans made the most of the shortages to impose hunger on the Athenians, which contributed to their eventual surrender. Following its defeat, while under the military and political control of Sparta, Athens lost its pre-war economic prosperity; the rest of the Peloponnese peninsula was likewise devastated by the huge economic cost of the war and poverty took hold.

Among many economic consequences of the war, it is worth highlighting that most members of the Peloponnesian League were forced to borrow money, in particular from the Persians, which afforded them an unexpected victory over their historical foes. More collateral damage came in the shape of increased piracy

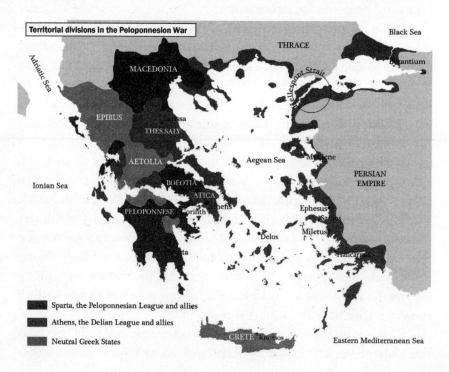

90

in seas that had previously been controlled by Athenian ships; this, along with the war's significant death toll, dealt a further setback to trade, due to a lack of manpower to work in fields and relaunch businesses. The regional economy was pushed into recession.

THE BISMARCKIAN SYSTEM

In 1871, Germany defeated France in the Franco-Prussian War, consolidating German unification and establishing the German Empire. The Frankfurt Peace Treaty awarded the wealthy French provinces of Alsace and Lorraine to Germany, and imposed harsh war reparations on France, which was left in political disarray. Otto von Bismarck was quick to take advantage. The German Chancellor used France's desire for peace to weaken its neighbour through the so-called 'Bismarckian System' of alliances. The main objective of these alliances was to isolate France. Between 1873 and 1877, Bismarck invested great political energy in ensuring that France's republican regime triumphed over the monarchists; his specific goal was to get rid of the French President Patrice de MacMahon and his monarchist allies. To this end, he encouraged the formation of a cordon sanitaire of liberal and anticlerical governments in Spain, Belgium and Italy, with the aim of supporting the French republicans and undermining MacMahon's monarchists. These interventions paved the way for the establishment of the French Third Republic. Bismarck's strategy was pragmatic: he played at kingmaker, forming and then dissolving republican governments according to his interests. His interference aroused suspicion among other European leaders, who were wary of his controlling aspirations.

From 1871 to 1878, Germany allied with Austria and Russia through the Three Emperors' League, a theoretical commitment to mutual defence between the three countries that eventually unravelled over territorial rivalries between Austria and Russia in the Balkans. Bismarck sought to resolve these issues at the Congress of Berlin in 1878, but Russia abandoned the league, leaving Germany and Austria to sign a Dual Alliance instead. This would become a Triple Alliance in 1882, when Italy was incorporated, by which time Russia had also sought to revive the Three Emperors' League. Bismarck also brokered Mediterranean Agreements between Great Britain, Italy and Austria. In 1890, Wilhelm I's successor, Emperor Wilhelm II, removed Bismarck from office and brought his system of alliances to an end. The rivalries and expansionist ambitions that would lead to the First World War had begun to form.

CHINA'S MULTIPLE NEIGHBOURS

China shares a land border with 14 different nations (North Korea, Russia, Mongolia, Kazakhstan, Kyrgyzstan, Tajikistan, Afghanistan, Pakistan, India, Nepal, Bhutan, Myanmar, Laos and Vietnam) and a sea border with Japan, South Korea, the Philippines and Vietnam – more than any other country. Recent stand-offs between Beijing and its maritime neighbours has attracted US attention, with the Americans keen to halt China's charge for global power. The South China Sea contains several chains of islets surrounded by uninhabited keys, atolls and sandbanks; although they are periodically flooded by the sea, they have a high strategic and economic value, for the area is believed to be rich in natural resources, a third of the world's maritime traffic passes through the area and the waters hold significant fishing stocks.

China, Vietnam, Malaysia, Indonesia, the Philippines, Brunei and Taiwan have claims to sovereignty of the sea and its islets, while Indonesia, Singapore, Thailand and Cambodia have lesser interests. All are alert to Chinese developments. Beijing has increased its military presence in the region, as has Washington. Japan has also made its presence known, opposing Chinese claims and championing its own interests. The Philippines brought a dispute before the Permanent Court of Arbitration in The Hague in 2013, accusing China of violating international maritime law, based on the United Nations Convention on the Law of the Sea (UNCLOS) and asked the court to pronounce on the 'nine-dash line' in the shape of a U that marks out the Chinese government's claims in the South China Sea. Beijing had already warned that it would not recognise the authority of the court's verdict on this case, and when

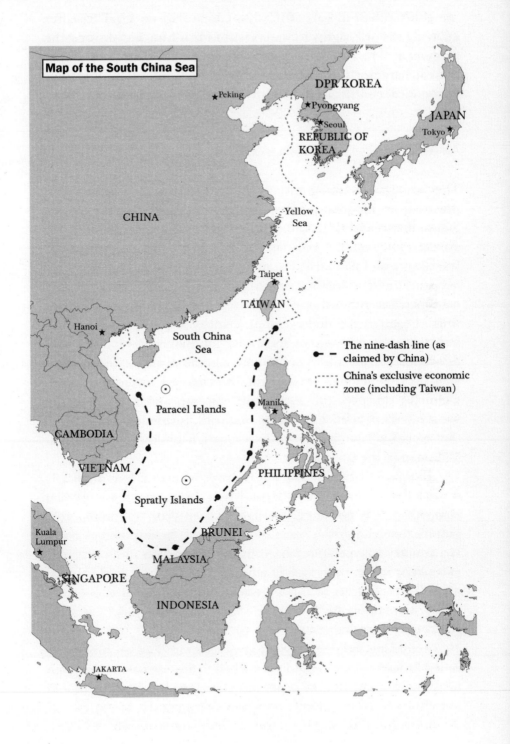

Map of the South China Sea

the court ruled, in July 2016, that China had no legal basis for applying historic rights to waters within this line, it dismissed the judgement. The ruling is legally binding, but the court has neither the capacity nor the resources to force its application, and thus geopolitical conflict in the South China Sea remains turbulent.

AN UPDATED CONCEPT OF 'NEIGHBOURHOOD'

The strategy of antagonising your neighbour has long been practised by the great powers, and the superpowers of the United States, Russia and China all do it today. At the regional level there are currently a number of major frictions, between Saudi Arabia and Iran; India and China; Pakistan and India; Algeria and Morocco; Venezuela and Colombia; South and North Korea. However, the concept of 'neighbourhood' has been transformed by globalisation, which began in the mid-twentieth century and accelerated in the late 1980s, as a result of increased international relations and developments in information and communications technology. Globalisation, though fundamentally economic in nature, is also technological, political, social and cultural, and it has fostered great interdependence between countries, turning the world into the 'global village' predicted by Canadian philosopher Marshall McLuhan in the late 1960s.

In this globalised world, any country, no matter how physically distant from another, is a virtual neighbour and a theoretical competitor. It is no longer enough to keep your traditional geographical neighbours at bay; supremacy must be disputed globally. If a country is hyper-specialised in the production of a particular product or in a certain area of advanced technology, its main rival might be thousands of miles from its borders, but this does not make competition any less fierce – in a globalised world, everyone can beggar everyone else.

According to Greek mythology, there was once an innkeeper called Procrustes who would offer a bed to anyone passing through his remote area. If they were too short for the bed, he would stretch them to fit it and if they were too long, he would cut off the protruding parts. This dark parable is used to refer to those who cannot tolerate others standing out – as soon as they realise someone is atypical they take measures to impose the 'norm' to do whatever is necessary to achieve their goal.

WHEN YOUR NEIGHBOUR IS A POWERFUL AND RUTHLESS RIVAL

Your neighbour doesn't have to be a historic adversary or an invader with whom you've had numerous armed conflicts; it may simply be a rival for economic, religious, ideological and geopolitical dominance. Even then, you can still maintain diplomatic and commercial relations, and your neighbour may even form part of the same political and military alliance. Greece and Turkey are both members of NATO and the UN, but they still view one another with a suspicion that periodically threatens to come to a head.

In early June 2017, Saudi Arabia became hostile towards Qatar, a neighbour with which it has much in common. The two nations are both Sunni Muslim and oil-rich, which has historically meant that relations between them have been friendly. However, Doha refused to succumb to Riyadh's regional power plays, which prompted the Saudis to accuse Qatar of supporting extremist groups in the region; behind the Saudi accusations lay a struggle for religious supremacy in the Muslim world. Saudi Arabia is the epicentre of the hard-line Wahhabi movement and has invested vast sums of petrodollars in promoting its expansion, while Qatar is loyal to another movement, the Muslim Brotherhood.[6]

Saudi Arabia has the advantage of disproportionate force in this competition; with 30 million inhabitants and an army of almost half a million, it has the strength to crush Qatar, which has a population of just two million and 11,000 soldiers. This rivalry, in which a cocktail of religion, economics and geopolitics is aggravated by outside interests, has the potential to trigger great instability across a region that is historically unstable.

Throughout the centuries, countries have tried to maintain superiority over their neighbours in order to neuter them as a military or economic threat. They have also sought to exploit them as markets for their products, and for this purpose have sought to ensure relative stability, but whenever a neighbour seems to be a threat, the first course of action is to attempt to foster internal strife by creating or encouraging subversive groups. Heightened tensions have typically led to armed conflict, of varying degrees of intensity. In a world in which states compete globally and everyone is a 'neighbour', the means for weakening the neighbour remain the same – economic, political, diplomatic and military – and all are employed in order to exert power and achieve supremacy over others, in order to maintain the status quo.

A state should never entirely trust the goodwill of its neighbours. Even when not orchestrating the tension, a country will always be somewhat cheered by political division, separatist movements, social unrest or riots in a neighbour, and perhaps even by its collapse, which will allow the more stable state to gain regional control.

All of this assumes that one state's misfortune does not harm a neighbour's economy, security and stability. States generally prefer neighbours to be stable enough to serve as a reliable market but volatile enough not to progress too significantly. This is preferable to chaos, for a neighbour in disarray is lost as a market and might send an exodus of people spilling out across the region or become a catalyst for widespread social unrest.

Rule 5

FEIGN AND CONCEAL

How to be a master of deception

'Things do not pass for what they are, but
for what they seem'

– Baltasar Gracián

'Feign what you're not; conceal what you are.' The seventeenth-century diplomat Cardinal Mazarin provided many examples of how to benefit from this strategy in his writings on political rule, most of which can also be applied to geopolitics. As Pedro Herranz – a political commissar during the Spanish Civil War – said, 'International politics has always been a game of cards: players must be careful not to show their hands if they want to win tricks.' A good poker face is key in geopolitics, because it allows you to feign friendship with everybody.

THE ART OF TRICKERY

Throughout history, spies have been like one state concealed inside another; they feign an existence in another country in order to obtain information that will be of benefit to their own. British journalist and writer Max Hastings tells of Soviet spies in the Second World War who pretended to be capitalist entrepreneurs in enemy countries in order to better hide the fact that they were gathering intelligence for the communists. The Soviet spies were applying Lenin's maxim that communists had to be prepared to use all manner of ruses, schemes and underhand strategies, including denying or concealing the truth, to achieve their ideological goals. This is not so different from the *taqiyya* (concealment), discussed especially in Shia Islamic texts, or the *kitman* (omission) often employed by Salafist jihadis in order to evade discovery before committing a terrorist attack.

Deliberately causing confusion by pretending to be or allowing people to believe you are one thing while actually being another is a geopolitical strategy that enables countries to develop out of sight before revealing themselves once they are strong enough to hold their own. Whether the strategy is to feign or to conceal, it is essential to be a master of deception. In his work *In Praise of Folly*, Erasmus wrote, 'opportune faked foolishness is the height of wisdom'. On occasion it can be beneficial to seem weak or poor so as not to attract envy or enemies, and this is also the case for states: it can be better to hide your resources so that others don't seek to seize them.

To paraphrase Machiavelli, who called politics 'the art of deception', we might say that in geopolitics, deception is the ultimate art.

THE TEACHINGS OF SUN TZU

In *The Art of War*, Chinese general and military strategist Sun Tzu presents numerous scenarios in which it is advisable to feign and conceal. For him, warfare was all about deceit: when you can, feign you cannot; when you are active, fake being passive; if you are near, pretend you are far; if you are far, pretend you are near; offer bait to lure your adversary into a trap; simulate disorder and surprise him; affect adverse conditions to encourage his arrogance.

The Chinese leader Mao Zedong acknowledged the influence of Sun Tzu's thinking on his victory over Chiang Kai-shek and the Kuomintang in 1949. Tzu's military treatise strongly influenced Mao's writings on guerrilla warfare, which were key to communist uprisings all over the world.

Modern China has undoubtedly feigned and concealed. One of the most important communist leaders of the twentieth century was Deng Xiaoping, instigator of the Great Leap Forward, the policy that sought to reform the Chinese economy. Having been purged by the party during the Cultural Revolution instigated by Mao to limit reform, Deng returned to politics in 1978 following Mao's death. He introduced reforms of a capitalist nature, but maintained the communist discourse, turning China into a regional leader and great world power in less than 40 years. Twenty or even ten years ago, no one imagined China might ever represent a challenge to the United States, or at least not one significant enough for Washington to realign its foreign policy priorities away from Europe and the Middle East and towards Asia-Pacific, as finally began to happen with the Obama administration.

However, despite this, at world summits on climate change, for example, China still presents itself as a country that is on the road to development. Its most recent leaders, Hu Jintao (2003–13) and his successor Xi Jinping, have consistently reminded international forums that China is still developing and must be allowed to behave accordingly. But is it really a developing country? Deng Xiaoping said, 'hide your strength, await your moment', which seems to be what China has been doing since the 1980s. In a speech delivered to the United Nations in 1974, Deng reminded his audience that China was a 'socialist country' and 'on the road to development'. Since then, the Chinese economy has become sixty-four times stronger, maintaining annual growth of between 7 and 10 per cent. It is now the world's second largest economy and has surpassed the largest, the United States, in terms of purchase power parity – a popular way of comparing economies using adjusted prices for goods – with the differential likely to grow in the coming years.

In terms of military spending, China is second on the worldwide list behind the USA, spending 2 per cent of its GDP on defence,[7] and research by the Stockholm International Peace Research Institute (SIPRI) suggests that China's defence spending is on an upward trajectory. Chinese-created organisations and South–South cooperation forums (which aim to stimulate trade and collaboration between countries of the developing Global South), such as the Shanghai Cooperation Organisation (SCO),[8] the BRICS Bank, the China Development Bank and the Asian Infrastructure Investment Bank, could soon come to overshadow international organisations founded by the USA and other Western countries, such as the IMF and the World Bank.

However, it still remains true that China is a country in development. Hundreds of thousands of people in rural areas and on the outskirts of large cities live in poverty. The Chinese state claims that its priority is to focus on domestic affairs and to encourage economic growth and wealth in the interior of the country. According to some analysts, the relative slowdown the Chinese economy has suffered in recent years has been a deliberate attempt to make the distribution of wealth more even across the population, in order to consolidate a middle class that will bring stability to the country and temper perceptions of injustice that might cause social unrest.

Largest military budgets in 2016

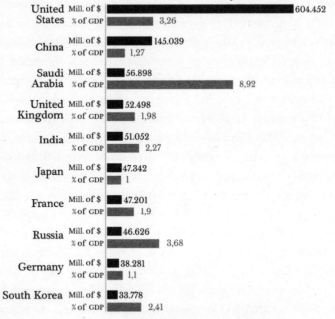

According to International Institute for Strategic Studies, *Military Balance 2017*

United States	Mill. of $	604.452
	% of GDP	3,26
China	Mill. of $	145.039
	% of GDP	1,27
Saudi Arabia	Mill. of $	56.898
	% of GDP	8,92
United Kingdom	Mill. of $	52.498
	% of GDP	1,98
India	Mill. of $	51.052
	% of GDP	2,27
Japan	Mill. of $	47.342
	% of GDP	1
France	Mill. of $	47.201
	% of GDP	1,9
Russia	Mill. of $	46.626
	% of GDP	3,68
Germany	Mill. of $	38.281
	% of GDP	1,1
South Korea	Mill. of $	33.778
	% of GDP	2,41

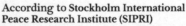

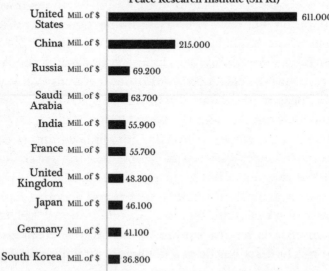

According to Stockholm International Peace Research Institute (SIPRI)

United States	Mill. of $	611.000
China	Mill. of $	215.000
Russia	Mill. of $	69.200
Saudi Arabia	Mill. of $	63.700
India	Mill. of $	55.900
France	Mill. of $	55.700
United Kingdom	Mill. of $	48.300
Japan	Mill. of $	46.100
Germany	Mill. of $	41.100
South Korea	Mill. of $	36.800

It could be that China has adopted a strategy whereby it can act as a world superpower without having to assume the accompanying responsibilities. One of the major current global geopolitical concerns is whether China's awakening will be peaceful or aggressive. In March 2014, Xi Jinping compared China to a lion stirring, albeit one that is 'peaceful, friendly and civilised',[9] but it is suspected of hiding its true intentions behind the smokescreen of its development.

Wherever the truth may lie, China is a good example of the feign and conceal strategy, as befits a country with a long and rich history and a culture of astuteness and patience. As Erasmus said, by way of Euripides, 'The wise man has two tongues, one to speak the truth with, the other for saying what he thinks fits the occasion.' That wisdom seems to apply to modern China's geopolitical strategy.

WHAT THE TRUTH HIDES

Many international military interventions have involved true intentions being hidden behind humanitarian or ecological concerns, or concerns about a fabricated 'enemy'. The invasion of Iraq was justified by the supposed existence of weapons of mass destruction. What was it really about? Control of oil. When limits and quotas on the production of certain materials, or the freezing of assets, are imposed on a state, this can be a tactic designed to stall its economic growth, and the placing of special tariffs on products can be done to protect the economy of a competitor. The 'war on terror' declared by George W. Bush in 2001 sought to create a supposed common global enemy: 'international' terrorism, which remains inadequate as a concept and is yet to be properly defined.

Any act of state intervention begs the question of what its true motivations are. Before any economic, military, ecological or humanitarian intervention takes place, we are presented with goals and reasons but, even when there is some truth to them, that is often not the whole story. The real reasons will also fit the political, economic and geopolitical agenda of the intervening country, an agenda that is unlikely to be noble.

Rule 6

THE BREAKING POINT

How to find and exploit an enemy's greatest weakness

'Supreme excellence consists in breaking
the enemy's resistance without fighting'

— Sun Tzu

Every people, nation or empire has experienced internal weaknesses and power struggles that outside adversaries have sought to take advantage of. Nationalist or separatist tendencies, social differences or radical movements, adequately manipulated from the shadows, can become an Achilles heel that a rival can push to breaking point.

The Chinese strategists Liang and Xiangsui speak of the importance of locating and targeting an enemy's weakness, and of how this can destabilise even the strongest power. A breaking point can be reached through guerrilla activism, terrorism or warfare. In all of these methods, the focal point of attack should be whatever is liable to cause the adversary the greatest psychological damage. In an era in which some Western countries are having to confront jihadi terrorism, it is worth recalling the words of the military strategist Pierre Servent, who said that although terrorists may be nebulous, they will always target civilians and public opinion, for these are the weak spots in democratic societies.

The United States Capitalises on Spanish Weakness

No matter how powerful and invincible they might seem, every superpower has a breaking point, which might become apparent at any time. One example of this is the Spanish–American War of 1898. At the Berlin Conference of 1884–5, the major European powers shared out African territories between themselves to take as colonies, as they had already done in Asia. Meanwhile, the USA, not having been party to these arrangements, began its own expansionist charge by focusing on the Caribbean. Several US presidents made offers to buy Cuba, which was attractive due to its strategic, agricultural and economic worth, but Spain always turned them down. The Glorious Revolution in Spain in 1868 had seen the birth of a nationalist movement in Cuba, which grew with the emergence of a Cuban middle class and was intensified by political and commercial frustrations over the restrictions imposed by Madrid. Periodic uprisings followed, the most significant being the Ten Years War (1868–78), the Little War (1879–80) and the War of Independence (1895–8). These were accompanied by media campaigns from Washington, which depicted the Cuban revolutionaries as freedom fighters, and from Madrid, which depicted the US government as intent on annexing the island despite having no connection to it.

In 1898, Washington used the need to protect the interests of US citizens living in Cuba as an excuse for intervention and sent a battleship to the island. When it was sunk following an explosion in Havana's harbour, the Spanish–American War began, a conflict that would end in victory for the USA and send the Spanish Empire into interminable decline. Spain lost Cuba, Puerto Rico and the Philippines in what became known in Spain as 'the Disaster of '98'.

Washington was able to exploit Spanish vulnerability at a time when it was experiencing a political and financial crisis following the Glorious Revolution that had deposed Queen Isabella. The US also stoked up nationalist feeling in Cuba to further weaken its relationship with its metropole. In this way the White House achieved its ultimate aim of exerting influence over the island.

GERMANY SENDS LENIN TO RUSSIA

The 'breaking point' tactic is often applied in conjunction with the strategy of 'sowing seeds of discord', which entails aggravating political, social and religious rivalries within a country. This is what Germany did to Russia during the First World War. Kaiser Wilhelm II's regime had for some time been trying to weaken its opponents through internal destabilisation, offering support to independence movements in Ireland, India, Egypt and Morocco. Russia, a state that was strategically critical to Germany achieving victory in the Great War, required a different tactic. Germany's troops were divided at the time between the western and eastern fronts. When the United States entered the conflict in 1917 in support of the British, Germany needed to withdraw forces from the east to strengthen the French border. In Russia, Tsar Nicholas II had been forced to abdicate in March 1917 by the bourgeoisie, but that hadn't stopped the Russians from continuing the war with Germany. Lenin had been exiled in Switzerland for over ten years, but the Kaiser thought a Russian government led by such a revolutionary would be more inclined to surrender. Germany made a pact with Lenin assuring him safe passage into Russian territory. The mere presence of Lenin in St Petersburg in April 1917 served to kick-start the socialist movement, which in less than a year took hold of the entire country, and pulled Russia out of the war.

Although the scheme did not result in Germany winning the war, it illustrates a successful deployment of a breaking-point strategy. Germany had been following the advice of the Prussian strategist Carl von Clausewitz, who said, 'Russia is not a country that can be conquered, that is to say truly occupied … A country like that can only be defeated by its own weakness, and through acts of internal discord.'

THE US ENTRY INTO THE SECOND WORLD WAR

During the Second World War, Washington reached the conclusion that it would have to fight against Germany in order to protect its own interests. If Hitler won the war and formed a united Europe, to which Russia's resources might even be added, it would only be a matter of time before that new Europe set its sights on the USA, both as an economic competitor and as a potential military adversary. It was understood that Hitler had already drafted plans to conquer the Americas once Europe was under control and the energy reserves of Asia and Europe had been secured, beginning with an invasion of South America. The White House could not allow such a prospect to develop, but chose not to intervene in the war until Europe had sufficiently weakened itself through the conflict, to ensure that no single European country emerged as a threat to American interests and that Europe would have no choice but to accept US offers of help. Once again, the major power of the day had successfully reshuffled the pack, keeping the best cards for itself.

VULNERABLE CENTRES OF GEOPOLITICAL GRAVITY

All states have centres of gravity: focal points that are so vital that they can bring everything crashing down if meddled with. According to political scientist Zbigniew Brzezinski, US global supremacy is directly dependent on how long and how effectively Washington can maintain its dominance over Europe and Asia. His theory is that Eurasia is the axis of global geopolitics: whichever power rules it controls two of the three most advanced and economically productive regions on Earth, and thereby rules the world.

As with individuals and families, every society has a weak point that can be exploited by adversaries to bring about its downfall. The best defence against this is to identify your breaking point yourself. By being aware of your own vulnerability, you can seek to hide it and protect it from others.

Rule 7

DIVIDE AND RULE

How to weaken your enemies by spreading disharmony

'Although an enemy army has many troops, an expert can divide them, so that they cannot help each other when attacked'

– SUN BIN

Breaking up existing power structures and stopping smaller entities from uniting is a strategy that dates back to at least the Roman Empire. It is summed up in Julius Caesar's maxim of 'divide and rule', and the strategy is the subject of considerable academic study, with most findings recognising its effectiveness.

During the First World War, Britain created an Arab revolt to defeat the Ottoman Empire, which was allied to Germany – it tipped the balance of the war in favour of the Allies. During the Second World War, Churchill did everything in his power to cause Russia to break its pact with Hitler and force the Russians to fight alongside the Allies. Later in the war, the major powers wished to avoid a strong Arab Muslim leadership, so encouraged rivalries between possible leaders. In India, the British Empire maintained regional borders between different ethnic groups, the better to provoke frictions and territorial disputes, preventing these groups from uniting to claim independence. When India did become independent after the war, the frictions remained, and British India ended up being divided into six states.

As a consequence of the Yom Kippur War (6–25 October 1973), the Arab members of the Organization of the Petroleum Exporting Countries placed an embargo on exports of oil to the USA and the Netherlands, and several countries nationalised their energy sectors. In seven years, the price of oil went from three dollars per barrel to thirty-five dollars. From then on, Washington began to stoke divisions between the members of OPEC in order to prevent further pacts that might raise the price of oil, of which the USA was the main global consumer.

As Olivier Entraygues writes in his analysis of the British general and strategist J.F.C. Fuller's writings, Great Britain has always been hostile to the idea of Europe being dominated by a single power. While not always seeking to crush its adversaries, Britain has repeatedly sought to reduce the power of emerging rivals so that balance is restored.

DIVIDING THE ARABS

On 15 June 1915, in order to take advantage of Arab discontent with Turkish rule, the British signed a secret agreement with Sharif Hussein bin Ali al-Hashimi, Emir of Mecca and Medina. Britain committed to the creation of an Arab state stretching from Syria to the Red Sea and the Gulf of Persia, and from Damascus to Mecca, in exchange for Arab help in defeating the Ottoman Empire; Hussein declared war on the Ottomans in June 1916, and proclaimed himself King of Hejaz five months later.

On 8 January 1918, US President Woodrow Wilson published his Fourteen Points, which would form the basis of peace negotiations between the Triple Entente and the Central Empire at the Treaty of Versailles. The twelfth point stated that the Arabs, along with other peoples previously subjected to Ottoman rule, 'should be assured an undoubted security of life and an absolutely unmolested opportunity of autonomous development'. However, when the Emir Faisal – named King of Syria by the British – put his arguments for Arab independence before the Paris Peace Conference in 1919, his speech met with a cool response. The Hashemite prince had believed he had the support of the Allied countries, having loyally served their cause, but his demands clashed with French ambitions in Syria.

Considering the vast territories that Sir Henry McMahon, the British High Commissioner in Cairo, had promised Faisal's father Sharif Hussein, the son's demands were modest – he merely sought immediate and total independence for the Arab Kingdom of Greater Syria (today's Syria, Lebanon, Jordan, Israel and the Palestinian National Authority) and Hejaz, in exchange for which he would accept foreign mediation in Palestine and recognise British claims for control of Mesopotamia.

In the event, Faisal was proclaimed King of the Arab Kingdom of Greater Syria by the Syrian National Congress, only to be ousted by the French a few months later. Sharif Hussein, who had kept all the letters he'd exchanged with McMahon, knew Britain had broken its promises. But worse was to follow, for at the same time as negotiating with Hussein, London also signed a treaty with Central Arabia, headed by Abdulaziz Al Saúd, also known as Ibn Saud, in which Britain agreed to pay him a considerable sum of money each month. Once the war for Arab unification was over in 1932, having resulted in half a million deaths and twice as many displaced people, Saud seized the holy places of Mecca and Medina and created today's Saudi Arabia. Prior to that, the British had plotted to prevent the Saudis from unifying the whole of the Arab peninsula by restricting access to the Indian Ocean from the Persian Gulf as much as they could. The whole exercise was a sham arranged to allow Britain and France to take control of certain territories that contained some of the largest and most profitable hydrocarbon reserves in the world. The self-declared Islamic State, which proclaimed itself a caliphate in June 2014, has recently sought to establish the great Arab state that was foiled by the Sykes–Picot Agreement of 1916,[10] when London, Paris and Washington refused to allow the establishment of this state.

A similar example of deceit occurred in San Remo in April 1920, when France, Great Britain and Italy reached various agreements whereby they not only shared out the spoils of the fallen Ottoman Empire, but also divided up eastern Anatolia between the Armenians and the Kurds. The Kurds were afforded a territory to the south of the Armenian area, centred on the city of Diyarbakır, with complete independence from the Ottoman Empire and the opportunity to create their own state. However, their hopes were dashed when Turkey made Mustafa Kemal Atatürk its first president in 1923; one of his first decisions was to revoke this Kurdish right. The European powers that had made the promise made no attempt to intervene.

LIBYA DIVIDED

In an article concerned with the thousands of emails from Hillary Clinton that were leaked to the press during her 2016 US presidential campaign, Brad Hoff considers the reasons for the American

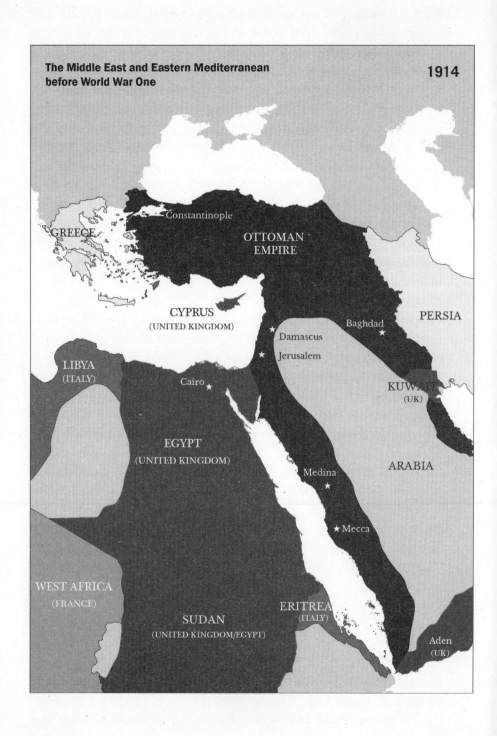

The Middle East and Eastern Mediterranean before World War One

1914

GREECE

Constantinople

OTTOMAN EMPIRE

PERSIA

CYPRUS
(UNITED KINGDOM)

Baghdad

Damascus

Jerusalem

LIBYA
(ITALY)

Cairo

KUWAIT
(UK)

EGYPT
(UNITED KINGDOM)

ARABIA

Medina

Mecca

WEST AFRICA
(FRANCE)

ERITREA
(ITALY)

SUDAN
(UNITED KINGDOM/EGYPT)

Aden
(UK)

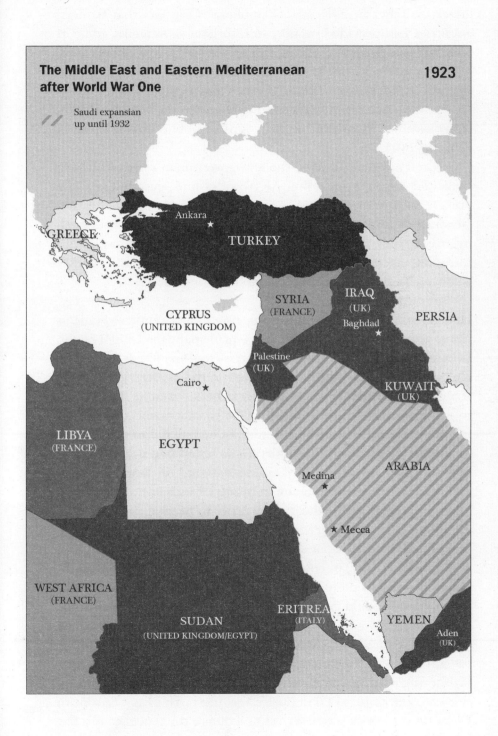

The Middle East and Eastern Mediterranean
after World War One

1923

Saudi expansian
up until 1932

GREECE

TURKEY

Ankara

CYPRUS
(UNITED KINGDOM)

SYRIA
(FRANCE)

IRAQ
(UK)
Baghdad

PERSIA

Palestine
(UK)

KUWAIT
(UK)

LIBYA
(FRANCE)

Cairo

EGYPT

Medina

ARABIA

★ Mecca

WEST AFRICA
(FRANCE)

SUDAN
(UNITED KINGDOM/EGYPT)

ERITREA
(ITALY)

YEMEN

Aden
(UK)

attack on Libya in 2011.[11] Hoff emphasises the fact that Western countries had provided support to insurgent movements, some of which are suspected of having ties to al-Qaeda, just as they have done elsewhere in the Middle East. In the case of Libya, special operations forces from Britain, France and Egypt trained militias on the border between Libya and Egypt and in the suburbs of Benghazi within a month of the first signs of public protest there in February 2011.

Foreign forces supplied the anti-government rebels with weapons and supplies, including AK-47 rifles and ammunition. The French newspaper *Libération* reported in 2011 that the Direction Générale de la Sécurité Extérieure (DGSE), France's external intelligence agency, had dropped parachutes laden with weaponry including machine guns, assault rifles, hand grenades and MILAN anti-tank guided missiles, to Gaddafi's opponents.

How do you divide and rule in the twenty-first century? François Thual argues that the major powers – principally the United States, Great Britain and France – and the largest multinationals (which are also among the major economic powers in the modern world) have compartmentalised the world in order to better exercise their power, to maximise profit and control access to raw materials. According to the French strategist, it would not be fanciful to suggest that in another generation's time, thirty or so brand new states will have been born in the name of asserting national or denominational identities. The current situation in countries such as Iraq, Syria and Libya suggests that this theory may prove to be true, and the same situation could even apply to large European countries, where the centrifugal forces of separatism are growing ever stronger.

Robert D. Kaplan considers that the more united Europe is, the more tension there will be with Washington. The only way in which Europe could currently become a serious competitor to the United States would be by forming what Churchill once called a 'United States of Europe', implementing a genuinely unified foreign policy and a potent common security and defence policy, with a single army and a unified intelligence service. The closest this has ever come to taking place was the birth of the European Constitution, which was never ratified due to the reticence of a few powerful countries such as France. At present, the United Kingdom is on course to leave the EU and there are also mounting tensions over the issue of refugees, which has left the idea of a United States of Europe feeling increasingly like a pipe dream.

In Kaplan's view, the United States will never allow Europe to be truly united, as that would put Washington at a major geopolitical and economic disadvantage. Nevertheless, it remains to be seen how this situation will develop in the future, given that Europe has always been the White House's ally and that a weak Europe would be of little use to Washington at a time when it is facing new and particular challenges. In a globalised world, in which threats to international peace and security can only be tackled collectively, the United States must keep its allies on side. Europe, too, is aware that each member state should not carry too much weight individually in the international community. In order to further their own interests, countries are better off remaining united. One threat to this is the situation often dubbed 'two-speed' Europe, whereby a small block of countries would pursue tighter integration between themselves, leaving other EU members behind. If this comes to pass, it would be a further obstacle to a genuinely united Europe.

If you can't eliminate all your enemies at once, you must eliminate them one by one. Dividing them is a logical place to start, and it has proven a highly effective geopolitical strategy. However, sometimes attempts to foster disharmony can have the opposite effect, uniting your enemies rather than dividing them. The Greek historian Xenophon in the fifth to sixth centuries BC advised that 'a leader displeasing all his subordinates at the same time seems a grave error to me, for spreading terror among so many will inevitably earn him enemies, and displeasing everyone at once will inevitably see them unite in a conspiracy against him'.

THE BALANCE OF POWER

Dominant powers have long sought to maintain the balance of power wherever they have strategic interests; preventing any one country from gaining in strength minimises the chance of having to deal with a competitor. One of Britain's primary motivations in the two world wars, for example, was making sure no one nation came to rule over the whole continent, and London has always been prepared to help weaker countries fight potentially dominant forces in Europe.

In the Middle East, the Obama administration allowed Shia-majority Iran to gain influence over Iraq, Syria, Lebanon, Yemen and Bahrain, which caused alarm among Sunni-majority countries in the region, as well as in Israel. It is likely the Trump administration will seek to rebalance power in the region, though this will be hard to achieve through peaceful means. Knowing how the great powers operate, it would not be fanciful to suggest that Trump is merely carrying on the game Obama started. Having allowed Iran and Shia Islam to strengthen in the Middle East, Washington will now turn against them, thus ensuring confrontation in the region. As long as the Arab and Muslim world remains disunited it cannot control the entire oil market and the region's choke points; this has been one of the key geostrategies of the Western powers in this part of the world for the past century. As George Friedman points out, regional power struggles that consume energies and distract countries from confronting the USA are in Washington's interests.

According to Thual, Germany employs a curious geopolitical strategy in seeking to control Eastern Europe in order to prevent a Russian resurgence. It therefore keeps a close watch on the Baltics, Central Europe and the Balkans, and tries to ensure that Serbia is kept away from the Adriatic coast. The Germans have also tried to maintain good relations with Turkey to ensure access to the Black Sea.

Fareed Zakaria offers some basic rules that explain how countries achieve balanced power dynamics; although they refer to Europe they can be applied universally. One strategy is that of Britain, which acts as a counterweight to emerging powers. Another is that of Bismarck, who engaged with all the powers to ensure Germany had a better relationship with each of them than they had with each other. For his part, Kissinger believed there are two kinds of threat to established power balances: when an important country increases its might to the extent that it threatens to become a hegemony (as could be the case with Russia); and when a state of secondary standing wishes to join the top tier and demands adjustments to allow for a new power dynamic (China and India would currently be the closest examples of this). According to this theory, a rebalancing of power is currently taking place, with a hegemonic power (the USA), a weakened Europe and a handful of other powers, such as China, India and Russia, keen to increase their influence over the rest of the world. In theory, common and interdependent interests should prevent tensions from exploding, but history would teach us that it is only a matter of time before changing power dynamics raise the spectre of war.

Rule 8

PUPPETMASTERY

How to wield power through indirect influence and action

'The world is governed by very different personages from what is imagined by those who are not behind the scenes'

– BENJAMIN DISRAELI

'Indirect rule' refers to the way in which major powers use their might to defend their interests without appearing to impose their will – the means by which powerful countries have dominated less developed countries through culture and economics has come to be known as 'neocolonialism'. According to historian Michael Coffey, in the aftermath of the Second World War, Soviet Minister for Foreign Affairs Vyacheslav Molotov saw the Marshall Plan, the US initiative to help Europe recover, as a pretext for Anglo-American domination of the continent. He was right insofar as it was as much a means of ensuring that Washington could count on Europe as an ally as it was about rebuilding the continent.

The subtle implications of indirect rule play a huge role on the international stage. Whenever a direct approach proves ineffective, indirect strategies come into play. As Brzezinski points out, Washington's global influence is to a large extent based on its indirect support of foreign elites, which end up becoming dependent on it. The US government is a particularly skilled indirect ruler. To ensure that its energy needs and strategic interests prevail, Washington applies the classic pressures of imperialism, while at the same time employing an array of less direct tactics that range from exerting economic influence to establishing a military or security presence. These tactics are cloaked in a series of mantras, relating to the conservation of landscapes and biodiversity, sustainable development, democracy, good government or the promotion of human rights.

According to Lorot and Thual, low-intensity conflicts are routinely used by major powers to strengthen their hold over weaker countries. Strategist George Friedman points out that the Saudi royal family and other Gulf monarchies continue to control Arab oil because the White House prefers it that way – as 'weak' and unpopular institutions, they will always be dependent on US support.

Amin Maalouf says, 'modernisation becomes suspect as soon as it is perceived as a Trojan Horse introduced by another culture that is both alien and overbearing'. He adds that many people 'see globalisation as synonymous with Americanisation', an idea that relates to 'McDonaldisation', a term coined by the sociologist George Ritzer.[12] Though not intended as an overt criticism of McDonald's, Ritzer uses the US fast-food chain as an example of a tendency in modern society to want things that are immediate, identical and available at any time.

China also makes use of indirect rule; Liang and Xiangsui offer an interesting perspective in their argument that 'Chinese cultural strategy favours the indirect rule strategy, much as it seeks to subjugate the enemy or achieve victory without combat.' Indirect rule must be carried out without arousing suspicion; Marenches highlights the cunning in infiltrating the other party's thinking to such a degree that they believe themselves to be the architect of a course of action that you have nudged them to take.

INDIRECT RULE THROUGH ART AND CULTURE

According to its Bureau of Economic Analysis, the arts and culture sector in the United States has been expanding steadily since 1999. It has grown by 3 per cent every year since 2012, contributing over 700 billion dollars annually to the US economy, almost 4.5 per cent of its GDP. Arts and culture is also the second largest sector in terms of exports; it includes the performing arts, information services, architecture, advertising and the fine arts, but filmmaking is by some margin its largest area. According to the European Audiovisual Observatory, the global market for motion pictures is structured in such a way that US productions command a 70 per cent share, with the EU accounting for 26.2 per cent and the rest of the world the remaining 3.8 per cent.

An industry that dominates the global market and spends billions every year on making films, as well as exporting stories, is spreading American values around the world; models of justice, education, government and consumption. Hollywood exports a vision of the world, in which the identity of goodies and baddies is unambiguous. During the Cold War, film villains tended to be Soviets, but now they are terrorists.

The Pentagon has long played a significant part in US film production. In 1927, production of the silent film *Wings*, in which Gary Cooper has a minor role, was assisted by the US Army in its recreation of First World War airborne battle scenes. When the US entered the Second World War, the collaboration became closer, with films serving as propaganda to encourage Americans to enlist and to sway public opinion in favour of war.

The collaboration did not end in 1945; four years later, the Pentagon produced an instruction manual for cooperation between the entertainment industry and the US armed forces. According to the guidelines, if a production met certain criteria, it would be given free access to army bases and offered assistance and resources, such as tanks, helicopters, submarines, aircraft carriers and the use of soldiers for extras. All film producers had to do was fulfil the requisites, which included a stipulation that scripts contributed a positive image of the armed forces, helping with recruitment and retention of personnel, and that it tallied with US government policy. Producers were free to choose whether to accept these conditions or not, but it was nevertheless a veiled way of subsidising a certain type of filmmaking that promoted a certain discourse.

In early July 2017, Tom Secker and Matthew Alford published an article on the Insurge Intelligence webpage[13] in which they concluded that the US military and intelligence agencies had been influential in 800 successful films and over a thousand television programmes. Making use of the Freedom of Information Act, Secker and Alford studied thousands of pages of Pentagon and CIA documents that showed how, over the years, the US government manipulated plots and prevented films that were critical of the military or the secret services from being made. The military has had a hand in some of the most popular films of recent times and as a matter of policy will refuse to provide support, and will even seek to change the script of, any film dealing with the Vietnam War, the Iran–Contra affair or suicide within the armed services.

Hollywood thus serves as a propaganda machine for US national security interests, fostering a mentality that is agreeable to war in a society that is already supportive of the use of military force abroad.

RULE BY FEAR

Another form of indirect control is rule by fear, in which terror of a supposed threat is instilled in a population. Though the threat may be real, it is magnified to such an extent that people voluntarily submit to the will of those manipulating them; the perfect execution of this strategy will have people not only accepting whatever restrictions are imposed on them but actually requesting them.

Social psychologist Philip Zimbardo is in no doubt that fear is the best psychological weapon a state possesses for manipulating its people – its use can see citizens willingly sacrifice fundamental freedoms in exchange for governmental promises of security. According to Zimbardo, the Bush administration began the war on terror following the 9/11 terrorist attacks in order to tackle the perceived threat to its national security. Zimbardo further suggests that fear has formed the ideological basis of practically every attempt by a government to seek popular or military approval for campaigns of aggression or repression, and can be used to justify torture and executions, as happened during the dictatorships of the 1960s and 1970s in Brazil, Greece and elsewhere.

Fear also compels societies to look more favourably on increased military spending, which benefits the military industries that prop up the economies of numerous countries, not least the permanent members of the UN Security Council. According to *Jane's Defence Weekly*, in 2016 the world's leading arms exporters were the United States (23.3 billion dollars), Russia (6.3 billion), Germany (4.4 billion), France (4.3 billion), United Kingdom (4.2 billion), Israel (2.4 billion), Canada (2.0 billion) and China (1.4 billion).[14] These figures are incomplete – even in countries supposedly committed to open democracy it is relatively easy to disguise arms deals as logistics equipment, combat support or dual-use technologies – but they give a good indication and broadly tally with SIPRI data for the period between 2013 and 2017, when the US exported 34 per cent of the world's weapons, Russia 22 per cent, France 6.7 per cent, Germany 5.8 per cent, China 5.7 per cent and the UK 4.8 per cent.[15]

Since the end of the Second World War, the major powers have been careful to keep their military actions as distanced from their own borders as possible. As long as domestic populations are not exposed to the horrors of war they can be relied on to not oppose the mass manufacture of arms, which they are told are vital for their protection.

THE POWER OF LARGE GLOBAL PRESSURE GROUPS

An example of how large global pressure groups seek to influence public opinion and events around the world was put under the spotlight in August 2016 when 'hacktivist' website DCLeaks revealed 2,576 internal documents from George Soros's Open Society Foundations (OFS).[16] Soros is a financial speculator who now runs a global network of non-governmental organisations located in some forty different countries, funnelling money into a range of different organisations, from the American Democratic Party to pro-Palestinian groups and the Black Lives Matter movement. The massive leak of internal information showed, among other things, an involvement in the affairs of Ukraine, before, during and after the controversial change of government in Ukraine in 2014.

And yet, although the authenticity of the leaked documents has never been in doubt, the aims and origins of DCLeaks have been called into question. The group explicitly states on its website – which has subsequently been taken down – that it believes George Soros to have been the architect and promoter of almost every revolution and *coup d'état* to have taken place anywhere in the world in the last twenty-five years. Besides the stated aim of revealing Soros's alleged ploys to influence global politics and social affairs, the DCLeaks homepage claimed its objective was to provide access to the inner workings of the OSF and related organisations, exposing Soros's work schemes, strategies, priorities and other activities.

But perhaps the most contentious aspect of all this is who exactly is behind DCLeaks. While its website declared it to be a US concern made up of 'hacktivists', US intelligence and specialist cybersecurity companies consider it highly likely that the DCLeaks hackers are in fact operatives of the GRU, a Russian military intelligence agency. For many, though, Soros remains a controversial

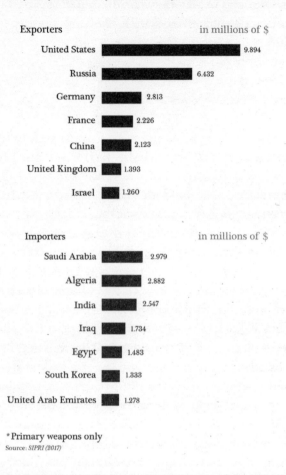

The principal arms* exporters and importers in 2016

Exporters — in millions of $

United States	9.894
Russia	6.432
Germany	2.813
France	2.226
China	2.123
United Kingdom	1.393
Israel	1.260

Importers — in millions of $

Saudi Arabia	2.979
Algeria	2.882
India	2.547
Iraq	1.734
Egypt	1.483
South Korea	1.333
United Arab Emirates	1.278

* Primary weapons only
Source: *SIPRI (2017)*

figure. Those on the right mistrust his anti-nationalist stance, and condemn his use of his vast wealth to promote progressive and liberal-minded movements all over the world.

On the other side of the political spectrum from George Soros is US billionaire Robert Mercer. He and his family were major donors to the Trump campaign in 2015–16, and are thought to have contributed a sum of around 36 million dollars to political activity in the lead up to this US election – including donations to political not-for-profits, which are not required to publish their donor list, but are allowed to be politically active.

Mercer was also the major investor in the shadowy data analytics firm Cambridge Analytica, which, in 2017, was exposed as having harvested the data of millions of Facebook users in order to target them on behalf of the Leave.EU campaign in the run up to the UK's EU referendum. The question is how far the interference of this data firm, controlled by a US billionaire, affected the outcome of a major political turning point in Europe.

Interference in electoral processes

In late December 2016, at a time when alleged interference by the Russian intelligence services in the US presidential elections was front-page news, journalist Shane Dixon Kavanaugh published an article on Vocotive.com that brought to light a study by the political analyst Dov Levin of the Institute for Politics and Strategy at Carnegie-Mellon University. It focused on repeated US attempts to influence the outcome of elections in other countries; after consulting a multitude of sources, including declassified US intelligence service documents, the memoirs of former CIA agents, congressional reports into intelligence service activities, diplomatic archives from the Cold War period and academic studies, Levin concluded that, between 1946 and 2000, the White House covertly interfered in eighty-one elections in forty-five countries, ranging from the Philippines in the 1950s to Nicaragua in the 1990s, when the CIA leaked information to undermine the Sandinistas. Furthermore, these numbers did not include Washington's numerous attempts to enforce regime change whenever a candidate opposed to their interests was elected. The initiatives were varied and adapted to suit the circumstances. They included spreading propaganda, providing support to preferred parties and candidates, offering financial backing or threatening to withdraw it from those already being supported.

Although the majority of these interventions in foreign electoral processes took place within the context of the Cold War in order to counteract Soviet influence on left-wing parties, Levin found that the US continued to meddle in elections long after 1991, including in the Russian elections in 1996. Moscow, of course, also has history in this practice; Levin concluded that the Russians tried to influence elections in other countries on thirty-six occasions between 1946 and 2000.

The last known case of this took place in May 2017, just before the second round of the French presidential election, when tens of thousands of emails from the centrist candidate Emmanuel Macron that had been stolen a few weeks earlier were revealed on social media. The aim of the leak was to undermine Macron to the benefit of his opponent, the far-right Marine Le Pen. This episode, which came to be called 'MacronLeaks', was credited to the Kremlin by some, while others thought it might have been a 'false flag' operation, carried out by Macron supporters with the intention that it would be attributed to Moscow in order to undermine Le Pen, who had the explicit support of the Kremlin.[17] Unlike the 2016 US presidential election campaign, during which leaked emails belonging to Hillary Clinton were judged to be authentic, the Macron leaks were said to be a mixture of genuine emails and fakes.

INDIRECT RULE THROUGH THE SPREAD OF DEMOCRACY

One of the most controversial organisations in the USA is the National Endowment for Democracy (NED). Created in 1983 during Ronald Reagan's presidency, its stated aim is to promote democracy throughout the world. During the Cold War, the United States financed a range of initiatives and organisations to advance human rights and political pluralism in the USSR. In its first years of existence, the NED focused its efforts on Poland and other countries in Eastern Europe. After George H. W. Bush became president in 1989, the NED widened its financial support further, for organisations in Armenia, Crimea and Lithuania.

Following whatever turn rivalries between Washington and Moscow took, the NED also engaged with political developments in the Americas. In 1984 it financed a candidate for the Panamanian presidency who was loyal to General Noriega and favoured by the CIA. In 1990 it sponsored the presidential campaign of right-winger Marc Bazin in Haiti. In the early 1990s it provided significant sums of money to the Cuban American National Foundation, which opposed Fidel Castro. The Venezuelan government has repeatedly denounced similar meddling in its affairs from the NED, accusing it of financing groups hostile to Hugo Chávez.

In much of the world, the NED carries out its mission by acting through other US entities that depend on it economically, including Freedom House, the National Democratic Institute for International Affairs and the International Republican Institute. The NED's detractors claim that, although it is technically a private entity, most of its funding comes from US Congress and that it is clearly a tool used by Washington to pursue US interests and geopolitical goals. Its most ardent critics are in no doubt that the NED and the organisations it funds have been used to sow seeds of discord in countries that follow policies disapproved of by the White House. The NED has provided financial and logistical support to media outlets, political parties, trade unions and civic organisations opposed to governments in power; in other words, it has been doing what the CIA is often accused of, but in a more transparent fashion.

Rule 9

LAWFARE

How the law is used to justify acts of war

'There is no greater tyranny than that which is exercised within the shade of the law and with the colours of justice'

— MONTESQUIEU

In the nineteenth century, Bismarck said that all governments determine their actions purely according to their own interests, though they dress them up with legal considerations. In 1975, Australian professors John Carlson and Neville Yeomans coined the term 'lawfare' to describe a transition from a war with weapons to a war with words. This expression achieved a degree of notoriety in 2001 thanks to an essay by Charles J. Dunlap,[18] who defines 'lawfare' as the use of law as a weapon of war. A general in the US Judicial Corps, he was referring to the Taliban's manipulation of international law, but he also shone a light on a tactic that has been employed for centuries. In any conflict, both sides have always sought to justify the war, be it from a religious, moral or judicial perspective.

EVOLUTION AND APPLICATION

In 2011, NATO acted in Libya under a United Nations mandate that invoked the principle of the 'responsibility to protect', ahead of a supposed imminent attack on the civil population of Benghazi. The application of this mandate, the sole aim of which was the protection of civilians, was used to support the Libyan rebels and ended up causing a change of government. Gaddafi's regime was undoubtedly violating the human rights of its citizens, but oil interests were also at play. Prior to the outbreak of civil war, Libya produced almost 1.6 million barrels per day, 2 per cent of global production, and European oil companies had significant interests in the country.

Why intervene in certain conflicts and not in others? What legitimises an intervention? Lawfare is less about George W. Bush's ill-defined 'war on terror' than it is the hiding behind internationally accepted legal principles in order to achieve geopolitical and geoeconomic aims. It allows states to distort the law to protect themselves and legitimise their actions.

Countries have long sought to establish agreed principles to justify going to war. Cicero maintained that the legitimacy of confrontation was dependent on concepts of morality, which planted the germ of the idea of the 'just war'. Similar theories were explored in the medieval period by Christian thinkers including Augustine of Hippo, Thomas Aquinas, Francisco de Vitoria, Francisco Suárez and Hugo Grotius, who sought to develop criteria for determining when declaring war was legitimate and to establish certain limits in practising it. Attempts legally to formalise the use of force led, in the nineteenth and twentieth centuries, to the creating of international law and the idea of the United Nations.

With the arrival of the concept of states the principle of morality gave way to one of sovereignty, which in turn gave rise to two further principles: state independence and non-interference in the internal affairs of other states. According to the concept of the just war, these principles can only be overridden in order to protect populations from violations committed by their own government. Historically, such interventions had generally sought to defend non-nationals abroad; in the nineteenth century, a prerequisite for the international community to recognise the sovereignty of a state was its ability to guarantee internal order and protect the lives and property of foreign nationals there. Between 1813 and 1927, the US took military action to protect US citizens abroad on at least seventy occasions. Other notable cases were the Boxer Rebellion in China (1899–1901) and the Congo Crisis (1964), when a coalition of states intervened to protect foreign nationals from various countries.

In the twenty-first century, another 'principle' has emerged alongside self-defence and self-preservation: the responsibility to protect. At first glance, there might seem to be nothing objectionable in seeking to protect those who are being persecuted by their own governments, but the problem is that responsibility to protect is hard to define. As Kissinger said, concepts of democracy, human rights and international law are so open to interpretation that both sides in a conflict can happily fling them at each other like battle cries.

Humanitarian intervention is closely connected to the idea of the responsibility of sovereignty. If a state cannot or will not protect its own people, or is itself the perpetrator of mass and systematic violence and human rights abuses, the responsibility to protect defaults to the United Nations, legitimised to intervene in the affairs of states. But while it is the duty of the United Nations to maintain world peace and international security, it is its Security Council that decides what constitutes a threat to international security. The major criticism of the doctrine is that it is impossible to apply objectively. The five permanent members of the UN Security Council, who have a right to veto, can decide where and how to defend human rights in other states, but their decision is inevitably dependent on their own geopolitical and economic interests, and this is when the lawfare strategy comes into play. The use of this strategy causes military interventions that are aimed at gaining or maintaining influence and power in a particular place to be championed. Such proposals generate intense debate at the UN, because acting in the name of one grandiose principle to the detriment of another is somewhat arbitrary, to say the least.

Libya was the first country where the responsibility to protect was invoked with the approval of Resolution 1973 of the Security Council, with ten votes in favour and five abstentions (including from Russia and China). However, the resolution was so clearly misinterpreted that the whole principle doctrine was called into question. The distortion was such that, during a conference in June 2017 at the Diplomatic School in Madrid, the Moroccan judge Mohamed Bennouna, one of fifteen magistrates on the International Justice Tribunal, said that 'the concept of responsibility to protect died in 2011 when we went to Libya in the name of the security of its population, to kill Gaddafi'.[19]

Why has the principle not been invoked in Syria? The conflict is different, but the waves of refugees attest to the fact that the civilian population is not being safeguarded but is rather being exposed to systematic attacks on cities, hospitals and refugee camps. However, this case makes it evident that the responsibility to protect is not a principle used objectively by the UN Security Council to protect civilian populations from human rights violations. Russia has

139

economic interests and strong geopolitical commitments in Syria, which it does not want to lose to the US or Europe. Meanwhile, Iran considers the Syrian leader, Bashar al-Assad, to be its only Arab ally in the region. Having a good relationship with Syria enables Tehran to be in contact with Hezbollah in Lebanon, through which it can threaten Israel. On the other side is the United States, intent on halting the advance of Islamic State. Turkey has interests in Syria too, as does Israel, as well as France and Great Britain, the 'creators' of this part of the world who divided it up after the First World War. Needless to say, though all sides might say they are fighting terrorist groups, the one thing they are not doing is showing any responsibility to protect civilian populations.

According to the Global Centre for the Responsibility to Protect,[20] at the time of writing, crimes on a massive scale are taking place in Syria, Sudan, Myanmar, North Korea, Iraq, Yemen and Eritrea, and urgent action is required. In South Sudan, the situation is critical and it is predicted that massacres and atrocities will almost certainly take place unless they are prevented. The risk of crimes being committed against the civilian population is also high in the Democratic Republic of the Congo, Israel and the Occupied Palestinian Territories, Nigeria, Central African Republic, Burundi and the Philippines, but such places do not concern the mainstream media or prompt the UN Security Council to invoke its responsibility to protect.

It is not just the misuse of the responsibility to protect in Libya and a lack of legislative clarity that undermine the doctrine, but also the fact that its deployment is so dependent on the will of states, which use it exclusively to defend their own positions. Principles that should be immovable pillars that relate to the sanctity of human life are in reality subject to double standards and employed as just another way of protecting national interests.

Of course, once war breaks out, the law plays second fiddle. As soon as hostilities commence, countries have only one objective in mind: winning the war. The past has taught them that the winners can write a version of history that will be kind to them. With this in mind, they have no hesitation in employing any means they deem to be effective, even if they have to violate the international laws they have signed and ratified.

It is worth recalling the response of the Roman militarist and politician Gaius Marius when he was reproached for defying Roman law to award citizenship to barbarian merchants who had fought under him against Gaul: he said, 'The law speaks too softly to be heard in such a noise of war.'

THE HYPOCRISY OF THE UNITED NATIONS

The United Nations Charter, signed on 26 June 1945, states the aim of developing friendly relations among nations, based on respect for the principle of equal rights (article 1) and on the principle of the sovereign equality of all its members (article 2). But if one thing is true about the UN, it is that it does not operate according to democratic principles: there can be no equality among members as long as permanent members of the Security Council exist and are afforded the powerful privilege of the right to veto. They use it whenever their national interests, or even those of their allies, might be affected. According to the Belgian historian Jacques de Launay, the right to veto exists because when the United States proposed the clause during the Yalta Conference, Churchill thought it sounded like a good way of protecting the interests of the British Empire and the Soviet Union saw it as a trump card that it might continually abuse.

In October 2016, the Gambia announced its withdrawal from the International Criminal Court (ICC), headquartered in The Hague, becoming the third African nation to do so in the space of a week, after South Africa[21] and Burundi. All three gave the same reason: that the ICC is focused on, or at least prioritises, the prosecution of Africans. They went so far as to label it 'the International Caucasian Court' and to accuse it of pursuing a neocolonial agenda. The Gambian Minister of Information, Sheriff Bojang, said, 'There are many Western countries, at least thirty, that have committed heinous war crimes against independent sovereign states and their citizens since the creation of the ICC, and not a single Western war criminal has been indicted.'

The ICC has certainly not been without controversy since it was created as a United Nations initiative on 17 July 1998. As an independent judiciary outside the structure of the UN, the ICC theoretically marked a major advance in the universal protection of human rights, with the court afforded responsibility for judging crimes against humanity and war crimes, such as genocide.

Those who argue that the ICC has been overly inclined to judge African affairs while ignoring atrocities committed in other parts of the world have plenty of evidence to back up their claims. On 4 March 2009, the ICC ordered the arrest of the President of Sudan, Omar al-Bashir, for five crimes against humanity and two war crimes, as a consequence of acts perpetrated by his Sudanese government against the civilian population of Darfur between 2003 and 2008. The next head of state issued with an ICC arrest warrant was Gaddafi in Libya; his case was closed upon his death in 2011. Thomas Lubanga Dyilo, leader of the Union of Congolese Patriots, was sentenced by the ICC on 10 July 2012 to 14 years in prison for war crimes and enlisting child soldiers in the region of Ituri between 2002 and 2003. Imprisoned alongside him in the ICC's detention facilities was Charles Taylor, President of Liberia between 1997 and 2003 and sentenced to fifty years imprisonment in May 2012 by the Special Court for Sierra Leone.

The fact that some of the most powerful and influential countries in the world, such as the USA, China, Russia and Israel, have not signed or ratified the Rome Statute that led to the creation of the ICC is a major issue. The fact that these countries are unwilling to subject themselves to an international judiciary is considered by many to be a prime example of the idea that international laws apply only to the weak. The weak know that when it comes down to it, powerful nations will never accept being judged by an international organism, even if they themselves clamoured for its creation and are among its most distinguished members.

Article 126 of the Rome Statute explains that the ICC only applies to states that sign and ratify it, meaning that it has no jurisdiction over any country that has not done so. In the specific case of Russia, on 16 November 2016, President Putin announced his decision to revoke his country's signing of the Rome Statute – performed in 2000, though never ratified – apparently motivated by an ICC communication that judged the Crimea to be a territory under Russian occupation.

The weak do not lack reasons to criticise the powerful. On 2 August 2002 the US Congress, showing absolute disregard for international law, approved the American Service-Members' Protection Act, which forbade any US entity from collaborating with the ICC, preventing the court from carrying out investigations on US soil, and denied US military assistance to the ICC. As if that were not enough, the Act expressly authorised the president's use of 'all means necessary and appropriate to bring about the release of certain US and allied persons who may be detained or tried by the ICC'. Unsurprisingly, this law was deemed to be completely at odds with the founding principles of the ICC. Suffice to say, in November 2016 when the ICC public prosecution office said it had strong reason to believe US troops deployed in Afghanistan had been involved in war crimes, specifically acts of torture and other mistreatments of prisoners held in secret internment camps, there were no repercussions. In the end, Spanish politician Manuel Fraga may have been right when he said 'the search for perfect social order has always provided justification for the worst abuses'.

THE MANIPULATION OF DEMOCRACY

In ancient Greece, public speaking, as the means by which leaders attracted the support they needed to endorse their activities, was a major part of the democratic process. Political satirists would subsequently pick their speeches apart, much as the media provides political commentary today. During the Cold War, the Soviet Union encouraged movements that opposed colonialism, dictatorships and right-wing governments and sponsored the establishment of populist democracies with the geopolitical aim of spreading Soviet ideology. The whole process was merely a different form of imperialism, in this case one supported and justified by an ideology. According to historian Barbara W. Tuchman, the Soviet leader Nikita Khrushchev proclaimed that 'wars of liberation' would be the vehicle by which the communist cause would be advanced, and declared that these 'just wars', regardless of where they took place, would have the full support of the USSR.

It is important to remember that during the Cold War the White House differentiated between left-wing dictatorships, which were bad, and right-wing ones, which were good, or at least tolerable. The highly influential Kirkpatrick Doctrine, drafted and passionately defended by Jeane Kirkpatrick, the US Ambassador to the United Nations under Ronald Reagan, drew a curious distinction between regimes in pro-Soviet countries, which were considered 'totalitarian', and those in pro-Western countries, which were defined as 'authoritarian'. Kirkpatrick claimed that the former not only had a greater propensity to exert influence on their neighbours, but that they also controlled the thoughts of their own populations through propaganda, espionage and political repression. In contrast, authoritarian dictatorships limited themselves to controlling, orientating and punishing people's conduct without seeking to control their traditions, such as religion and the family. Other high-ranking Americans, including Vernon Walters and Henry Kissinger, agreed with her that the principal difference between the two types of dictatorship was that right-wing dictatorships had the potential to become democracies, while the left-wing ones could only be removed through violence.

Based on this classification, the US administration supported dictatorships and hardline movements in the so-called 'Third World' whenever they were anti-communist in nature and could, therefore, play a role in Washington's geopolitical game with Moscow – examples included Afghanistan, Angola, Argentina, the Philippines, Guatemala and Nicaragua.

Little has changed since then. Western governments regularly declare their unreserved support for democracy and reject dictatorship or authoritarianism, yet several democratically elected governments deemed to be unhelpful to Western interests have been ousted in recent years, with varying degrees of outside involvement. Some of these regime changes have led to military dictatorships, such as in Thailand, where a military junta cut short Thaksin Shinawatra's mandate, and in Egypt, where the Muslim Brotherhood won at the ballot box but was replaced by General el-Sisi. Although it did not end in dictatorship, the legitimately elected Viktor Yanukovych in Ukraine was expelled from power primarily as a consequence of US and Russian geopolitical rivalries.

In other words, whether a dictatorship is supported or demonised depends on what geopolitical interests are at play. The wider world either attacks or turns a blind eye to authoritarian and repressive regimes, according to what benefits they offer. Gulf monarchies, for example, which entirely lack democratic principles, are highly coveted as commercial partners due to their fabulous wealth.

WHY ISRAEL WILL NOT GIVE BACK THE GOLAN HEIGHTS

Israel seized the Golan Heights from Syria as a consequence of the Six-Day War in June 1967, though the United Nations has never recognised Israel's right to ownership: a Security Council resolution in 1981 declared Israel's claims to be unsubstantiated by international law. Since then, Tel Aviv has systematically ignored the UN and international law and prioritised its own national interests. To Israel, the Golan Heights are of huge strategic importance: they are the country's main water source and, being relatively unpopulated, represent an area where Jewish settlements might be built to satisfy future demand. It would be disastrous for Israel if the land were to fall back into the hands of Syria, a country Israel has technically been at war with since the Yom Kippur War in 1973, because it provides a buffer zone in the event of a Syrian attack. If the land were returned to its neighbour, Israel fears that Palestinian terrorist groups would settle there and be well placed to attack Israeli territory.

BUSH AND THE WAR ON TERROR

A few hours after the terrorist attacks of 11 September 2001, the US President George W. Bush delivered a message to the nation from the Oval Office in which he put forward the case for proactive strikes against terrorists and anyone who helped them. According to Richard A. Clarke, after the speech the Defense Secretary Donald Rumsfeld pointed out that international law allowed for the use of force as prevention but not as retribution, to which Bush angrily replied: 'I don't care what the international lawyers say, we're going to kick some ass.' The US showed a similar

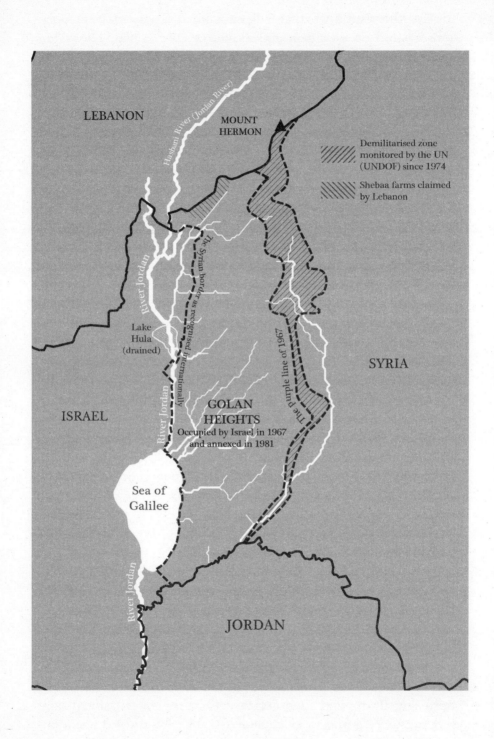

disregard for international law when it installed secret CIA prisons around the world or employed torture when interrogating suspects. As Fareed Zakaria has stated, for several years the Bush administration boasted of its disdain for treaties and multinational organisations.

The terrorism card has been played numerous times in the defence of such behaviour, but the US Department of State's Foreign Terrorist Organizations and State Sponsors of Terrorism lists are extremely arbitrary. To begin with, there is no internationally recognised definition of terrorism, which means that a group or individual can appear on one country's lists but not on others. The Albanian-Kosovan UÇK periodically appears and disappears from the US list, and Cuba, having been on the list since 1982, vanished from it in 2015. The lists are often used to apply sanctions for reasons that bear no correspondence to their stated aim and seem an arbitrary means of applying geopolitical pressure. According to Clarke, during the Iran–Iraq War (1980–88) the Reagan administration took Iraq off the list of nations that promoted terrorism, specifically so that Baghdad could access loans to develop exports endorsed by the US government.

The French analysts Labévière and Thual describe how, in the aftermath of the 9/11 terrorist attacks, the Bush administration ramped up the global terror alert based on an apparent threat from organisations such as al-Qaeda, Hamas and Hezbollah; this led the Pentagon to operate a 'global response' that normalised the notion of 'preventive war' and served to promote long-term US goals more than it encouraged international cooperation in counterterrorism. International relations became militarised in a way that they had not been since the end of the Cold War. Speaking in 2003, the British journalist Seumas Milne pointed out that Tony Blair had assured the British electorate that far fewer civilians would die as a consequence of the invasion of Iraq by US and UK forces than would in a single year of Saddam Hussein's government. Amnesty International has estimated that the number of annual deaths related to political repression was in the low hundreds at the time; in the five years following the invasion, estimates put the number of civilian deaths between 150,000 and a million.

In April 2017, US President Donald Trump decided to attack a Syrian airbase, arguing that a plane that had left from it the previous day had sprayed sarin gas on the civilian population.[22] He acted in accordance with Article II Section 2 of the US Constitution, which affords the president the powers of commander in chief of the US armed forces. This was not the first time a US administration had interpreted the constitution in whatever way it saw fit in order to justify the use of military force overseas without a mandate from Congress. The same thing had happened with Libya in 2011, for example.

The key question is, what constitutes a crisis extreme and urgent enough to justify acting with force? The president's powers are much broader than they might at first appear; the law is flexible enough that the White House need only really concern itself with mobilising public opinion, by magnifying the importance of an event in order to argue that it demands an immediate and rigorous response. The Oval Office likes to argue that congressional approval should not be required for a military operation of limited scope, even when it may be particularly potent. Another habitual argument is the justification of a strike on humanitarian grounds, as was the case with Trump in Syria. Ultimately, if a strike is desired, it can always be legitimised in the name of national security, which is such an ambiguous concept that it can be applied to almost anything.

International laws are often controversial, but one thing they can do is make it harder to justify military intervention abroad. In theory, except in cases of self-defence, a military operation can only be carried out on foreign soil after a UN Security Council resolution has been passed; in practice, the UN is routinely bypassed.

In the case of Syria, not only did the US lack a UN resolution, but it was also difficult to explain convincingly how a gas attack thousands of miles away from US soil could have any immediate impact on US national security, which left the increasingly implausible humanitarian argument. It is difficult not to conclude that the US acted for reasons disconnected to the sarin attack and which had more to do with domestic politics and the desire to send a message to China and Russia, their great geopolitical rivals, and to a lesser degree to Iran, increasingly influential in the Middle East and a rival to Washington's main regional allies.

The UN Security Council did issue a resolution, on 20 November 2015, which authorised a coordinated response to the activities of al-Qaeda, Islamic State and its affiliates in Syria. The justification was that these were terrorist groups that represented an unprecedented global threat to peace and international security. It was an ambiguous resolution in that it did not specify either what action might legitimately be taken against these terrorist groups, or which countries or international organisations were entitled to take it. And in no sense did it authorise any country or international organisation to attack the armed forces or infrastructure of the sovereign state of Syria.[23]

CHINA'S VIEW OF INTERNATIONAL LAW

According to the Chinese militarists Peng Guangqian and Yao Youzhi, international laws can be summarised by ten basic principles:

1. Mutual respect for sovereignty and territorial integrity (the current situation in Syria calls the application of this principle into serious question).
2. Non-aggression towards others (this is respected less and less, as recent conflicts in the South China Sea demonstrate).
3. Non-interference in the internal affairs of others (this is one of the guarantees China offers to countries in negotiations, thanks to its right to veto at the UN Security Council).
4. Equality and mutual benefit (weaker countries are much less likely to be respected, especially when there are conflicting interests at play).
5. Peaceful coexistence (economic and geopolitical interests ensure little peace and much competition).
6. The non-employment of force or the absence of the threat of its employment (China is a nuclear power, so the threat of force is a constant: it underpins the entire geopolitical game and is a fundamental pillar of deterrence).

7. National self-determination (this depends on the definition of 'nation': many nations are only recognised as such when it suits the interests of the powerful).

8. Respect for human rights and basic freedoms (China, perhaps more than any other country, stands accused of not adhering to these concepts, which are routinely used as geopolitical tools wherever an intervention is deemed convenient).

9. International cooperation and honest fulfilment of international obligations (this is always dependent on the interests of the moment: competition will always trump cooperation).

10. Peaceful resolution of international disputes (this is pursued as long as war is not deemed to be more beneficial).

Guangqian and Youzhi also provide three situations in which war might be a legitimate option: a state exercising its right to self-defence; military action conducted under a UN Security Council mandate; and an independence or national liberation movement fighting against colonialism or foreign rule within the framework of the right to national self-rule. The last of these is tailored to a Chinese mentality and fits with actions that Beijing has supported in third-party countries, many of them African states fighting against colonisers. China would probably not consider it equally 'legitimate' if the Tibetans or the Uyghurs, for example, were to launch a movement to fight for independence.

VIOLATION OF INTERNATIONAL LEGISLATION: OUTER SPACE

The Outer Space Treaty in 1967 stipulated that outer space belongs to all of humanity, meaning that it cannot be appropriated by any nation 'by means of use or occupation, or by any other means', regardless of a project's level of scientific or economic development; it should remain accessible to the entire international community for peaceful use and exploration. This treaty has been signed by 129 countries, although twenty-four of them have yet to ratify it. It was extended to include the Moon Accord (1979), which governs the activities of states on the Moon and other celestial bodies, establishing regulations for the future exploration and exploitation of any natural resources found there.

Despite this, in October 2007 President George W. Bush signed an order giving the US the right to deny access to space to any rival that might use it for hostile aims. At a meeting of the UN General Assembly in November 2016, Washington also rejected the establishment of any other treaty that might limit its own use of space. During this session, the passing of a resolution to prevent an arms race in outer space was discussed. Four countries abstained including the US.

Despite other international treaties that prevent it, the US is also actively seeking to win the race to exploit asteroids. In 2015 President Obama signed a legislative proposal allowing for the mining of space objects that was subsequently approved by Congress, enshrining in law the right of the US to exploit asteroids for its own benefit; the US Commercial Space Launch Competitiveness Act expressly allows US citizens to 'engage in commercial exploration for and commercial recovery of space resources', giving asteroid mining companies the right to claim the riches of outer space.

THE INTERPRETATION OF THE LAW

Robert D. Kaplan has argued that the concept of international law proposed in the Netherlands in the seventeenth century, according to which all states are treated as equal and war is justified only in the defence of sovereignty, is essentially utopian; he points out that the dividing line between war and peace can be fluid and that international accords are only established when they are in the interests of the states that have the power to make them happen.

Liang and Xiangsui likewise believe that the rejection or recognition of international laws by individual countries depends largely on their own interests. Smaller countries hope to use the laws to protect themselves, while larger powers employ them to keep the smaller ones in check. In other words, countries can be divided into two camps when it comes to international relations: the weaker countries that believe international relations should be based on respect for international law, and the stronger ones that think the geopolitical weight of each country is what counts. As a result, international legislation is neither respected by strong states nor enforced by weaker ones.

Rule 10

DON'T DO FOR YOURSELF WHAT OTHERS CAN DO FOR YOU

How to get others to do your dirty work

'I'd rather have 1 per cent of the effort of a hundred men than 100 per cent of my own effort'

– JEAN PAUL GETTY

In any major operation, a common strategy is to trick others into putting all the effort in. The rule is to never do for yourself what others can do for you, especially when it comes to actions that would reflect badly on you. Others can be paid to do whatever is required, though the strategy is even more effective if they are coaxed into acting through trickery and subterfuge. If skilfully handled, the shameful act will be carried out without anyone detecting your involvement.

THE EMPLOYMENT OF CORSAIRS

From at least the thirteenth century, this strategy was applied at sea by using both people and ships. State authorities gave certain sailors a 'letter of marque and reprisal', the authorisation to obstruct, attack, sack or even sink the merchant ships of rival countries, all for the benefit of the nation. This was piracy dressed up as a legal activity. Countries used the strategy in times of war to weaken the economies of their enemies and force them to use squadrons of their naval fleets to protect maritime routes. It allowed countries to temporarily increase their naval capacity without any outlay, for these corsairs were paid with the goods they captured.

In the seventeenth and eighteenth centuries, corsair ships constituted a sizeable portion of the overall fleets of the major powers. It was a lucrative business with the blessing of the authorities; every country had laws governing how the booty was shared, the usual practice being that profits from selling captured ships and goods were distributed equally between the captain and crew, the owner of the boat and the government of the contracting country.

Corsairs were theoretically supposed to adhere to a certain discipline, following guidelines that governed their operations. In practice, they tended to have the freedom to carry out attacks wherever they saw fit. The paperwork that made their business official usually stated that hostile acts against foreign ships should comply with the laws and customs of war, but the authorities did not regulate these actions unless it suited them to do so. The corsairs also enjoyed the advantage of being thought of as part of the structure of the armed forces, even if those they acted against did not always concede them this privilege.

More than half of the renowned corsairs operated under the auspices of the British crown, though Spain, France, the Netherlands and some Latin American countries also used the practice. Francis Drake was the archetypal corsair. He was at various times an explorer, a slaver, an acclaimed navigator, a politician and an admiral in the English navy. Spain, having suffered multiple attacks led by him, saw him only as a pirate, no matter that he was on the payroll of the English state. In England he was considered a hero, and Queen Elizabeth I awarded him a knighthood for services to his country.

Corsair activity reached a peak between the sixteenth and eighteenth centuries; during the War of Independence, the Americans bolstered their naval fleet with corsair ships, and at the end of the eighteenth century, in the aftermath of the French Revolution, French corsairs targeted American and British ships in the Atlantic Ocean and the Caribbean Sea. They continued to be employed into the nineteenth century with some regularity, and in the American Civil War, corsairs acted on behalf of both the north and the south.

We can see a modern-day equivalent of corsairs in the private military companies that have proliferated since the end of the Cold War. Governments contract private companies and confer upon them the right to use force in order to benefit the nation, and they are protected by a legal legitimacy that seems highly questionable.

THE MODERN MERCENARIES: PRIVATE SECURITY FIRMS

Commercial military service providers (CMSPs), known as 'contractors', are increasingly used to perform actions a state cannot or does not want to undertake with its own resources. The first private military company was Watchguard International, founded in 1965 by David Stirling (creator of Britain's SAS) and John Woodhouse.[24] The company performed its first operation during the civil war in North Yemen.

The deployment of CMSPs has increased in recent decades for a number of reasons: countries have reduced their military quotas; there has been an increase in low intensity, asymmetric conflicts; and Western countries are reluctant to engage their own armed forces, due to the negative reactions at home to reported casualties.

Though typically deployed in conflict zones, CMSPs are branching out into other fields, such as the fight against narco-trafficking and piracy, the protection of humanitarian aid deliveries by NGOs and the UN, and counter-terrorism operations in Afghanistan, Pakistan and Iraq (where in 2007, for example, more contractors were mobilised than conventional soldiers). The companies tend to belong to or be linked to groups with political and economic power. Their registered addresses are usually in tax havens, they generate billions of dollars every year and are able to purchase the latest weapons and military technology, providing a boost to multinational arms manufacturers. Their employees, whose average age is between thirty-five and forty, usually consist of people who have worked in the armed forces, the intelligence services or the police, although there are also some former gang members.

For states, employing CMSPs instead of their own armed forces has numerous advantages. CMSPs are more economical because their contracts are short term, they require no social security payments and there is no cost in training them. Furthermore, they inspire confidence, for the majority are cross-checked professionals, who are reliably efficient due to their experience. They can be trusted to act in confidentiality on covert operations and are unconcerned by public opinion. They have ready availability and can provide either flexibility or specialisation. Most importantly, they enable states to sidestep political and legal constraints and responsibilities.

But CMSPs also have their downsides: their lack of respect for international law in war is well known. Despite the numerous scandals in which employees of these companies have been involved, there is still no framework through which they can be compelled to answer to national or international law. They also often ignore international labour legislation, contracting personnel from developing countries on reduced salaries and without providing social benefits.

Most of all, CMSPs bypass due democratic procedure regarding the use of physical force, particularly when they engage in clandestine operations. Until now, efforts made to regulate them have failed due to legal differences between countries, the globalisation of the industry and multiple interested parties. A 1977 amendment to the Geneva Convention relating to mercenaries does not cover CMSPs, principally because they do not exactly fit the definition provided for 'mercenary'. The same can be said of the United Nations Convention against the Recruitment, Use, Financing and Training of Mercenaries in 1989. The most recent effort to regulate the private security industry is the Montréal Document (2008), which is a list of seventy 'recommendations' on how to operate in conflict zones, monitor behaviour and punish violations of international law.

INDIRECT WARFARE

Third parties have always been employed to perform some of the most arduous and unpleasant tasks in war campaigns, from tactical operations to heinous acts such as summary executions. After the First World War, communist Russia decided to make guerrilla tactics part of its war machine. At the 1928 Party Congress meeting in Moscow, it was suggested that there should be a guerrilla warfare division, in the event of war; in 1933, the *Instructions for Guerrilla Warfare* manual was released and incorporated into Red Army strategy. When the German–Russian conflict began in 1941, the first guerrilla groups were already being organised. Their activities began in Serbia and were coordinated by Russia, with input from the British. The aim was to wear the Germans down and force them to divert resources and troops to maintain control of the Balkans. Tito, the future President of Yugoslavia, was sent from Moscow to take charge of one of the main guerrilla groups. According to Max Hastings, the Allies encouraged such guerrilla activity throughout the Nazi-occupied territories.

Third parties have also routinely been employed to commit acts that are atrocious even within the tumultuous context of war. According to the historian Eugene Rogan, during the Armenian genocide the Ottomans released a number of convicted murderers from prison and mobilised them into bands of 'butchers'. And during the 1980s and 1990s, it is believed that the CIA employed mercenaries to lay bombs in Fidel Castro's Cuba, paying them between 2,000 and 5,000 dollars per bomb plus travel expenses.

FALSE FLAG OPERATIONS

An array of schemes, traps and tricks are deployed in conflict. As Winston Churchill said, 'In wartime, truth is so precious that she should always be attended by a bodyguard of lies.' One tactic often used by powerful states and entities is to undertake actions specifically to blame them on someone else. These covert actions are known as 'false flag operations', a term that derives from the military practice of getting troops to carry a different country's flag to mislead the enemy. The target of blame may be a sworn enemy, someone you would like to turn into an adversary or someone that you would like someone else to consider an adversary. Sometimes the party being framed is merely a scapegoat, chosen at random.

False flag operations can take many forms: terrorist attacks, military attacks or acts of sabotage. They may be carried out in a physical space or, as is increasingly the case, via telecommunications systems and cyberspace. These days, they are aimed at influencing decision-making in political circles as much as on the battlefield.

Because they are covert, false flag operations are typically planned, managed and executed by the intelligence services using their own agents, members of army special forces or personnel specifically contracted for the job. In some cases, especially in countries that lack democratic systems, there is evidence of the secret services enacting false flag operations as if they are operating in a parallel state. In the volatile world of espionage, false flag techniques are widely used to recruit agents or to persuade third parties to carry out actions without knowing their true objectives.

Given that false flag operations are performed under the utmost secrecy, many are almost impossible to prove and end up confined to the murky world of conspiracy theories. And even when the true order of events is known, it can remain difficult to determine what happened. Some of these private operations are properly documented, thanks to the thorough research of journalists or because information has been declassified. In some cases, schemes have been revealed by remorseful perpetrators on their deathbeds, or by other intelligence services wishing to benefit when knowledge of their rivals' actions goes public. It is common for a false flag operation in politics, whether an act of terrorism or some kind of subversive activity, to then be used to justify a country going to war. As Stalin is reputed to have said, 'The easiest way to gain control of a population is to carry out acts of terror. The population will clamour for such [restrictive] laws if their personal security is threatened.'

In the specific case of subversion, when one country wishes to undermine the unity of another, false flag groups may be employed to spread false rumours or encourage certain lines of thinking. False flag initiatives can also be used to put populations on a war footing, ensuring popular support for, or at the very least passive acceptance of, a proposed intervention. The most common technique for mobilising citizens is to demonise the enemy, by misrepresenting them to the point that they can be fought with maximum ferocity. This tends to be achieved by spreading lies or divulging false information to make the public indignant, engaging in psychological warfare and manipulating the media. The human mind is easy to manipulate: we tend to believe what we want to believe or what fits with our preconceived ideas; simple but insistent messages eventually sink in and we have an inherent need to resolve the doubts that trouble us.

In operational terms, false flag operations must be performed using the art of deception, in order to deliberately mislead others into acting in ways that favour the instigator. As a military tactic, false flag manoeuvres often take the form of 'pseudo operations', performed by military forces dressed in the enemy's uniform, whether to gain information about a terrain or adversary's activities, or to eliminate opposition leaders. As Napoleon said, 'One spy in the right place is worth twenty thousand men on the battlefield.'

Historical examples of false flag operations abound, despite the fact that only a small minority of them ever reach the public domain. One of the most notorious is the great fire of Rome in AD 64, started by Nero but blamed on the Christians. In the twentieth century, differing degrees of evidence exist in relation to false flag operations carried out by nations including Russia, Japan, Germany, Britain, Turkey, the US, Algeria, Bosnia, Indonesia and Serbia. There have also been persistent rumours of multiple false flag operations in the recent conflicts in Libya, Iraq and Syria. Few countries, be they dictatorships or democracies and regardless of government ideology, have never resorted to using such tactics. One might even argue that autocratic regimes have less need of them given that they are able to act without paying heed to local populations or political opposition.

LEADING FROM BEHIND

In recent times, perhaps scarred by previous failed ventures, Washington has moved away from direct intervention and become markedly more indirect, generally employing third parties to achieve its objectives. According to Richard A. Clarke, the US used the Pakistani army information services as intermediaries in Afghanistan during the Soviet–Afghan War (1979–89). Backed by money supplied by the US, the Saudi government and charity organisations, the Pakistanis were able to turn nineteenth-century-style Afghan warriors and a few thousand Arab volunteers into a formidable fighting unit. Without being involved directly, the US spent some 600 million dollars each year on the war.

This change of approach was honed further in 2001, when the US invaded Afghanistan in response to the 9/11 terrorist attacks. To expel the Taliban from power, the US employed militia from the Afghan Northern Alliance, overseen by a relatively small number of their own special operations soldiers. More recently, the US has turned to Kurds in the fight against Islamic State in the volatile battlefields of Syria and Iraq. George Friedman approves of this approach and believes the US should establish alliances in which other countries would bear the brunt of conflict, with Washington supporting them through economic incentives, military technology and the promise that, if needed, it will provide direct military support. This policy can be summed up by what President Barack Obama called 'leading from behind', in other words remaining in charge but in a near-imperceptible manner.

Synergy

Acting in conjunction with someone else can bring results that are more than just a sum of two parts; the extra impact a partnership can produce is known as 'synergy'. It is employed as a geopolitical strategy by states wanting to have a larger impact than they can in isolation. It translates into the formation of alliances and coalitions between countries, whether permanent or circumstantial. These partnerships range from established international groupings, such as the UN and NATO, to supranational organisations in which a loss of sovereignty is traded for a common benefit, such as the European Union. The alliances serve diverse purposes, including security, mutual defence, economic advantage, and political and military cooperation.

Even the superpowers feel obliged to join some associations; albeit on the condition that they get to lead them, as the US usually does. According to Zbigniew Brzezinski, US global supremacy is underpinned by an elaborate system of alliances and coalitions around the globe. Some of these unions seem to unite countries and organisations that have very different aims, but a common enemy or sudden shared interest. In *World Order*, Kissinger suggests the hypothetical example of limited cooperation, or at least tacit agreement, between Iran and the Taliban and even al-Qaeda, in order to confront a common adversary: the USA. Iran's Islamic Revolution in 1979 might thus be interpreted as a framework for cooperation across the Sunni–Shia divide in the name of championing broader, anti-Western interests. Such cooperation could include Shia-led Iran supplying arms to jihadi groups that are affiliated to Sunni organisations such as Hamas, to act against Israel, as well as to the Taliban in Afghanistan. Kissinger points out that some reports suggest the Sunni-affiliated al-Qaeda may be able to operate out of Iran.

Alliances and unions are occasionally forced into existence by the emergence of a powerful external threat, both at the state level or internally, due to terrorism. In the period leading up to the First World War, Bismarck understood that a dominant state at the heart of Europe would run the constant risk of inducing coalitions to form against it, as had happened with the regimes of Louis XIV in the eighteenth century and Napoleon in the early nineteenth century. Throughout the ages, London has managed to oppose any power from dominating the continent by forming military alliances against the emerging common enemy.

Rule 11

CREATING AN ENEMY

How to invent a convenient 'threat'

'A wise man gets more use from his enemies
than a fool does from his friends'

– BALTASAR GRACIÁN

Human groups seem always to have felt the need to have an adversary, perhaps to strengthen unity within their society or to serve as a target for their ambitions. If an enemy doesn't exist, you therefore have to invent one.

When people become convinced of the existence of a threat to their lives or social order, a sense of heightened solidarity can be fostered, which facilitates subordination to a ruling class and an acceptance of exceptional collective measures that would not otherwise be consented to, including the removal of rights and freedoms. If skilfully directed, the strategy can make even the most peaceful people support war in the name of defending their nation, though the real reasons for going to war may be nothing of the sort.

Another common reason for creating an enemy is to distract a society from its domestic problems. This happens most often under authoritarian regimes, which seek to justify their existence by creating a sense of unity and fear in a population through persuading them that they are facing an imminent attack. Recent historical examples include Argentina's military junta going to war with Britain over the Falkland Islands in 1982, and Cuba and North Korea, where inhabitants are mentally prepared for their country to be attacked by the US at any moment. The strategy allows governments to keep their populations under strict control and serves as an excuse to expand armies and intelligence services.

NATO REINVENTS ITSELF

Since the end of the Warsaw Pact in 1991, NATO has sought to reinvent itself in order to justify its continued existence. It has gradually expanded its field of operations to encompass the entire world, removing the physical limitations specified by the treaty

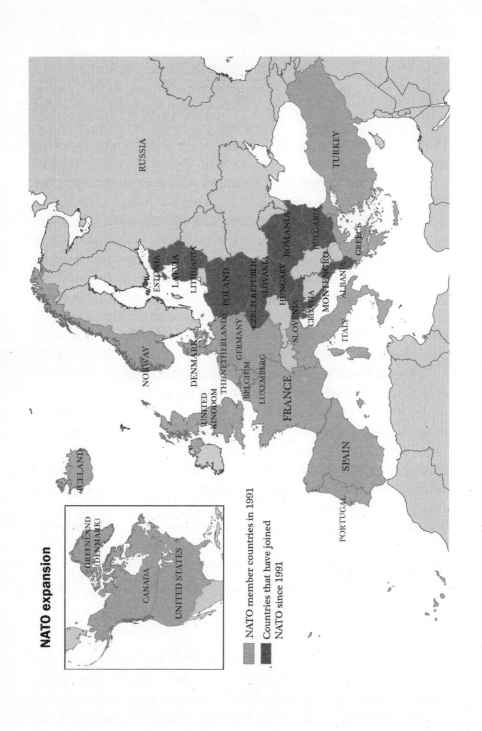

NATO expansion

RUSSIA

TURKEY

ESTONIA
LATVIA
LITHUANIA
POLAND
CZECH REPUBLIC
SLOVAKIA
HUNGARY
ROMANIA
BULGARIA
SLOVENIA
CROATIA
MONTENEGRO
ALBANIA
GREECE

NORWAY

DENMARK

UNITED KINGDOM

THE NETHERLANDS
GERMANY
BELGIUM
LUXEMBERG
FRANCE

ITALY

ICELAND

SPAIN

PORTUGAL

GREENLAND (DENMARK)

CANADA

UNITED STATES

NATO member countries in 1991

Countries that have joined NATO since 1991

that created it: the Washington Treaty in 1949 (also known as the North Atlantic Treaty) limited it to the territories belonging to its member states. However, after interventions in the Balkans – Bosnia, Kosovo and Serbia – came interventions in Afghanistan and Libya. Most importantly, it has found an old enemy to lock horns with again: new tensions with Russia have allowed it to argue for renewed spending and troop deployments, while at the same time attempting to encircle Russia by welcoming former Soviet states into its bosom.

The current hostility of Western countries towards Moscow has been fostered by Washington, which has two main aims: to contain Russia's emergence as a rival power, and to create an enemy for European allies to rally together against, which will ensure their subordination to the US because Europe relies on the US for protection and weapons. The Kremlin has its own geopolitical aspirations, but the USA's principal geopolitical strategy is to prevent alliance between Russia and other European countries. As George Friedman says, such a coalition would produce a powerhouse that it would be very hard to contain.

A Russian–European union would mean a superpower with the capacities (whether in terms of technology, natural resources, energy, population, markets, culture, military or nuclear means) to threaten the US government. This might explain why the White House used Ukraine to provoke a clash between Europe and Russia. Washington managed to convince European state leaders of Russia's evils, and these leaders campaigned to push public opinion in their countries towards anti-Russian policies. Whether through gullibility or weakness, those leaders have walked into a well-prepared trap, and growing tension and the mutual flexing of military muscle could lead to an incident that sparks war. Such a battle would take place on European soil and have catastrophic consequences for the continent.

THE MILITARY-INDUSTRIAL COMPLEX, MOTHER OF ALL ENEMIES

The military industry has regularly been criticised for relentlessly inciting a fear of enemies in order to guarantee its own existence. Chris Hedges, a veteran US war correspondent, has said that

Washington's permanent war economy sustains itself by inspiring fear – of the communists during the Cold War and of the jihadi today.[25]

Iran and North Korea are the current chosen enemies. Presenting them as being on the brink of attacking their regional rivals ensures that surrounding states buy large amounts of weaponry and helps to fuel an arms race in the region. Saudi Arabia's fear of Iran led it to become the second largest arms importer in the world between 2013 and 2017 (behind India, a country with a population 40 times larger), and the largest in 2014 and 2016. The United Arab Emirates, with a population of just nine million, was the fourth largest importer (Egypt was third) between 2013 and 2017. South Korea was the eighth highest between 2008 and 2017, driven by the hypothetical threat of an invasion from its northern neighbour, despite the fact that 25,000 American soldiers are stationed in South Korea, meaning any attack by North Korea would directly draw the US into war.

As the main arms supplier to all of these countries, the US profits handsomely from this situation. In a list of the USA's biggest arms customers, Saudi Arabia is first, the United Arab Emirates second and South Korea fourth.

The other great enemy today, radical Islam, is portrayed by some as the destroyer of the Western world. For many years, communism served as the primary threat to both the Western and Muslim worlds; after the fall of the Soviet Union they were each forced to find a new adversary, and they found each other.

THE CREATION AND DEMONISATION OF AN ENEMY: GADDAFI IN LIBYA

Great Britain demonstrated how to demonise an adversary in order to gain public support for a military attack in the days before the international offensive against Libya, launched on 19 March 2011. On 2 March, the English journalist Justin Marozzi wrote an article in the *Daily Mail*, saying that Gaddafi had chemical weapons and was ready to use them against his own people.[26] His theory was that the Libyan opposition, which was fighting Gaddafi in order to bring democracy to Libya, would soon be massacred. Marozzi provided details of the terrible effects these weapons could have, stating that the information came from 'a growing number of military men and Western intelligence experts'. He included a few concrete facts, such as that Gaddafi had promised to get rid of this type of weapon in 2003 in order to be welcomed into the international community, but said the tyrant had kept ten tonnes of chemical products with which to manufacture mustard gas and 650 tonnes of other materials that could be used to make a variety of chemical weapons.

In terms of biological weapons, a Libyan former justice minister confirmed that Gaddafi still had anthrax, nerve agents such as sarin and, possibly, a genetically modified smallpox virus. Marozzi suggested that Gaddafi also had a thousand tonnes of uranium dust that would enable him to build an atomic bomb. He also claimed that Gaddafi had maintained friendly relations with countries such as North Korea, Iran and Iraq, all part of US President George W. Bush's 'axis of evil'. This, Marozzi argued, was enough to cast serious doubt on Gaddafi's 2003 promise to disarm. Marozzi emphasised how badly armed and equipped the opposition forces were, as if pleading for them to be supplied with the means to take on the dictator. The article was instrumental in encouraging Western citizens and rulers to favour an attack on Gaddafi's regime, though Libya did not ultimately use any of the weapons described, either against its own population or international forces.

Brad Hoff offers another example concerning Libya in an article about the Hillary Clinton emails leaked during the US presidential campaign.[27] He says that, as part of the media strategy designed to demonise Gaddafi and gain popular support for attacking Libya, rumours were spread that Gaddafi's forces were committing mass rape as a weapon of war (for which Viagra pills had even been supplied to troops). Several journalists reported this story, despite the fact that international organisations such as Amnesty International had declared the accusations to be false.

There were also accusations that Gaddafi had planted dead bodies in sites NATO had bombed, in order to frame Western countries for the killings. This too was proved to be false.

Rule 12

LIE BIG AND SOME OF IT WILL STICK

How to win the truth wars

'A lie told often enough becomes the truth'

— Vladimir Lenin

Public opinion has always been important, but winning 'hearts and minds' has become increasingly crucial in modern times. The term 'populism' has its critics, given that all parties in a democracy seek to be popular. To triumph in a democracy, you need more votes than your opponents, and you will get them by winning the support of the most populous section of society. If you want to capture people's support, you need to offer them something attractive: you catch more flies with honey than with vinegar. To do this, politicians tend to rely on populist strategies that proclaim greater social justice, though these electoral pledges are often forgotten as soon as the party is sworn in.

One way of convincing society of something is to repeat the idea to the point of saturation. This was the strategy employed by Joseph Goebbels, Minister of Propaganda in Nazi Germany between 1933 and 1945, known to believe that, 'the bigger the lie, the more it will be believed' and 'a lie told a thousand times becomes the truth'.[28] The media is the instrument through which lies are repeated, which means that the fabled freedom of the press is often taken advantage of to manipulate the public. In Lenin's opinion, 'freedom of the press means freedom to buy up newspapers, to buy writers, to bribe, buy and fake "public opinion" for the benefit of the bourgeoisie'.

Propaganda has over the years been used by governments of all kinds.[29] According to Pierre Gallois, the Soviet Union made it one of the main components of its system of governance. And William J. Casey, Director of the CIA from 1981 to 1987, is believed to have said, 'We'll know our disinformation program is complete when everything the American public believes is false.' Propaganda comes into its own in times of war. Marenches thought of disinformation as one of the secret weapons of modern warfare, while Fuller believed that propaganda warfare was a legitimate means of controlling the minds of the masses and inflaming public opinion against

175

an enemy, as well as winning over neutrals and subverting public opinion within the enemy.

The prevalence of new technologies and our modern addiction to immediacy mean that populations risk being brainwashed by the avalanche of information they receive without analysis or context, with public opinion overly influenced by whatever appears in the media. The floods of surveys, statistics and opinion polls, the results of which are easily manipulated, have the same impact. When the truth is discovered and damaging information cannot be denied, states react by attacking the source. This is what happened after WikiLeaks revealed Hillary Clinton's emails: the main focus was on who put the information in the public domain rather than on the content of the emails.

PROPAGANDA AND THE MANIPULATION OF THE MASSES

Edward Louis Bernays, nephew of Sigmund Freud, is considered to be the father of modern propaganda and public relations. His theories, which were set out in a book called *Propaganda* (1928), hold true today. In the first chapter he judges the conscious and intelligent manipulation of the habits and views of the masses to be an important element of social democracy operated by an invisible government, the true power behind the throne. Bernays advances his claim further by saying that our opinions are governed by people of whom we have, for the most part, never heard. It is they who pull the strings that control people's minds, who control social forces and conceive of new ways to harness and steer the world.

Harold Dwight Lasswell, a pioneer in communication theory, delved deeper into techniques used to manipulate the masses during the First World War. One of the ideas in his book *Propaganda Technique in the World War* (1927) is that propaganda is essentially the use of the media to infuse a particular idea in the population's conscience, in order to push public opinion in a certain direction without having to resort to violence. All of which suggests that if you worry you're being brainwashed, you've probably been brainwashed into having that worry.

176

THE THOUSAND COLOURS OF THE KALEIDOSCOPE

In his poem 'Las dos linternas' ('The Two Lanterns'), the Spanish poet Ramón de Campoamor says, 'the world is the colour of the glass it is seen through', but it could be said today that the world is the colour of the glass we are allowed to see it through. The filter depends increasingly on which newspaper you read, which TV channel you watch or which social media feeds you follow; media outlets create an artificial and self-serving reality that rarely coincides with objective truth.

Put another way, the world can either be viewed with the naked eye or through a telescope or microscope; these are equally valid ways of seeing. By inundating ourselves with information, however, we may have the impression we are placing our eyes over a microscope or peering through a telescope, when in fact we are faced with a kaleidoscope of mirrors – attractive, diverting and hypnotising, but unclear. What we think of as reality is a mere entertainment staged to prevent us from seeing what's happening behind the scenes. As Noam Chomsky says, 'the picture of the world that's presented to the public has only the remotest relation to reality. The truth of the matter is buried under edifice after edifice of lies upon lies.'[30] The truth is hidden by simultaneously withholding information and providing it in excess.

JEFFERSON'S ADVICE ON THE PRESS

In 1807, seventeen-year-old John Norvell sent a letter to the third president of the United States, Thomas Jefferson, seeking advice on how a newspaper ought to function: 'It would be a great favor, too, to have your opinion of the manner in which a newspaper, to be most extensively beneficial, should be conducted, as I expect to become the publisher of one for a few years,' he wrote. Jefferson answered him via a letter in which he took the opportunity to launch a bitter attack on the press of the day:

> To your request of my opinion of the manner in which a newspaper should be conducted so as to be most useful, I should answer

'by restraining it to true facts and sound principles only', yet I fear such a paper would find few subscribers. Nothing can now be believed which is seen in a newspaper. Truth itself becomes suspicious by being put into that polluted vehicle. The real extent of this state of misinformation is known only to those who are in situations to confront facts within their knowledge with the lies of the day. I really look with commiseration over the great body of my fellow citizens, who, reading newspapers, live and die in the belief that they have known something of what has been passing in the world in their time. I will add that the man who never looks into a newspaper is better informed than he who reads them; inasmuch as he who knows nothing is nearer to truth than he whose mind is filled with falsehoods and errors.[31]

These words not only remain valid today, they are arguably truer than ever. In the early nineteenth century, many people got their information solely from the printed press, whereas now there is also radio, television, cinema, the Internet and social media. In the modern world, practically everyone, at least in the more developed countries, is inundated with more information every day than their ancestors would have received in a lifetime. But we must not confuse having more information with being wiser; the larger the volume of information, the greater the likelihood of disinformation.

THE PRINCIPLES OF PROPAGANDA

The following principles of propaganda are attributed to Joseph Goebbels:

1. Simplification and the single enemy: adopt a single idea, a single symbol. Make all adversity the responsibility of a single entity.
2. Method of contagion: join diverse enemies into a single category or individual. Adversaries must constitute a singular entity.
3. Transposition: project your own mistakes and shortcomings onto the adversary, answer attack with attack.
4. Exaggerate and misrepresent: turn any anecdote, no matter how small, into a grave threat.

5. Vulgarise: all propaganda must have popular appeal; adapt it to suit the least intelligent people being targeted. The larger the group that needs convincing, the smaller the mental effort required to understand the message should be.

6. Orchestration: propaganda should limit itself to a small number of ideas that are repeated endlessly, presented again and again from different perspectives, but always converging on the same concept. There should be no cracks in the argument, no doubts.

7. Renovation: one must issue new information and arguments at such a pace that, by the time the adversary can respond, the public is already interested in something else. The adversary's responses must never be allowed to cancel out the accusations.

8. Credibility: build arguments from varied sources and through fragmented information.

9. Silencing: keep quiet on matters for which you have no answers and hide news that favours the adversary, while employing counter-programming with the help of the media.

10. Transfusion: as a general rule, propaganda operates from a pre-existing sentiment, whether a national mythology or a blend of traditional hatreds and prejudices.

11. Unanimity: manage to convince the many that they think 'like everyone else', creating an impression of unity.

Many of these principles are still applied today, and several are deeply engrained.

THE TEN STRATEGIES OF MEDIA MANIPULATION

Though frequently credited to Noam Chomsky, these ten strategies of media manipulation were devised by the French writer Sylvain Timsit, who published them in 2002.[32] The fact that they are mistakenly attributed to Chomsky is a perfect example of media disinformation: it seems to have begun with an error, intentional or otherwise, by the Pressenza news agency. People kept returning to the Pressenza source to reference the strategies and used the same credit, and so the mistake was perpetuated. This happens increasingly with news stories, as media outlets employ very few experts or analysts. When combined with the race to be the first to break the story, the result is that news loses validity and much of what reaches consumers is incomplete, twisted or simply wrong.

The following is an abridged breakdown of Timsit's strategies:

1. Distract from the important: distraction as the primary element of social control. The strategy consists of diverting the public's attention away from important problems and decisions taken by the political and economic elites by constantly bombarding them with distractions and irrelevant information, while at the same time dissuading people from taking an interest in knowing anything essential.

2. Create problems, then offer solutions: this strategy, also known as 'problem–reaction–solution', consists of creating a problem to cause a certain reaction in the public, with the aim of having the public clamour for the measures that the ruling class wants to impose. It can range from unleashing urban violence to perpetrating bloody terrorist attacks, or creating an economic crisis with the purpose of having people demand greater security, even to the detriment of their own liberties, or a cutback in social services spending. It might also be called the 'strategy of constructive chaos', for it involves creating chaos, violence and destruction, at least on the surface, in order to be given free rein to implement a new social model without facing any popular opposition, the people themselves having demanded a return to 'normality'.

3. Graduality: an extreme measure can be accepted by being drip-fed over a number of years. Introduced gradually, an idea that might otherwise have sparked a revolution will be meekly tolerated.

4. Delay time: flag up an unpopular decision as being 'painful but necessary' in the future, thus gaining immediate public acceptance of something that will be applied later. If the public have more time to get used to it, they will ultimately accept the change with resignation.

5. Address the public as if they are young children: the more you want to trick the audience, the more you must adopt a puerile tone, employ basic language and use messages that can be understood by even the most intellectually limited mind.

6. Use emotion more than reflection: employ emotion to provoke a short-circuit in rational analysis, deactivating people's critical faculties. It is then easy to plant ideas, desires, fears, terrors and compulsions, or to induce certain behaviours.

7. Keep the public ignorant and unremarkable: make sure the public is incapable of understanding the techniques and methods used to control and enslave them, beginning with a lack of education for the lower classes so they remain submissive to the elites.

8. Encourage the public to look favourably on mediocrity: promote the notion that it is cool to be stupid, vulgar and uncultured. Reality TV is a prime example of this.

9. Reinforce self-blame: make individuals believe that they alone are responsible for their own misfortune, due to them being stupid, unskilled or not trying hard enough. They will thus remain in a depressed state that will inhibit their actions and ensure there will be no revolution.

10. Get to know individuals better than they know themselves: technology now makes it possible for someone else to gather data and gain a fuller understanding of an individual than they have of themselves, making it easier for those pulling the strings to control them.

PROPAGANDA IN THE REAGAN ERA

According to several recently declassified documents, the Reagan administration devised a programme of psychological intervention to counter Soviet propaganda, which was fairly prevalent in Western countries at the time. Fine-tuned over the years, Washington's psychological campaign was aimed at influencing public opinion in target countries as well as among US citizens, in particular to overcome the 'Vietnam syndrome' and gain popular support for activities that benefited US interests.[33]

The task of developing and implementing this ambitious programme was entrusted to a team in the CIA, led by Walter Raymond Jr, that specialised in covert operations. Concerned about Soviet penetration into South and Central America, Washington carried out a number of propaganda campaigns in Costa Rica, Cuba, El Salvador, Guatemala, Honduras, Nicaragua, Panama and Peru, before rolling the programme out into other countries that were deemed to be of high strategic interest to the US, such as Afghanistan and the Philippines. In some of the declassified documents, reference is made to attempts to influence the global political party Socialist International, as well as leaders of European political parties with socialist and social democratic ideologies, with the aim of steering them towards a line more agreeable to Washington's interests. A key component of the programme was the identification of areas where these target countries were vulnerable. News was manipulated, with some news invented and other news suppressed, through connivance with local journalists and editors whenever possible.

The programme became official in January 1983, when President Reagan signed the National Security Decision Directive 77, the Management of Public Diplomacy Relative to National Security, which outlined the need to strengthen public diplomacy. The objective remained the same: to convince the public, national and international, of the positivity, integrity and advantages of US foreign policy.

RUSSIA PLAYS AT DISINFORMATION TOO

In June 2015, American journalist Adrian Chen revealed that a Russian company called Internet Research Agency was employed by the Kremlin to wield influence on the Internet and social media by spreading false and distorted information.[34] According to Chen, this company, which employed hundreds of well-paid twenty-somethings to work as Internet trolls, had been responsible for one of the most notorious cases of fake news ever seen in the US. The case occurred on 11 September 2014, in the small town of

St Mary Parish, Louisiana. On the thirteenth anniversary of the twin tower terrorist attacks, alarmist text messages announced a serious accident at the Columbian Chemicals processing plant in St Mary Parish and urged citizens to 'take shelter' and 'check local media'. In a matter of minutes, hundreds of messages on Twitter from a multitude of different accounts provided details that seemed irrefutable, including eyewitness statements, images of the chemical facility being devoured by flames and security camera footage from a nearby petrol station showing the explosion and a dense column of black smoke rising in the distance. A YouTube video, made with such care that nobody could have suspected it was false, showed a man watching the news unfold on TV. A Wikipedia page went up with links to video clips and witness statements were attributed to real residents of the town. Mainstream media outlets, journalists and politicians were bombarded with Twitter messages about the disaster. A screenshot of the CNN homepage, doctored to show coverage of the event, appeared, and links were posted to cloned versions of television channels and newspapers in Louisiana. Shortly afterwards an elaborate YouTube video appeared, in which Islamic State claimed responsibility for the attack.

This wasn't the first time such a thing had happened. There had been a number of smaller dress rehearsals in the second half of the previous year, of which the most significant took place on 13 December 2013, when news spread on Twitter of an Ebola outbreak in Atlanta. As with the St Mary Parish case, there were faked news reports and false videos accompanied by hashtags that trended for several hours. Those responsible for the hoax went to such great lengths to foster authenticity that they constructed and spread a video in which healthcare professionals dressed in protective clothing transported a victim from Atlanta International Airport.

THE CNN EFFECT

The theory that the media can dictate foreign policy, the so-called 'CNN effect', first arose in the 1990s. The immediacy of international media creates its own reality, given that it is the TV channels that decide what is news and what isn't. CNN has become a driving force behind world opinion, wielding significant influence over some countries' domestic and foreign policies. According to a number of studies, its repetition of footage of events such as the Tiananmen Square protests in China in 1989, the fall of the Berlin Wall, the First Gulf War and the Battle of Mogadishu, had a significant impact on government decisions. George H. W. Bush has said he sent 28,000 US troops to help deliver humanitarian aid during Somalia's civil war in 1992 after watching television footage of starving children. But other studies argue that the media reflects rather than frames the political agenda of governments.[35] With Operation Restore Hope in Somalia, for example, the White House wished to draw public attention to the country because it was planning an intervention, and the media complied.

Then there is the question of who controls the media. In a complex society in which urgency and immediacy rule, conscientious, reliable, comparative and impartial analysis has become increasingly difficult to find. Most media outlets rely on information sources that are of dubious reliability and skilfully manipulated by vested interests. Apart from a few exceptions, media platforms offer partial information rather than genuine journalism and favour striking headlines over factual rigour. Powerful forces drag coverage in one direction and towards an exclusive way of thinking.

In recent years the most influential media platforms in the world have become concentrated in just a few hands, which gives their owners immense power and the capacity to rattle – and indeed bring down – governments, companies and people. According to some studies, just six companies now directly or indirectly possess 95 per cent of the world's main television, radio and written media: 1,500 newspapers, 1,100 magazines, 2,400 publishing houses, 1,500 television channels and 9,000 radio stations. Other research that includes cinema concludes the main media conglomerates to be the following (listed in approximate order of size, for knowing their true economic might is practically impossible given their large networks of companies and subsidiaries):

- Comcast, USA; number one in the world
- The Walt Disney Company, USA; second in the world

- Time Warner, USA; third in the world
- Twenty-First Century Fox, USA; fourth in the world
- CBS Corporation, USA
- Viacom, USA
- Bertelsmann, Germany
- Globo Group, Brazil; number one in Latin America
- Hearst Corporation, USA
- Lagardère Group, France
- News Corp, USA
- Televisa Group, Mexico
- Sony Corporation, Japan (although its communications business is based in the USA through its affiliate Sony Corporation of America)
- Vivendi, France

THE BOGEYMAN

One technique employed to control and subjugate populations is to instil an irrational and paralysing fear that can only be overcome by protection from the powerful. This is the geopolitical equivalent of parents telling their children stories of the bogeyman, a shadowy figure who kidnaps children. In geopolitics, such threats are used by powerful states to remind weaker ones of the disadvantages of going it alone in a mean world, or to stir up emotions in its own population.

One of the most spurious threats is that of 'global terrorism'. In reality, it only affects a few countries in the world. Countries such as Venezuela, Mexico and Honduras, for example, have very different security concerns, and in many other states, terrorism is hardly on the agenda. The same is true of concepts such as the 'proliferation of weapons of mass destruction', which erroneously implies that there is a global nuclear arms race; besides those that already have them, only North Korea and Iran could realistically be said to be seeking them.

'Organised crime' is another example of a problem that, although serious for weak or corrupt governments and failed states, is essentially a social hazard in most advanced countries. Countries that claim it to be some kind of existential threat could make a bigger effort to tighten the loopholes exploited by criminals if they really wanted to put an end to organised crime.

As the US journalist and editor Henry Louis Mencken put it, 'The whole aim of practical politics is to keep the populace alarmed (and hence clamorous to be led to safety) by menacing it with an endless series of hobgoblins, all of them imaginary.'

Rule 13

WEAPONS OF MASS COMMUNICATION

How to control the message to win hearts and minds

'The mass media serve as a system for communicating messages and symbols to the general populace. It is their function to amuse, entertain, and inform, and to inculcate individuals with the values, beliefs, and codes of behavior that will integrate them into the institutional structures of the larger society.'

– NOAM CHOMSKY

The constant avalanche of information to which we are subjected in the modern world creates the illusion that we are responsible for our own opinions. Although we may believe we are thinking independently and drawing conclusions for ourselves, this constant bombardment of news makes thinking with clarity impossible.

THE WAR OF DISINFORMATION

Even the most expert analyst can get things wrong, not through ignorance of the subject but through ignorance of the source of the information they are analysing. The information that reaches the public is always, in one way or another, partial, distorted, subjective or intentionally manipulated. Even for those who are aware of the situation, breaking free is difficult. Acquiring alternative information is complicated and can also be costly. Above all, it requires time, a luxury few people permit themselves in the fast-paced era in which we live.

News coverage of the conflicts in Syria and Iraq offers an example of the way in which a dominant idea can be imposed by the media. News of these two conflicts has been controlled by Al Jazeera (Qatar), the BBC (UK), CNN (USA), France 24 (France) and Sky News (UK), which as well as having their own platforms also provide reports for other television channels around the world. To this list we might add the Reuters news agency (based in London and part of the powerful Thomson Reuters group). In other words, they are either from the English-speaking world or two other countries – Qatar and France – which have their own agenda when it comes to the conflicts.

Increasingly few media outlets have the capacity to employ their own reporters and correspondents; they merely acquire the news from the major news agencies and tweak it to suit their audience, typically without cross-checking it with other sources.

As a result, the principal international news agencies have a huge influence on the messages that reach citizens. For example, most news about North Korea is provided to the world by the BBC and Reuters, which rely on information provided by the South Korean intelligence services, meaning impartiality is impossible.

MEDIA MANIPULATION OF WARS

Modern-day media propaganda and information operations go hand in hand with military ventures. Although in theory the former supplements the latter, they are often treated with equal importance and a war is often first won at home, by gaining the population's support or consent. When fed a series of basic but insistent ideas, people become convinced of the need for confrontation and prepared for the eventual losses inevitably incurred.

One of the first steps is the demonisation of the adversary. Even if they were already of dubious reputation, they become positively satanic; new gory details, invented or magnified as required, come to light in order to generate outrage. The aim is to convince the public that the evil leader or regime has brought intervention on itself and that the government has no choice but to act against such a monster to put a stop to the awful crimes that are being committed against humanity.

As we've already seen, another key objective is to hide the true motivation for going to war. Strategic interests, which tend to be a mixture of the economic, the geopolitical and the personal, are concealed behind the declared need to defend people whose rights are being abused. If anyone is bold enough to oppose the venture, they may be accused of betrayal. During the Vietnam War, the US government line was that anyone who refused to support the troops was a communist sympathiser.

During the Nuremberg trials, Hitler's chief lieutenant Hermann Göring had the following conversation with the US military psychologist Gustave M. Gilbert:

> GÖRING: Why, of course, the people don't want war. Why would
> some poor slob on a farm want to risk his life in a war

when the best that he can get out of it is to come back
to his farm in one piece? Naturally, the common people
don't want war; neither in Russia, nor in England, nor
in America, nor for that matter in Germany. That is
understood. But, after all, it is the leaders of the country
who determine the policy and it is always a simple
matter to drag the people along, whether it is a democracy, or a fascist dictatorship, or a parliament, or a
communist dictatorship.

GILBERT: There is one difference. In a democracy the people
have some say in the matter through their elected representatives, and in the United States only congress
can declare wars.

GÖRING: Voice or no voice, the people can always be brought
to the bidding of the leaders. That is easy. All you
have to do is tell them they are being attacked, and
denounce the pacifists for lack of patriotism and exposing the country to danger. It works the same in
any country.[36]

THE SPANISH–AMERICAN WAR: THE BIRTH OF THE TABLOID PRESS

During the Spanish–American War of 1898, the press played
a key role in mobilising the US population. In the 1890s, a new
form of sales–obsessed journalism, then known as 'yellow journalism', had been born. Newspapers magnified any occurrence or
incident in Cuba, no matter how insignificant, and even invented
news when there was none, to keep the public constantly hooked.
There was heated competition between the main newspapers to
be the first to publish the most striking or scandalous news. This
professional rivalry turned personal in some cases, as between
Joseph Pulitzer, editor of *New York World*, and William Randolph
Hearst, editor of the *New York Journal*. Hearst's Havana correspondent had been instructed to file gory news stories, but reported
back that Cuba was tranquil. According to legend, Hearst replied
with an uncompromising order, 'You furnish the pictures and I'll
furnish the war.'

The US tabloid press relentlessly pushed its message until the population demanded the US government go to war with Spain over Cuba. Stories of atrocities committed on the island by the Spanish authorities were exaggerated or fabricated in order to steer popular opinion towards a belief in the need to defend human rights there.[37] The climax was the aggressive and disproportional media campaign that followed the sinking of the battleship USS *Maine* on 15 February 1898. The origin of the explosion that destroyed the US navy vessel, which had been sent to Cuba to protect US interests on the island, was never clarified, which didn't stop Hearst and Pulitzer from attributing blame to the Spanish. They portrayed them as savages and criminals, repeating the motto 'Remember the *Maine*! To hell with Spain!' until it entered the popular psyche and became a rallying call for those in favour of war. Eventually there was popular support for a war that Washington had long sought to start for commercial and geopolitical reasons.

THE MEDIA WORKS FOR THE INTELLIGENCE SERVICES

Rumours abound of media outlets and journalists working with intelligence services, and some of the most brilliant journalistic investigations are said to have been the fruit of deliberate leaks from intelligence or police sources. However, proving this is nigh-on impossible given the inherent secrecy, and trying to expose it can put reporters' lives at risk. This is not just a throwback to tensions generated by the Cold War: it is rumoured that countless journalists all over Europe are today influenced by the governments of certain countries, and to a much larger degree than we might imagine. In the US, many CIA investigators, former agents and journalists[38] have come to the conclusion that the CIA, from its creation until the present day, has exerted a huge influence on American and foreign media, in order to make the information that is transmitted to the public more favourable to US interests.

One example of such activity is Operation Mockingbird, which was rolled out by the CIA in the early 1950s. At the time, the CIA was a legacy organisation of the Office of Strategic Services, which had nurtured a network of sympathetic journalists in Europe during

the Second World War.[39] After the war, the Department of State created the Office of Policy Coordination, which merged with the Office of Special Projects in 1948 and became the fastest growing department within the nascent CIA, expanding from 302 members in 1949 to 2,812 by 1952, with its budget increasing from 4.7 million dollars to 82 million within the same time frame. It began to wield enormous influence: some researchers have suggested it targeted journalists, columnists, writers and editors from as many as 800 news outlets, including prestigious names such as the *New York Times*, *Newsweek*, CBS and *The Times*.

Operation Mockingbird entailed the CIA making contact with an influential journalist or editor, who would then be responsible for recruiting other reporters, some of whom were not necessarily aware of the ultimate source or purpose of their instructions. These journalists were often of such high standing that their opinions were republished by hundreds of media outlets.[40] To help them write their stories, the CIA provided journalists with classified information, which they would later pass off as their own findings. Another form of compensation came by way of public or private advertising contracts: newspapers and television channels that served the interests of the intelligence services experienced significant increases in advertising revenue. After a while, they became so dependent on this that they couldn't imagine giving it up.

Attempting to have the media transmit news, information and analysis that is favourable to the government is routine work for intelligence agencies; it is not confined to traditional print media, but also affects television, radio, cinema and literature, with the Internet and social media also increasingly becoming significant battlegrounds.

THE COMPLICATED PROCESS OF EXERCISING FREEDOM OF EXPRESSION

In the modern world, technological advances such as smartphones, the Internet, social networks and satellite communications ought to allow for a greater variety of opinions, including some that diverge from those of the establishment. However, the opposite would appear to be true and freedom of expression seems to be more compromised.

We are subjected to a tremendous amount of media pressure. Freud foresaw this when he noted that 'culture is something imposed on a reluctant majority by a minority that managed to gain possession of the instruments of power and coercion'. Despite the freedoms we enjoy, we live in a world in which anyone whose opinion we don't want to hear is ostracised, in which a person can be socially 'assassinated' for suggesting alternative ways of thinking, in which those who triumph are those whose opinions are automatically accepted and in which anyone who questions established and prevailing attitudes is invariably not only silenced but crushed.

THE SPIRAL OF SILENCE

The spiral of silence theory remains as valid today as when it was first outlined by German political scientist Elisabeth Noelle-Neumann in 1977. She understood public opinion as being a pre-determined and self-serving vision of reality that is imposed upon a society;

individuals have no choice but to follow the dominant attitudes of the day, even if their way of thinking is at odds with it. According to Noelle-Neumann, social pressure has such a strong grip on people that few dare to have different opinions from those that are dominant, out of fear of being ostracised or marginalised. Her central argument is that, in a society where unconventional or politically incorrect opinions are systematically silenced by the media, it is the individuals themselves who, seeing that their opinions aren't reflected, choose not to express them in public, so as not to risk social exclusion.

This phenomenon had previously been explored by Alexis de Tocqueville, one of the fathers of classic sociology, in considering attitudes towards the church in mid-eighteenth-century France: 'Those who continue to believe in the doctrines of the church are afraid of being left on their own with their faithfulness and, fearing society more than error, declare that they share the opinion of the majority.'

According to Chilean journalist Rubén Dittus, the spiral of silence can be summarised as four basic assumptions: society threatens to marginalise any individual that strays from the mainstream; people are innately afraid of being isolated; as a consequence of this fear, they seek to latch onto popular opinions; and as a result of these calculations, they adjust or repress their own opinions.[41]

This leads people to express what they really think in more indirect ways. One of these today is commenting on online news stories. In this virtual and anonymised space they feel able to say things they dare not express anywhere their views might be overheard or recorded. It can be interesting to analyse how others react to these outpourings of unfiltered opinion. The obvious conclusion is that public opinion differs considerably from what might be assumed to be the majority view. The other conclusion is that there is a rare sincerity to these comments, which are made anonymously and without fear of stigmatisation. They perhaps provide some indication of how afraid people are to say what they think in societies that are supposedly democratic and free.

This situation has practical repercussions, as the outcome of recent elections and referenda in a number of countries has shown. Mainstream media outlets expect a certain result, find polls to back it up – and are then surprised by the actual outcome. Shocking results can occur when people vote not for the choice that was being imposed on them, but for what they actually want, safe in the knowledge that their opinion will remain confidential.

TOTEM AND TABOO

The theories outlined by Sigmund Freud in *Totem and Taboo* in 1913 continue to be valid today, even in societies in which citizens can theoretically exercise complete freedom. Freud concluded that throughout history groups have had their totems, representations of the sacred values with which the community identifies, and they have had their taboos, things that are forbidden because they are considered harmful or incompatible with the group's traditions and culture. The former are the origin of religions, while the latter become laws and moral norms.

The words 'totem' and 'taboo' sound like they belong to the past, but they carry more weight in the modern world than might be expected. Societies continue to have 'sacred' things and 'forbidden' things; in some cases these statuses are acquired extraordinarily fast, and much more quickly than in previous eras. There are some subjects today about which it is practically impossible to offer an alternative vision, even if this is backed up with scientific research, without running the risk of being socially marginalised or ruthlessly criticised on social networks.

The triumph of singular thinking means it is easier to fill someone's mind with pre-conceived ideas than to allow ideas to be born and germinate by themselves, especially if these ideas might then run counter to the interests of the dominant class. It is often the case that those who make the most noise about defending freedom of thought are the same people who seek to restrict it. As Noam Chomsky said, 'If we don't believe in freedom of expression for people we despise, we don't believe in it at all.'

Rule 14

THE USES AND ABUSES OF THE POOR

How the masses are used as pawns in geopolitical power plays

'Both Islam and Christianity knew how to speak to the poor and attract them to their bosom'

— Amin Maalouf

Governments routinely justify their decisions by saying they are acting for the benefit of the poor, the marginalised or the socially excluded. The official line is that the social, economic and political development of less fortunate people and countries is pursued by the highest international institutions and the wealthiest of powers. The reality, however, is that apparently altruistic actions are often employed in pursuit of much less worthy geopolitical aims. Many a revolution has been started in the name of the poor, only for those behind it to assume power and usher in an even more repressive regime. Turbulent times, economic crises and social upheaval are routinely taken advantage of by extremists seeking power, whether they be those who champion a 'revolution of the people' or the xenophobes and nationalists who speak of 'them and us'.

Political movements and institutional religions have long taken advantage of the poor, the excluded, the hungry and the humiliated, often with the excuse of providing material or spiritual 'salvation'. These people are lured in by the promise of a better future and the possibility of attaining and enjoying what others already possess. The perception of injustice is more common today than ever before, thanks to a media that shows what is enjoyed everywhere in the world. If you have got nothing or very little to lose, you will likely opt for the hope of gaining something, however slim.

THE MANIPULATION OF SLAVERY

Some historians view the anti-slavery element of the American Civil War (1861–5) to have primarily been a strategic argument to win the support of a section of the population, and consequently increase the number of soldiers in combat, rather than the product of Abraham Lincoln's idealism. Some of his declarations can be seen to suggest that he doubted the viability of abolishing slavery in the short term and racial equality in general. The main point of contention between the north and the south was arguably the criteria used for setting tariffs; Lincoln advocated protectionism rather than the free trade policy that was favoured by the south, which he thought benefited British interests. In some ways, the conflict can be viewed as a struggle for economic power between a southern economy based on agriculture that required slave labour to remain profitable, and an industrialised northern economy in which slavery was not only unnecessary, but a burden on the new society that was emerging.

Throughout its prolonged existence, slavery was an integral part of the economic models of the societies employing it. The first references to social stratification that included slaves are found in Sumerian writings dating from around 3500 BC. The practice of slavery was common until the late twentieth century, and it still goes on in some form today.

When primitive societies first began to accumulate riches and have a surplus of goods, this gave rise to a desire to use other people of a lower social distinction for less attractive tasks. Prosperous societies realised it was more attractive to enslave captured adversaries than to kill them, as they'd been doing until then. This context changed with the Industrial Revolution, when the mechanisation of production and field labour meant that human manpower ceased to have the same importance; in fact it became more onerous to keep slaves than machines.

IDEOLOGIES THAT KEEP POVERTY ALIVE

In times of plenty, those who harbour extremist views move underground and bide their time, waiting and hoping for the inevitable crisis. When it comes, the extremist movement rises to the surface and tries to take advantage of social, economic and political unrest to style itself as the voice of change, the mouthpiece and saviour of the people. The only real aim is to win power so the movement can further its own interests, but it will camouflage this aim with a smokescreen of populist discourse.

If they do ever end up in power, these movements tend to keep as many people as possible dependent on state welfare, whether directly or indirectly. They also tend to impose an ideologised education programme that enables them to exert a heavy influence on people and eliminate nonconforming voices. For countries that have the misfortune to fall into the hands of such regimes, it becomes very difficult to escape them.

Wars and Revolutions in the Name of the Poor

War and revolution are nurtured by laying the groundwork for the manipulation of the downtrodden. Lenin said that the guerrilla cause is sustained by the pauper, the manual labourer and the unemployed, and indeed he used the poor to force a regime change, from Tsarism to communism. The underlying causes of the Russian Revolution were class inequality, poverty, social and political unrest, incompetent Tsarist rule and repression – exemplified by Bloody Sunday on 22 January 1905 in St Petersburg, when the Russian Imperial Guard crushed a workers' protest and killed hundreds of people, including women and children. However, the revolution was also orchestrated by Germany in order to destabilise Russia, with whom it was at war. As mentioned earlier, it was Berlin that organised Lenin's return from exile.

Like communist revolutions, those of the extreme right base themselves on supposed popular rule. They also take advantage of people and crises, but in a slightly different way: for the communists, the rich and privileged are the enemy that must be defeated, whereas far-right movements blame everything on foreigners and outsiders. The Nazis blamed Jews for Germany's poverty after the First World War and would eventually stigmatise anything that wasn't of the 'Aryan race'. In present-day Europe, some people are quick to blame immigrants and refugees for economic and social crisis, establishing a link between migration and security that populist political parties attempt to use for electoral gain.

THE USEFULNESS OF THE POOR TO THE STATE

The poor are not just used in domestic social upheaval; they are also employed strategically to defend state interests abroad. Some states present themselves as champions of universal justice, in much the same way as they might make an imaginary distinction between good and evil in order to justify military interventions that they claim promote peace, democracy, human rights and the eradication of poverty. These aims may indeed be sought, at least partially, but behind them lie geopolitical interests of far greater import.

In May 1798, the French government sent a large army, led by Napoleon, to conquer Egypt. This ambition was not new: the German philosopher Gottfried Wilhelm Leibniz had, a century earlier, suggested to Louis XIV that France ruling Egypt would undermine Dutch authority in the region. By 1798, France's main enemy was Britain, and the plan was to attack London through Egypt and India. Although the geopolitical objective was to undermine British influence and power, liberating the poor was the justification for the intervention. A year earlier, the French consul to Egypt had said that the time had come to act because the Egyptian people were victims of an oppressive and corrupt government. As Professor Anthony F. Lang explains, the ideas of the French Revolution were used to help create a narrative around the duty to liberate those who were unjustly oppressed by backward and uncivilised governments.

Another way of justifying an invasion is to claim it is intended to deliver humanitarian aid. France uses this strategy in its current dealings with some African countries, in particular those it once colonised, maintaining close economic ties and influencing policy through aid, the presence of French companies and military partnerships. As the political geographer Jacques Lévy explains, France's presence in Africa in the post-colonial period has enabled French companies to obtain agricultural and mining produce and to have exclusive access to a financial system governed by French pricing, with the complicity of private French companies and African governments.[42] There are French military missions, including EU or UN missions, all over Africa, which allow France to monitor its geopolitical interests in the region. These missions range from those in Central African Republic, where Paris was part of Operation Sangaris between 2013 and 2016,[43] and the EU Military Operation in Central African Republic since January 2014, to those in Mali and its bordering countries – Operations Serval and Barkhane. France's main objective is not to fight jihadism or develop local economies and democracies, but to maintain French geopolitical influence in the region and protect commercial operations, such as the extraction of uranium in Niger.

Humanitarian aid, though fundamentally important in the medium term, has the side effect of modifying short-term food and consumption habits, and fortunes have long been made by taking advantage of chaos, disaster, war and poverty wherever need is most urgent. There is always someone keen to profit from the desperate; in the refugee camps of Africa, the Middle East and now Europe, poor people seeking protection are exploited by groups that appropriate aid and sell it to those for whom it was intended to be distributed for free, or establish criminal businesses such as prostitution and drug trafficking rings. As Jean Paul Sartre said, 'disorder is the greatest servant to established order … All confused destruction weakens the weak, enriches the rich and increases the power of the powerful.'

In June 2017, The Sentry, an organisation founded by actor George Clooney and activist John Prendergast to supervise aid distribution in armed conflicts, published a report accusing generals and high-ranking South Sudanese officials of openly profiting while their violence-ravaged country suffered a dramatic humanitarian crisis. One of the accused was Malek Reuben Riak, a lieutenant general in the government's People's Liberation Army, who had an annual salary of just over 40,000 dollars and a current account at the Kenya Commercial Bank that saw three million dollars' worth of activity between January 2012 and 2016, including 700,000-dollar cash deposits. This money came from opaque deals struck with foreign companies established in South Sudan,[44] where the war had expelled two and a half million people from their homes and caused 100,000 people to die of starvation.

Combining the concepts of 'intervention' and 'humanitarian aid' results in 'humanitarian intervention', a term that the British sociologist Martin Shaw argues has come to be used as an excuse for the West to carry out military operations. These initiatives may be more or less justified in terms of assisting the helpless, and they may even genuinely seek to promote development and ensure human security, but the big question remains as to why operations are carried out in some countries and not others. The lack of transparency about these decisions recalls the question of why 'responsibility to protect' applied in Libya but not in Syria or Southern Sudan. The humanitarian aid argument has also been used to justify interventions that had clear military and geopolitical aims in Bosnia, Kosovo, Afghanistan and Iraq. Colin Powell, then US Secretary of State, explicitly alluded to this when he encouraged NGOs to go to Afghanistan and serve as a 'multiplying force' for the White House.[45]

The relationship between military force and humanitarian aid is complicated. It is difficult to justify military intervention from a humanitarian point of view, because humanitarian principles are based on neutrality, impartiality and independence; if a humanitarian organisation subordinates itself to military objectives, it undermines its own principles. In order to fully realise their missions, humanitarian groups sometimes need military force to protect their safety, though these collaborations do compromise their values and are open to abuse. For example, if the military helps facilitate a vaccination programme, it may also use that mission to gather logistical information, often on the direct instructions of intelligence agencies.

SOCIAL MEDIA AND REVOLUTION

Revolution can be understood as a process of social, political, economic, cultural, religious and moral change brought about in a sudden, radical, intense and sometimes violent way. The inter-connectedness of contemporary society means that a new revolutionary movement would be more capable than ever of extending at great speed across the planet.

Marx's theories on class struggle can be applied to the current conflict that exists between rich and poor countries. There is a notable demographic disparity; disadvantaged countries experience vast population growth, while better-off countries have low birth rates and ageing populations. Modern forms of communication create a heightened sense of inequality because the marginalised are exposed to the lives of those who enjoy opulent lifestyles with minimal effort. Social media platforms such as Facebook and Instagram contribute to this; those whose lives are physically distant from such materialism suffer an illusion of generalised, easy splendour.

Such inequality prompts a sense of antagonism and frustration among those that have less and feel excluded by the powerful and dominant. In recent times, this has manifested itself in mass migratory movements. In the future, it could be expressed through violent class struggle on a global scale, most likely focused in large urban areas, where the majority of the world's population lives. It is an intriguing scenario, and a very worrying one too.

THE POSTMODERN TIGER

Robert D. Kaplan speaks of what he calls the 'new postmodern tiger': the crowd that bays at real and perceived injustices. It roars at what Martin Shaw dubs 'wars of transfer' – intrastate conflicts in which the civilian population becomes the target – social and political crises, government corruption and economic crises that lead to a lack of opportunity or jobs. In less developed countries, the tiger is powered by people who want change, while in advanced nations it is the frustrated young. The more developed countries, where the majority of the young have had access to higher education, is often where the tiger roars loudest. Feelings of frustration can be particularly acute in educated young people who perceive they will never get a job that suits their level of study and training, and that they will struggle to reach a certain level of income. Another tiger is powered by the elderly, who are worried about their own future and that of their offspring.

Populist movements and radical groups have always sought to rouse these tigers in order to launch revolutions.

Rule 15

SOWING SEEDS OF DISCORD

How to defeat your enemy from within

'The enemy with internal problems is ripe
to be conquered'

– NICCOLÒ MACHIAVELLI

If you can't defeat your enemy through military force, you can try to do so by sowing seeds of internal discord. The age-old recipes for divide and rule include the manipulation of minorities, the fostering of disagreements between political dissidents and the promotion of separatist movements. Any society, no matter how unified it appears on the surface, will contain people and groups who feel disgruntled, aggrieved or marginalised, as well as damaged people who may seek to cause harm to the collective. The disaffected can easily be drawn into quarrels that corrode the social base. If you want to conquer a country, it makes just as much sense to become familiar with its internal tensions as with its geography. Machiavelli advised that a good invasion strategy should begin with supporting local minorities so that they turn against the majority and weaken the country's power base.

A WELL-USED STRATEGY

In the nineteenth and early twentieth centuries, Great Britain and other European governments promoted Arab revolts in the Middle East in order to wear down the Ottoman Empire. France toyed with the ancient rivalry between two major Syrian cities, Aleppo and Damascus, while at the same time stirring up hostilities between Muslim minorities, in particular the Alawites and the Druze, against the Sunnis.

Walter Görlitz argued that several New York bankers financed the Russian Revolution because they hated Tsarism, due to the persecution of Jews after the death of Alexander II in 1881. Germany, aware that it would never emerge victorious from war in Europe without revolution in Russia, likewise encouraged it. The Kaiser trusted Lenin's assertion that if he came to power he would immediately broker peace with Germany and attack British imperialism, even sending the Russian army into India. With these prospects on the horizon, Germany lent between 40 and 80 million marks to Russian agents working against the Tsar during the First World War.

In the same war, Germany also came up with a scheme aimed at generating conflict between the USA and Mexico. A secret telegram sent by Arthur Zimmermann, the German Minister of Foreign Affairs, to the German ambassador in Mexico on 16 January 1917, suggested that a German–Mexican alliance be established in the event of the US entering the war; as reward for intervening against the US, Mexico would be given Texas, New Mexico and Arizona in the event of a German victory. The Zimmermann telegram was intercepted and deciphered by British intelligence agents.

In the 1920s, the German communist party worked tirelessly on behalf of the Soviet Union to try to debilitate the Weimar Republic. A few years later, Stalin had an interest in the Spanish Civil War lasting for as long as possible, because he believed that Russia's borders were safe from attack as long as the conflict continued. Specifically, he believed that if Franco was victorious, France, at the time an ally of Moscow, would become preoccupied with its southern flank and give Berlin the freedom to launch an invasion of Russia. Moscow already knew Hitler had plans to do this – the Soviets therefore sought to support Spain's Republican forces and encouraged democracies to follow suit.

During the Second World War, Section II of the Abwehr, the German military information service, was responsible for special missions, which included providing support to rebels, insurrections and saboteurs in foreign countries. There are countless other examples of intelligence agencies making strategic use of internal discord in rivals. Japanese agents were in regular contact with Indian, Malaysian and Burmese nationalist groups throughout 1941, offering them covert support for their independence ambitions. Tokyo sent a telegram to the Japanese consular general in Singapore in January 1941, issuing orders to stoke agitation and encourage political friction, as well as to ramp up propaganda and intelligence operations. The Japanese had also been busy encouraging disaffection among soldiers of the British Raj since 1939.

In the 1950s, with reunification with the South unforthcoming, North Vietnam resorted to fostering insurgency, followed by a so-called 'war of liberation'. During those same years, NATO drafted plans to support resistance movements throughout Europe in the event of defeat to its rival alliance, the Warsaw Pact.

During the Cold War, East Germany had 16,000 agents active in West Germany, as well as forty-five radio stations and various TV channels broadcasting programmes specifically aimed at the Federal Republic, where they also distributed communist newspapers, pamphlets and magazines. The Soviets maintained sixty-three communist parties in Western and neutral countries, as well as hundreds of action groups that were managed by fifteen global pro-communist organisations. The Soviets were masters in the art of fostering internal confrontation throughout the Cold War years. One of their tactics was to foster subversion in the West, through pacifist, disarmament, self-rule and social justice movements and protests against colonialism, racial segregation and nuclear power.

Democracies are just as likely as authoritarian regimes to employ these strategies. In the Cold War, the West sponsored demonstrations in the USSR about human rights issues, freedom of expression and press freedom. US money was involved in the overthrow of Chile's socialist President Salvador Allende in 1973. Additionally, US Democrats have used these tactics just as much as Republicans, though they are perhaps more skilled at hiding their true interests; according to Richard A. Clarke, in 1995 the Clinton administration approved a secret scheme to finance covert CIA activities aimed at encouraging subversion against the Iranian regime.

When Saddam Hussein attacked Iran in 1980, he claimed one of his motives was that the Ayatollah Khomeini had summoned the Shia majority in Iraq to rebel. Something similar could easily happen today if Tehran were to make use of the Shia minority living in Saudi Arabia on the banks of the Persian Gulf, the part of the country where the major oil wells are located. This possibility is of major concern to Riyadh, at a time when relations with Iran are particularly tense. The Iranians could do the same in Bahrain, where mobilising the Shia majority against their Sunni minority rulers would be relatively straightforward. As for threatening Iran, it is George Friedman's understanding that the country's geography makes it practically impossible to invade by conventional means: its frontiers are almost all surrounded by high and treacherous mountains. The US has therefore concentrated its efforts on seeking to incite a revolution similar to those that brought down governments in the Soviet Union.

As mentioned above, Clausewitz maintained that Russia was impossible to conquer through armed force and would only ever be defeated through internal feuding. This remains true today, to such an extent that the Kremlin suspects its major adversaries, led by the US, of seeking to sow seeds of discord through NGOs, collectives such as the feminist punk group Pussy Riot and media and social networks, by spreading accusations about a lack of political freedom.

Thual points out that Russia also suspects Western countries of indirectly assisting Islamist rebels in the North Caucasus, in Dagestan and Chechnya, and suspects Georgia of providing support to the Chechen rebellion. Russia's enemies have always encouraged Georgian nationalism as a means of weakening Russia in the Caucasus; every time Georgia has become independent, it has been tempted to subjugate its minorities, while Moscow has sought to use these same minorities to undermine Georgian rebels, such as in the Russo-Georgian War of 2008. China has similar concerns over Tibet, convinced that both India – home to around 200,000 Tibetans, including the Dalai Lama – and the United States, its great geopolitical and geoeconomical rival, are sponsoring separatist movements there.

George Friedman believes Washington's strategic objective regarding the Islamic world is to keep these countries mired in chaos and incapable of unity; as long as Muslims are fighting among themselves, the US is winning the battle. This perpetual disunity has also always been the British approach to Europe, for it has always disliked the idea of the continent being dominated by Germany or France.

THE USA SOWS SEEDS OF DISCORD IN CUBA

The US has never hesitated to sow the seeds of discord in any country with the temerity to stand up to it, Cuba being a prime example.

The CIA has attempted to employ all manner of sophistry against the island's communist regime over the years, including Operation Good Times, which was plotted but never carried out. This scheme aimed to disillusion the Cuban population by distributing pornographic images in which Fidel Castro appeared with a series of foreign women in a room full of imported food. The material was to have been printed on leaflets with the tagline '*Mi comida es diferente*' ('My food is different') and handed out in Havana. While this operation never came to fruition, others like it have almost definitely been employed by the US secret services. Through social media and the use of television, such operations can be effected in less than twenty-four hours, no matter how high the target's political or social standing.

The anti-Castro activity is merely the latest iteration in the US's long history of disruptive activity in Cuba. For almost a century before the US declared war with Spain over Cuba in 1898, various US administrations had provided support to dissidents and insurgents on the island. In 1809, President Thomas Jefferson took advantage of France's invasion of Spain to promote an uprising there. In 1814, his successor, James Madison, stimulated an insurrection against the Spanish authorities by Americans with properties on the island. James Knox Polk (US President 1845–9) stirred up another revolt by US property owners, which failed because it was not backed by the Cubans. Ulysses S. Grant openly supported Cuban insurrection during the Ten Years War (1868–78), which is considered the island's first fight for independence. Grover Cleveland (1885–9 and 1893–7), despite his apparently neutral stance, allowed insurgents to continue receiving provisions from the US. William McKinley (1897–1901) was a decisive supporter of Cuban independence.

In November 1895, the US recognised a Cuban government of insurgents as legitimate, with a US syndicate immediately providing a three-million-dollar loan. Washington also supplied the insurgents with artillery training. As hostilities between Spain and the US grew in 1898, Spain's diplomatic efforts meeting with US passivity, dozens of boats departed from US ports for Cuba's coasts, laden with supplies for Cuban insurgents. It is estimated that of around eighty shipments, only half were stopped at US ports and just 4 were intercepted by the Spanish navy before they reached Cuban soil.

SOWING SEEDS OF DISCORD AMONG THE DISCORDANT

In the 1920s, Cheka, the Soviet political and military intelligence service, carried out one of the most successful ever infiltrations of a dissident organisation: Operation Trust. Created in late 1917 by Felix Dzerzhinsky, a Polish communist revolutionary, Cheka (from the Russian initials of the first words in its full name, the All-Russian Extraordinary Commission for Combating Counter-Revolution and Sabotage) was given almost unlimited powers to combat movements that were opposed to the revolution or straying from official doctrine.

At the beginning of the 1920s, the Monarchist Organisation of Central Russia (MOTsR from its Russian initials) was founded in order to enable dissidents to infiltrate the new Bolshevik government and undermine it from the inside, with the ultimate aim of reinstalling the Romanov dynasty. By 1925, it had become a magnet for Russian dissidents, those loyal to the exiled Tsarists and supporters of European governments who were hostile to the new regime in Moscow. However, in reality the MOTsR was a ruse designed by Cheka to identify opponents of the Bolshevik government. By 1921, Lenin's Soviet leadership had come to realise that it would not be able to consolidate its grip on power while the nearly half a million supporters of the former regime, urged on by foreign intelligence services, still constituted a risk.

Through Soviet agents embedded in the MOTsR, and after acts of coercion convinced other members to join the Bolshevik ranks, the dissident group was soon controlled by Cheka, which enabled Moscow to neuter the most belligerent opposition. Operation Trust was a resounding success, managing to curtail the activities of the regime's enemies and helping strengthen the Soviet Union.

SPREADING DISCORD THROUGH THE POST

Between 1944 and 1945, the US Office of Strategic Services (OSS), the precursor to the CIA, carried out Operation Cornflakes, a mission aimed at demoralising the German population. The strategy consisted of sending fake letters containing anti-Hitler propaganda to the German population, which it was imagined they would read over breakfast. Whenever air raids targeted trains with postal wagons, a second wave of planes would drop sacks full of fake letters near the wreckage, the idea being that they would later be recovered by the Germans and delivered as genuine.

To carry out the deception, the OSS began to gather information from Nazi prisoners with experience of how the German postal service worked, in addition to details supplied by German exiles in the USA and information from the German telephone directory, through which they were able to identify millions of residential addresses. The envelopes were stuffed with subversive materials, but they looked authentic on the outside and bore stamps that were replicas of official ones. On closer inspection, however, these stamps showed Hitler's head in the form of a skull, and the lettering had been altered from 'Deutsches Reich' ('German Empire') to 'Futsches Reich' ('Ruined Empire').

The plot proved fairly unsuccessful. By that stage of the war the postal service was only functioning sporadically in much of the country and many homes had either been destroyed or abandoned. Spelling errors drew the attention of German post office staff, who informed the German intelligence service and the plot was uncovered.

CIA ACTIVITY IN SYRIA

According to a secret CIA document dated 14 September 1983,[46] the US intelligence agency carried out a number of activities during the Iran–Iraq War that were aimed at weakening Hafez al-Assad's Syrian regime. Syria represented a threat to US interests in Lebanon and the Gulf: it had switched off a major Iraqi oil pipeline,[47] which Iraq needed to be operational to ease economic pressure and force Iran to call an end to the war. Covert military manoeuvres were being orchestrated from three border states – Iraq, Israel and Turkey – to encourage countries to join forces against al-Assad.

The report also outlined how Syria could directly interfere with US interests in the Middle East by refusing to withdraw its forces from Lebanon, which would lead Israel to occupy the south of the country. The shutting down of the Iraqi–Syrian pipeline was also cited as the main cause of Iraq's financial ruin and a dangerous internationalisation of the Gulf War. It added that if the US wanted to play a significant role in Syria, given that diplomatic initiatives had failed, it would have to come through military threats that were not only credible but directly jeopardised al-Assad's position and power.

Another secret CIA document, dated 30 July 1986, was entitled 'Syria: Scenarios of Dramatic Political Change' and outlined different chains of events that might expel al-Assad from power and force radical change.[48] One scenario anticipated excessive government response to minor acts of Sunni dissidence, which might provoke more significant disturbances and even degenerate into civil war. The paper also recognised that Syria was integral to Moscow having any influence in the Middle East. If the Sunni majority were to take political control, the Soviet position would be compromised.

The document warned that a weak government in Damascus could lead to Syria becoming a base for terrorism. It also indicated that Washington would prefer a Sunni-controlled government, though warned of the risk of Sunni fundamentalists taking power, as they might seek to establish an Islamic republic, increase hostilities with Israel and provide support and sanctuary to terrorist groups; this warning remains relevant today.

THE US HAS PURSUED REGIME CHANGE IN SYRIA FOR YEARS

A dispatch sent by the US Embassy in Damascus to the US Secretary of State and the United Nations Security Council, dated 13 December 2006 and classified as 'secret', described Syria as economically stable with weak internal government opposition. Revealed by Wiki-Leaks in a link that has since been taken down,[49] it also highlighted a number of vulnerabilities that might be exploited, including widespread fear of Iranian influence. The cable claimed that Sunnis in Syria believed that Iranians were recruiting members of the minority Shia population and trying to convert the poorest Sunnis, while also gaining footholds through building mosques and setting up businesses. Tensions with Kurds were also flagged for possible exploitation, in Syria's north-east in particular, but also in Damascus and Aleppo.

Another vulnerability was said to be the growing number of extremists using Syria as a base, despite measures that the Syrian government had adopted to clamp down on groups connected to al-Qaeda. Curiously, the dispatch recommended that Islamists acting in the margins against the regime be left alone – although they were acknowledged to pose a significant long-term threat, it was difficult to judge what threat they posed to Syria at the time. The message concluded by advising that these vulnerabilities be seen as opportunities to interfere in government decision-making, maintain a sense of instability and force Syria to pay for its mistakes.

The US State Department was concerned that Iran's nuclear weapons capability would not only end Israel's regional nuclear monopoly, 'but could also prompt other adversaries, like Saudi Arabia and Egypt, to go nuclear as well'. Furthermore, 'Tehran would find it much easier to call on its allies in Syria and Hezbollah to strike Israel, knowing that its nuclear weapons would serve as a deterrent to Israel responding against Iran itself'. For all these reasons, 'bringing down Assad would not only be a massive boon to Israel's security, it would also ease Israel's understandable fear of losing its nuclear monopoly'.

The email continued: 'In short, the White House can ease the tension that has developed with Israel over Iran by doing the right thing in Syria … the opposition is not going away, nor is the regime going to accept a diplomatic solution from the outside. With his life and his family at risk, only the threat or use of force will change the Syrian dictator Bashar Assad's mind.'

Based on the notion that Iran could threaten Israel 'not through a direct attack, which in the thirty years of hostility between Iran and Israel has never occurred, but through its proxies', the suggested US strategy was to do likewise: to 'work with regional allies like Turkey, Saudi Arabia and Qatar to organize, train and arm Syrian rebel forces'. The email also suggested the Americans 'develop international support for a coalition air operation' while pointing out that 'Russia will never support such a mission, so there is no point operating through the UN Security Council'.

HOW THE US ENCOURAGES DISCORD IN UNCOOPERATIVE COUNTRIES

The Brazilian historian Luiz Alberto Moniz Bandeira, a specialist in foreign policy and international relations, is forthright in his analysis of how Washington has sought to impose its will on countries that stand in the way of its interests.[50] He argues that the USA's irrepressible quest for global domination leads it to employ whatever means are necessary against any country that refuses to yield to its wishes, wherever it is and regardless of its government's political affiliation. Moniz believes the White House is more determined than ever to force states to keep to their established trajectory, pointing out that hegemonic powers are more dangerous when their power is waning than emerging.

Washington uses its intelligence services, NGOs and foundations to conduct campaigns of psychological warfare, putting 'errant' countries back on track or destabilising governments that continue to defy it. Their tactics include magnifying internal discontent to generate disruption and unrest, while taking care to give the impression that discord is spontaneous and protest movements are well-meaning, to avoid any suspicion of outside manipulation. If a change of government is achieved, and especially if it appears to have come about through popular demand and democratic principles, the US mission has been accomplished. Moniz asserts that the USA uses the term 'political defiance' to describe toppling a government and taking control of its institutions in this way.

DISCORD IN CYBERSPACE

Cyberspace is increasingly used maliciously to psychologically manipulate an adversary, or even a theoretical ally, by provoking certain feelings or spreading particular narratives. The ultimate purpose is to manoeuvre populations in a specific direction, so that they force their governments to move in the same direction, even if it runs counter to their principles and values. Colonel Ángel Gómez de Ágreda, a European authority on geopolitics, calls such activities 'affection-based operations'. Unlike the physical aims of more traditional military actions, these types of operation principally target mood and mind. In the modern world, a population's mood can be the nucleus where decisions are made, the will to win is nurtured and morality is shaped. 'Information operations' is a term the US military uses for IT-based warfare designed to 'influence, disrupt, corrupt or usurp adversarial human and automated decision-making while protecting our own'. Psychological effects are often now prioritised over physical damage; an image can be more powerful than a heavily armed battalion and cyberspace is the modern-day battlefield.

RUSSIAN ESPIONAGE AND THE ART OF DISINFORMATION

On 30 March 2017, Thomas Rid presented a report to the US Senate Intelligence Committee on information operations that Russia might be performing in the country.[51] He defined these 'active measures' as covert or semi-covert activities aimed at influencing US political decision-making and said the source is almost always concealed or faked, with Russian intelligence agents hiding behind anonymity or false flags. Rid offered the committee another definition of the aim of disinformation operations by quoting Colonel Rolf Wagenbreth, who, as head of Department X in the East German Stasi, was something of a master in the field. He said, 'a powerful adversary can only be defeated … through a sophisticated, methodical, careful, and shrewd effort to exploit even the smallest cracks between our enemies … and within their elites'. Rid himself added, 'The tried and tested way of active measures is to use an adversary's existing weaknesses against himself, to drive wedges into pre-existing cracks. The more polarised a society, the more vulnerable it is.'

The Russian intelligence services were pioneers of disinformation in the early twentieth century and went on to become prolific in the mid-1960s, when active measures became standard practice and commanded vast resources. During the Cold War the Soviets carried out over 10,000 disinformation operations. According to Rid, the first large-scale cyber-espionage campaign between states was what the FBI enquiry termed the Moonlight Maze attack in late 1998, which targeted US government institutions including the Pentagon and NASA. In recent years the situation has intensified, with Russian campaigns of digital espionage now considered routine. Since 2015, Russian intelligence agents have combined digital espionage and active measures, in other words, hacking and leaking information. In May and June of 2015, the 'Saudi Cables' demonstrated an innovative new tactic: hacking a target, extracting compromising material, creating a specific web-page to leak it, supplying the documents to WikiLeaks as cover and then distributing the stolen information as widely as possible.

All the major powers are constantly trying to manipulate their citizens, in more or less covert ways. We cannot truly trust any information, even when we try to compare it to other sources. Information contamination is more widespread, better concealed and more generalised than ever before. We can become caught up in the question of who hacked and leaked the information, but should not fail to focus on its content. Leaked documents generally reveal highly compromising details about the real interests and duplicitous behaviour of our political leaders, even those who claim to be liberal, transparent and progressive.

Rule 16

RELIGIOUS FERVOUR

How to weaponise religion to gain power

'Religion is excellent stuff for keeping common people quiet. Religion is what keeps the poor man from murdering the rich'

— NAPOLEON BONAPARTE

Humankind has an innate attraction to the metaphysical, which has been used and abused throughout history. Joseph Goebbels, highly attuned to how human nature might be manipulated, was well aware that religion could be an important factor in geopolitical influence. He said, 'One has to recognise that the vegetative tendency towards the mystic exists. To not make use of it would be foolish.'

At the end of the nineteenth century, the French sociologist Gustave Le Bon carried out important studies into the behaviour of human collectives and established that, when acting in a group, the individual sacrifices intellectual power but is stimulated emotionally, and the collective psyche tends towards generalisation and thinking in symbolic terms. People who, whether acting out of self-interest, genuine conviction or a combination of the two, are able to excite the primary human feelings, have always been able to exert huge influence on large sections of the population, and one way this becomes manifest is in religious fervour.

Yet behind every religious war there is a fight for political or economic power. Incumbent or aspiring rulers have always used religious fervour to rally the masses and to help them achieve their aims. In other words, religion has never been the exclusive or main reason for a conflict, but rather an excuse. As Kissinger puts it, 'Religion is "weaponised" in the service of geopolitical objectives.'

From the time of the Romans, via the Crusades, to the current jihadi context, religion has been used to justify attacks against states or groups that are seen to be a threat to political and economic interests. This includes war camouflaged as some kind of mystical mission.

The so-called 'Quest for the Holy Grail', which first appeared in 1180 in the unfinished *Perceval, the Story of the Grail* by Chrétien de Troyes, was used as propaganda to summon European Christians to reconquer land occupied by Muslim infidels. In the sixteenth century, at the time of the Protestant Reformation, many feudal lords converted to Protestantism with the sole purpose of acquiring property belonging to the Catholic Church. Religion has served as a cover for all manner of cynical initiatives.

During the First World War, Sheikh ul-Islam, the Ottoman Empire's main religious leader, declared jihad on Russia, France and Britain, whom he accused of attacks aimed at crushing Islam. He proclaimed in the name of the Ottoman Empire that it was the religious duty of Muslims everywhere, including those living under British, French or Russian administrative rule, to immediately answer the call with their bodies and possessions. The order was given in the name of the Ottoman Empire, which presented itself as leader of the unified Muslim world, having expanded in all directions through armed conflicts disguised as holy wars.

Religion and geopolitics sometimes fuse into a belief in some kind of sacred calling, as when a nation deems itself to be the chosen one, which is the case with the USA today. According to the former Palestinian Foreign Minister Nabil Shaath, George W. Bush told those attending an Israeli–Palestinian peace summit in 2003 that he had authorised large-scale military interventions in Afghanistan and Iraq after being given the order by none other than God. This position should not come as a surprise – as Pierre M. Gallois pointed out, General Dwight D. Eisenhower declared in 1953 that 'destiny has laid upon our country the responsibility of the free world's leadership'.

Leaders often use religious-political codes to mobilise populations, in what is a fairly effective strategy. Machiavelli highlighted the importance of maintaining fear and respect for religion among troops, for they proved more obedient when threatened by punishment from a higher power. Marenches believed there is no greater weapon than the highly motivated individual warrior, and that nothing is more motivational than religious fanaticism with the promise of everlasting life for those who do not fear death. This is the understanding of today's Salafist jihadi groups that spur their followers on to wage war against the unfaithful and the unholy, despite the fact that the geopolitical ambitions behind the war are either vague or almost impossible to achieve. The jihadi discourse is identical to that used by the Knights Templar in the era of the Crusades: kill the unfaithful 'because that's what God wants', and then reach paradise and be absolved of your sins for having died fighting the unfaithful.

That said, although it has increased in recent years, sectarianism is not the main source of tension in the Middle East, and nor has it ever been. The conflict in Yemen, for example, is not religious per se: religious differences between Sunni and Shia are being used to justify interventions prompted by a clash of geopolitical interests and the leadership aspirations of two regional powers, Saudi Arabia and Iran.

JIHAD AS A CAUSE OF COMBAT

The prophet Muhammad, on his return to Medina after the Battle of Badr in 624, is supposed to have pronounced, 'We have returned from the small jihad to the big jihad.' The 'big jihad' refers to the individual's inner struggle to purify the ego. The Arabic word *jihad* literally means 'effort' and in Islamic tradition has a meaning that can be both religious and military: fighting one's base emotions and defending Islam against external aggression. This double meaning became outdated in the Middle Ages, when different types of jihad were established according to different interpretations of Muhammad's sayings.

The concept of jihad of the sword, meaning all manner of armed actions to ensure Islam's continued existence and to protect its lands when attacked, is the most controversial in that it is open to interpretation by those with vested interests; it has served to underpin numerous initiatives of conquest and has often been loaded with connotations similar to those of the term 'holy war', employed in the West to justify the Crusades, the real purpose of which was reconquering the Holy Lands and, in Spain, the recovery of land taken by the Saracens.

After Muhammad's death in 632, the caliphs that succeeded him held up jihad to unite different tribal groups, using religious feeling to channel the aggressions of tribal warriors who, thinking themselves implicated in a holy war, turned into mujahideen, 'people fighting a jihad'. This stirring up of religious fervour had a practical benefit, because expanding the faith through war boosted the economy through the riches won in conquests, which ensured the new doctrine quickly spread. Jihad has since been called on numerous occasions throughout history. At the end of the nineteenth century, when Russia appealed to a collective sense of Christian identity to persuade Armenians to join them in fighting the Turks, the Ottomans used Muslim solidarity to launch a jihad against Russia.

In Africa it has been common for rulers to declare jihad with the materialistic aim of controlling transport routes through the desert, which is what happened with the Sokoto Caliphate, founded in 1809 during the Fulani jihad against the Hausa Kingdom. During the first Tuareg rebellion in Mali (1916–17) a jihad was declared to help expel the French.

A call to jihad was also attempted during the Bosnian War (1992–5), with limited success: exact figures are disputed, but most estimates suggest that between 1,000 and 2,000 foreign mujahideen came to fight on behalf of Bosnian Muslims. The most recent declaration of jihad came from Islamic State in Syria and Iraq.

How to create a jihad

One aim of jihad is to bring about a new social model in which politics and religion become one. The Islamisation of society has regularly been used in the Muslim world as a means of reaching or maintaining power, with military action used to achieve internal control or external conquest. Muhammad al-Shaybani, an Islamic law scholar, drafted guidelines for jihad against unbelievers in the eighth century. His notions were further developed by the Spanish-Muslim philosopher Ibn Rushd (known in the Western world as Averroes) in his 1168 treatise *Jihad*.

The process begins when the ruling class, inspired by religious and historical factors and driven by political, nationalist, geopolitical and economic aspirations, decides to use the lower strata of society to help it pursue its aims, and declares a jihad. The imams and the *ulama* – the body of Islamic scholars – play a fundamental role in the jihad process. By preaching the strictest form of Islam, they spread radical ideas, which intellectuals reshape to make accessible to the general population. The intellectuals will likely be well educated and have university degrees, but not have gained the socio-occupational recognition they feel they deserve, so are frustrated. Faced with a lack of social mobility, they see jihad as a class struggle.

There is no shortage of young people prepared to join the ranks. In Tunisia, for instance, a country with 10 million inhabitants, some 7,000 people have left to join the ranks of Islamic State in Syria and Iraq; it is estimated that 40 per cent of them have completed some kind of university study. The level of frustration among the young in Tunisia is high due to a perception that the efforts they made in gaining their qualifications are not rewarded. Work opportunities are either monopolised by the elites or poorly paid, and unemployment rates are among the highest in the world, reaching 60 per cent among the young.

Those who supply the funds for jihad and provide shelter for its operatives tend to be pious members of the bourgeoisie. These qualified people are from conservative and middle-class backgrounds, are highly motivated by ideology and become involved with Islamist movements in part due to concerns that Western values are eroding their society.

The militant base consists of underprivileged individuals with no future prospects who, in the absence of state welfare, turn to Islamic organisations for help. Hamas and Hezbollah, for example, provide their followers with better social aid than the state. These individuals are the pawns, easily manoeuvred and always ready for revolution. They are ripe for the picking, and their recruitment merely involves rallying them to fight against injustice and oppression, and for a new social order that is more generous to them. Whether it is perceived or actual, their social marginalisation leads them to look beyond their daily reality for meaning. The jihadi dream is sold to them as a mixture of class struggle, sociopolitical revolution and religious war.

Lastly come the fanatics. Every religion has those who are convinced of the righteousness of the cause and overcome with religious fervour. Believing they must defend their religion at all costs, and with their lives if necessary, they are prepared to do whatever is asked of them, including suicide, because their faith is the most important aspect of their existence. No matter how far the socioeconomic conditions of majority Muslim countries improve, there will always be fanatics who want to take their society back to an fantasy past of untold splendour, in which all elements of life were governed by a extreme and strict view of Islam.

THE CRUSADES – THE CHRISTIAN JIHAD

The four Crusades that took place from the end of the tenth to the end of the thirteenth century were inspired by religious reasons, but had political, social and economic elements. Feudal lords saw the religious fervour that motivated thousands of people to join the fight against the infidels and took advantage of it to open up new trading routes to the east. These routes, which included a land passage to India that might even have led to China, would be impossible to use as long as they remained under Muslim control.

The foot soldier crusaders answered the call to arms based on their faith, but also a yearning for fame and fortune. Joining up was a means of improving one's social standing, through the riches and land promised by the recruiters; though in the popular imagination they were all gentlemen knights in armour, the majority of the crusaders were from the lower classes.

The history of this military-religious venture can be traced back to Muslim expansion in the early years of Islam's existence, which included seizing control of Jerusalem in 638. By 1074, Pope Gregory VII proposed offering assistance to Christians in the east who were suffering Muslim attacks, an idea his successor, Pope Urban II, would develop further; this led to the First Crusade (1095–9), which culminated in the re-conquest of Jerusalem. These campaigns mixed religious concerns with geopolitical thinking, and sought to protect pilgrims bound for the Holy Land, help the Byzantine Empire fight back and consolidate Papal supremacy. Pope Urban II, who died two weeks before Jerusalem was reconquered, showed how the skilful combining of religious fervour and military tactics could bring excellent results. This did not go unnoticed by al-Sulami, a Muslim cleric in Damascus, who knew no city in Syria was strong enough to withstand a Christian attack. He understood that the only way to resist would be to create a cause that every Muslim would be compelled to answer, a fight to defend the lands of those devoted to Islam: jihad.

Over subsequent years and centuries, the Holy Land became the stage for multiple battles. The religious convictions involved were undoubtedly genuine, but spiritual concerns have always combined with material interests in matters of Islamic jihad and

Christian holy war. The attitudes of both sides throughout these confrontations might be summarised by the cry that inspired the first charge of the crusaders in Anatolia: 'Stand fast together, trusting in Christ and the victory of the Holy Cross and today, please God, may we all gain many riches.'

The combination of religious fervour and armed combat also produced the first religious orders, the Christian equivalent of the mujahideen. The best example of this was the Poor Fellow-Soldiers of Christ and of the Temple of Solomon: the Knights Templar. A new order that was both militant and religious, the Knights Templar needed an ideological doctrine to satisfy misgivings about men putting people to the sword in the name of a religion that was ostensibly pacifistic. To settle this paradox, the concept of the just war was born.

In 1128, Baldwin II, King of Jerusalem, aware of the advantages that employing ascetic warrior monks in combat would bring, sent Hugues de Payens, the first Grand Master of the Knights Templar, to Europe to seek new recruits to swell their ranks and gather provisions for the Holy Land. He argued that sin and guilt resided not in the act of killing but in the intent: killing an enemy was only a sin if done out of hatred; there was no sin in killing with purity of spirit. On de Payens's bidding, Bernard of Clairvaux, abbot of the Cistercian order, wrote a work that would provide the grounding for the Templar's ideals, *In Praise of the New Knighthood*, written between 1126 and 1129. In this work, St Bernard provides rational reasoning for holy war and justification for the use of violence against the unfaithful:

> The knights of Christ can fight the battles of their Lord with complete tranquillity of conscience, fearing neither sin if they kill the enemy, nor the danger of being killed themselves. For to inflict death or to suffer death for Christ has nothing criminal about it, but rather brings an abundant claim to glory ... Killing is preferable to having the rod of sinners hanging over the heads of the just ... Certainly it is proper ... that they be thrown out of the Lord's city all these producers of iniquities, they who dream of snatching from the Christian people their estimable riches enclosed in Jerusalem, sullying the Holy Sites and taking control of God's sanctuary.

The warrior monks gradually lost ground to the Muslims, among whom leaders with tremendous religious fervour emerged. They inspired their troops to seize any lands from the Christian infidels that they considered to be the property of Islam.

Centuries later, tensions in the Middle East continued between Christianity and the officially Islamic Ottoman Empire. The Crimean War (1853–6) was sparked by a geopolitical issue: the control of the Black Sea access to the Mediterranean, but it was dressed up as the defence of Christian communities in Ottoman-controlled Jerusalem. Tsar Nicholas I positioned himself as the defender of Orthodox Christians living in territories ruled by the Ottomans, many of which were of strategic importance. The Ottomans considered their sovereignty to be under attack and firmly opposed the Tsar, which prompted Russia to enter the Balkans and so began the confrontations.

THE NORTH CAUCASUS

In recent history, Muslims in the North Caucasus have repeatedly been manipulated for geopolitical aims. The Caucasus, located between the Black Sea and the Caspian Sea, is the gateway to Europe from Asia and therefore of huge geopolitical importance. Russia's fight to control this area dates back to the time of Peter the Great, who expanded into the region in the eighteenth century to keep the Ottoman Empire at bay. The area has been a constant source of conflict ever since, with various powers using religious differences to pursue their own geopolitical goals.

In the nineteenth century, both the Ottoman and British empires stirred up conflict between Orthodox Christianity and Islam. London's main interest was to prevent, or at least hinder, Moscow's expansion towards the Mediterranean Sea, the Indian Ocean and Persia: if the Russians controlled the area, a vital artery connecting Europe to the Indies would be put at risk. For Istanbul, achieving a total Islamisation of the Caucasus was key to the dream of expansion that it pursued until the final days of its empire.

During the Second World War, Germany also had interests in the area. Controlling the region would provide access to oil resources in Baku and the possibility of expanding as far as Iran, which was coveted due to its strategic location and energy reserves. Berlin began courting Turkey to persuade it to participate in capturing the Caucasus; Hitler drew up a plan for winning independence for the Caucasian nations, through which he hoped to earn the loyalty of their hardened warriors and have them fight on the Axis side against the Allies and the Soviet Union. From there, Hitler could have taken over the Caucasus oil wells and encircled British India (with the other part of the pincer formed by Japan). With this in mind, the German secret services had some success in supporting Muslims in the North Caucasus in confrontations with Moscow, and managed to persuade some to enlist in the German army.

Stalin, fearing a Berlin-backed revolt in the region, elected to deport more than one and a half million Muslims from the North Caucasus towards Central Asia between November 1943 and March 1944. Without making any allowances, he deported the majority of Caucasians enlisted in the Red Army, at least half of whom died of typhus en route. Although Khrushchev allowed them to return to their homes in 1956, Stalin's deportation had aroused a hatred of all things Russian among North Caucasus Muslims that lives on today.

The region is still a tinderbox that Russia and the USA consider key to their geostrategic and economic interests. This is not only because of its position between Europe and Asia, but because it is a region rich in hydrocarbons and uranium deposits. With the experience of the Second World War still fresh, Moscow has long suspected that Washington would take advantage of regional instability to deny Russia its long-held ambition of expanding south. Losing control of the region would make Russia vulnerable to any attempt to cut off its energy supply lines. With this in mind, Russia has publicly accused pro-West Georgia of supporting al-Qaeda in Chechnya.

Russia's unconditional support of Iran in the development of its nuclear capacity may be motivated by the fear that, were Moscow to withdraw its backing, Tehran might react by giving support to the mujahideen fighting in the region, which Iran has thus far refrained from doing.

THE BAGHDAD PACT

On 24 February 1955, the Central Treaty Organization (CENTO), better known as the Baghdad Pact,[52] was established between Iraq and Turkey; they were joined shortly afterwards by Iran and the UK, with Pakistan signing up a year later. It also had the military and economic backing of the White House and, indirectly, the Atlantic Alliance, with Turkey acting as a link between the two organisations.

Washington and London were the driving forces behind this defence-focused organisation. The US did not participate directly so as not to antagonise Arab countries with which it had a fraught relationship, limiting itself to joining the military committee in 1958. For the British, CENTO was a way of exerting influence in the Middle East in a manner that would compensate somewhat for their loss of India, but the true purpose of CENTO was to have a military alliance in the region that would halt Soviet expansion. The US, the UK and NATO worked to stoke religious fervour among the Muslim members of the pact, in order to mobilise them against the Soviets, who had been making inroads in the region through aggressively supporting social justice projects.[53]

However, the Soviet Union played its hand well and the Baghdad Pact proved powerless to stop Moscow from extending its reach in the region through political agreements and military alliances. The Soviets came to exert great influence on Egypt, Iraq, Libya, Syria, Somalia and Yemen, establishing naval bases and deploying thousands of soldiers. Perhaps not coincidentally, these places are now the most unstable countries in the region; outside interference does lasting damage. We may also be seeing a rerun of the Cold War in the region – the USA, bitter about having lost out in these places first time round, is determined to make a belated mark. Religious fervour, specifically that of Sunni Muslims, is being manipulated once again, principally by Saudi Arabia and Turkey, in order to expel Russia from Syria and prevent it from establishing a foothold in Libya and Egypt. The problem is that the stirring up of religious fervour can unleash a monster that eventually turns on its creator.

AFGHANISTAN: THE CALL TO GLOBAL JIHAD

The Brezhnev Doctrine, which allowed for military intervention to help socialist regimes in difficulty, provided the official justification for the Soviet Union to enter Afghanistan in December 1979. Having signed a Treaty of Friendship, Cooperation and Good Neighbourliness with Afghanistan the year before, the USSR was able to claim that it was answering a call to defend the Afghan people against imperialist aggression.

The Soviet decision to intervene was influenced by the Iranian Revolution, which saw Iran become an Islamic republic in April 1979. Moscow worried that the Islamic fervour roused by the Ayatollah could spread to countries with majority Muslim populations south of the USSR. The Soviet intervention in Afghanistan thus sought to use the Hindu Kush mountain range as a natural barrier to prevent Islamism from making incursions into Soviet territory.

The vast social differences between Afghanistan's large urban centres and its rural zones were exacerbated due to Soviet education policies and the increased participation of women in different facets of society. By the time the Soviets withdrew in 1988, around 50 per cent of students and 18 per cent of state employees were women; these developments were considered sinful by some and the mujahideen used this to gain support for their radical ideology. They met the Soviet invasion with a major guerrilla warfare campaign and they were aided in this by Afghanistan's challenging mountainous landscape. The mujahideen lacked a definite leader and were not fighting to install a new social model; their principal driving force was a will to preserve ancient traditions and concepts of honour. No strong ideological ties, other than a fervent adherence to the Islamic faith, were formed between the different groups: their loyalty was solely to local leaders.

The US administration continued to employ the containment policy it had put into place at the beginning of the Cold War. Aimed at halting the advance of the Soviet Union and its sphere of influence, the US, aided by Saudi Arabia and Pakistan, sponsored a global jihad to which thousands of fighters from all over the world responded. The immediate result was the defeat of the USSR, but the consequences of exacerbating Islamic radicalism in the region are likely to be felt for a long time to come.

Rule 17

THE ESCAPE ROUTE

How to recognise that a desperate enemy is the most dangerous opponent

'Leave the door of reconciliation open for enemies'

— BALTASAR GRACIÁN

Machiavelli cautions against driving enemies to desperation because it makes people unpredictable and dangerous. Sun Tzu says 'If enemies are desperate, they come to win or die, so avoid confronting them. When you surround an army, leave an outlet free. If they lack everything, you must prevent their desperation. Do not press a desperate foe too hard.' Countries or people who can see no way out become doubly determined. The escape-route strategy makes sure a door is always left open for the enemy to beat a dignified retreat.

THE ERROR AT NORBA

The settlement of Norba was built by the Volsci overlooking the Pontine Marshes, thirty miles south-east of Rome.[54] Given its strategic position, Rome sought to colonise Norba from 492 BC and eventually won control after triumphing in the Roman–Volscian wars. Norba was also fought over during the First Latin War (498–493 BC) between the Roman Republic and the Latin League, with Rome again coming out on top. Later came Rome's first civil war (88–87 BC), which brought about Norba's demise. The civil war was sparked by the Roman general Sulla, who sought to return republican Rome to a dictatorship, and entered the Italian peninsula with an army of over 40,000 men. Local people had already heard of the fate that awaited conquered cities: inhabitants had been disarmed and dismembered and their cities pillaged. Faced with this prospect, the cities that had not yet fallen were not inclined to surrender and so resisted.

What made Norba stand out was its demise. When Sulla's troops burst into the city, its citizens committed mass suicide to avoid falling into enemy hands. They set fire to themselves and burned the city to ashes, preventing their conquerors from seizing their riches. Despite Sulla's efforts to rebuild it, Norba lost its geostrategic significance and was classified by Pliny the Elder as an extinct city. If the inhabitants had been offered an escape route, perhaps they would have surrendered, preserving the city's riches and strategic worth. Sulla would certainly have found it more profitable if he'd given Norba the chance to claim an honourable defeat. Roman conquerors did this elsewhere, offering populations certain rights if they surrendered and allowing them to keep their land in exchange for taxes and conscripts.

NUMANTINE RESISTANCE

If the Roman rulers had read the Chinese strategist Sun Bin's *The Art of War*, and specifically the passage that advises 'do not attack the desperate, wait until they have found a means of survival', they would not have forced the Iberian city of Numantia to offer the resistance it did. The city put up such a fight that the expression 'Numantine resistance' entered the Spanish lexicon to describe tenacious resistance in difficult circumstances.

The remains of this Celtiberian town are located close to modern-day Soria, in northern Spain. In the summer of 133 BC, the town was besieged by Roman troops led by Publius Cornelius Scipio Aemilianus, also known as Scipio Africanus Minor. The Celtiberians had been fending off the Romans for over twenty years, and the mighty Senate was beginning to feel humiliated at being unable to conquer this tiny town. Determined to settle the matter once and for all, they began by surrounding Numantia with moats, towers, stockades and ramparts. They then built a high, thick wall, almost ten kilometres long, with towers every thirty metres, and patrolled it with soldiers armed with crossbows and catapults. Seven camps were established to lay siege to the town and stop nearby tribes from coming to the assistance of the Numantines. The Romans were confident that the inhabitants would beg for mercy as soon as hunger and sickness took their toll. Military superiority was on their side: they had over 60,000 men and a dozen elephants, while the Numantines numbered no more than 2,500.

But the Numantines refused to succumb. They resisted until the last, then chose to commit suicide collectively rather than to surrender, and burned the town to rubble. All Scipio got from this hollow victory was fifty-odd Numantines his army managed to capture alive, while the defeated city entered into legend.

GEOPOLITICAL 'ESCAPE VALVES'

The pressure cooker that is international geopolitics requires a number of 'escape valves' to ease tension between the leading players and avoid open warfare. The proxy wars of the Cold War are one example. Such conflicts occur when two or more powers face off via a third party, thus avoiding direct confrontation. They usually take place using private security groups, mercenaries or spies, but during the Cold War whole countries were used; the Korea and Vietnam wars allowed both sides to let off steam without engaging in a direct confrontation that might have led to mutual destruction. Along with skilled diplomacy, they prevented Washington or Moscow from ever feeling trapped to the point of having to choose the nuclear option.

In the current geopolitical context, it is conceivable that North Korea, suffocated by international sanctions and pressured on all fronts, could commit some kind of unexpected act if not offered a diplomatic 'escape valve' to save face.

Rule 18

THE MR NICE GUY STRATEGY

How to rule with a smile

'You gain more from licking than biting'

— SPANISH PROVERB

The 'Mr Nice Guy' strategy consists of framing your demands as being for the common good, in order to exert your will without causing friction. It can become a subtle but tyrannical form of power, allowing a state total control without drawing protest and tension. The strategy involves never openly provoking or being seen kicking and screaming. Reasonable and unaggressive on the surface, Mr Nice Guy is able to move forward without resistance. When well-executed, this strategy is tremendously effective, disarming partners and opponents alike, for such evident goodwill is taken to be indicative of a belief in the general good. But Mr Nice Guy is, in fact, cynically and cunningly pursuing his own interests.

The user of this strategy is something of a chameleon, able to camouflage actions with posturing. Mr Nice Guy does not react to shows of strength, menace or pressure, but it is an 'active' rather than a passive non-reaction, ignoring all provocations and continuing to do as he pleases. It is possible to morally and intellectually neuter much more powerful adversaries in this way, unaccustomed as they are to having their threats ignored. Mr Nice Guy simply rises above them, takes care not to raise the tension and waits for the adversary, frustrated by a lack of reaction or response, to tire and give up. A parallel can be drawn between this tactic and the Chinese execution method of death by a thousand cuts. Employed in China for centuries before finally being outlawed in 1905, it kills without the victim realising it, through tiny wounds that merely irritate, but ultimately drain the body of blood.

SOFT POWER

In geopolitics, the 'Mr Nice Guy strategy' manifests itself through the use of soft rather than hard power. Introduced as a term by the American geopolitical scientist Joseph Nye in the late 1980s, 'soft power' is a country's ability to persuade other countries to do what it wants without resorting to force. In 2004, Nye applied it to US foreign policy after 9/11. He argues that, in order to force others to change their ways in the long term, a state must use a combination of soft and hard power.

If anyone has mastered the art of soft power, it is the White House. Aided by companies, foundations, universities and other civic institutions, the US has exported its values and beliefs to the rest of the world. We have already seen how its films are consumed all over the world, ensuring that its outlook is absorbed by others, and, as Nye has said, US security policy is based as much on winning hearts and minds as it is on winning wars. Kissinger said much the same thing when he stated, 'No foreign policy – no matter how ingenious – has any chance of success if it is born in the minds of a few and carried in the hearts of none.' In the modern world, an ever more complex international panorama means that soft power is of increasing importance. Wider access to information has obliged states to favour public diplomacy and cultural propaganda over sabre-rattling to achieve their foreign policy objectives.

The 'make nice' ambitions of the United States

According to the Brazilian historian Moniz Bandeira, every US president since the fall of the Berlin Wall and the disintegration of the Soviet Union, whether Republican or Democrat, has had one geopolitical goal in mind: world domination.[55] This comes from the conviction that Americans are an exceptional nation that is morally obliged to spread democracy, basic freedoms and human rights around the globe, against people's will and with the use of force if necessary.

This belief in the American people's 'manifest destiny' has led occupants of the White House to unquestioningly assume the role of global saviour and guardian of peace and security. As Moniz points out, it tallies with another of Kissinger's well-known phrases: 'America had a mission to bring about democracy – if necessary, by the use of force.' Since the United States came into being in 1776, only twenty-one years have passed during which it has not been involved in a war.

Behind a shamelessly flaunted altruistic façade lurk economic interests and entrenched geopolitical ambitions. Whether the incumbent president favours a friendly smile or a stern or hostile expression, it is always a mask: behind the scenes he is being controlled by an economic elite, which dictates foreign policy. Moniz asserts that major global decisions are ultimately taken by an exclusive club made up of high finance, the military-industrial complex, the intelligence services, families with large fortunes, religious organisations, the mighty multinationals and the energy industry. He claims that whenever Washington intervenes in world affairs, waving the flag of freedom and democracy while reinforcing its own dominant position, the result is the same: chaos, violence and humanitarian disaster.

Obama's eight years as president offer a prime example of the Mr Nice Guy strategy. A global media campaign that presented him as a friendly, modest and tolerant figure not only repaired the damage to US prestige caused by his predecessor, George W. Bush, but allowed the same hegemonic policies pursued by his predecessors to be glossed over and even excused. A scandal such as the National Security Agency (NSA) spying on European leaders became no more than a press anecdote, when it might otherwise have caused the streets of European capitals to fill with anti-American protests.

Moniz notes how Obama changed the wording of US foreign policy – officially ditching 'war on terror' or 'long war' for 'overseas contingency operations' – while in reality continuing to intervene in other countries just as before, and in some cases with increased vigour. This was often done through opaque or covert actions that used special operations forces and via drone attacks. Tens of thousands of bombs were dropped on Afghanistan, Iraq and Syria, and a huge number of arms were sold to Saudi Arabia. The Bureau of Investigative Journalism estimates that 373 drone attacks were carried out in Pakistani territory alone under the Obama administration, with between 2,089 and 3,406 people killed (of whom between 257 and 634 were civilians, and between sixty-six and seventy-eight were children). Some sources also suggest that, when reporting on drone attacks, the US government counts any man of military age as a 'combatant' rather than a civilian.[56]

Rule 19

THE CREATION OF NEED

How to sell arms

'Intelligence gathered by this and other governments leaves no doubt that the Iraq regime continues to possess and conceal some of the most lethal weapons ever devised'

– GEORGE W. BUSH

When a state has a lot of something, or can easily access it, creating a sense of need for that product elsewhere can bring riches and power. If there are no needs, they must be created: the most celebrated marketing gurus are those who can push products consumers never realised they needed. The same thing happens with armaments in geopolitics.

The Maslow pyramid establishes five levels of need: physiological, security, affiliation, recognition and self-fulfilment. According to this theory, once the human being has satisfied his or her basic needs, beginning with the physiological, the higher needs come into focus, concluding with self-fulfilment. This can be extrapolated to the international context; because countries have more or less pressing needs, other countries can exploit them to their own benefit, and can even encourage such needs to emerge. Every state, no matter how benevolent and peaceful, must protect itself from potential enemies. There will always be another state with a major arms industry ready to offer an arsenal of ingenious defence equipment that will likely never be used. If the vulnerable state is not convinced of the need to protect itself, a more powerful one may take the liberty of reminding it of the possibility of an imminent attack.

Creating a need often goes hand in hand with creating an enemy, and there is overlap with the 'beggar thy neighbour' strategy. Arms-selling countries stir up animosities and overemphasise threats, for they trade on fear: South Korea's fear of North Korea; Saudi Arabia and other Gulf countries' fear of Iran; Colombia's fear of Venezuela; Poland, the Baltic countries and Ukraine's fear of Russia; India's fear of China.

The US writer Eliot Weinberger recalls how, in order to convince public opinion of the need to invade Iraq in 2003, the US government disseminated a number of dubious 'facts'. One was that Iraq had bought concentrated uranium oxide from Niger, which

Weinberger believes to have been false. Another was that aluminium tubes suitable for use as centrifuges had been found, which was true, although that's not what they were being used for. Mobile biological laboratories were flagged up, though they proved to be producing helium for weather balloons. An apparent fleet of unmanned planes proved to be one, large, inoperable airship. Saddam did not have the labyrinth of underground bunkers he was alleged to have, and of the 400,000 bodies supposedly buried in unmarked mass graves, only 5,000 were ever found. In Weinberger's eyes, the most ridiculous part of all this was that the principal source of what Colin Powell, Secretary General of the United States between 2001 and 2005, claimed to be 'solid information' was an essay written by a postgraduate student a decade earlier.

According to a study by the Congressional Research Service, Washington sold 46 billion dollars' worth of arms in 2015 alone, and the Pentagon confirmed that in 2016 sales continued along the same line. Under the Obama administration, US companies conducted 278 billion dollars' worth of arms sales, more than double the business done during Bush's mandate. The majority of these weapons went to countries in the Middle East within the framework of a campaign to combat terrorism or protect countries from an attack by Iran. In fact, according to the Stockholm International Peace Research Institute (SIPRI), the principal arms purchasers between 2012 and 2016 were Saudi Arabia (according to some estimates, the US sold the Saudis up to 120 billion dollars of weaponry during the eight years of Obama's presidency), the United Arab Emirates and Turkey. Following in the slipstream of his predecessor, Trump closed a deal to sell the Saudis a further 110 billion dollars' worth of armaments in May 2017. One month later, with the Gulf region in crisis, he sold Qatar thirty-six F-15 fighter planes, which cost 12 billion dollars.

The fundamental human need for security is also exploited by states. The mainstream political discourses call for peace and gradual disarmament, which rings hollow when we know that the armaments industry is worth billions of dollars to the US every year. World leaders speak of peace at forums such as the United Nations, while increasing their defence budgets. There is no better way of advertising the virtues of your military products than by using them in whatever wars are currently underway; Syria is currently a veritable testing ground for new equipment.

Although the strategy of creating need can be applied to other sectors, such as technology, its military and geopolitical use provides the clearest example of how economic interests lead states to exploit situations for their own gain. The world powers, with their access to almost unlimited capacities of production, understand that large-scale manufacturing requires large-scale consumption, and that nothing consumes more than organised destruction, which also creates a need for massive reconstruction. War has always been a profitable business.

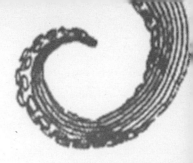

Rule 20

THE MADMAN

How to keep your rivals guessing

'Vary your behaviour. This confuses others,
especially competitors'

— BALTASAR GRACIÁN

Classical figures ranging from King David and Ulysses to the Arab mathematician and astronomer Alhazen all used the technique of pretending to be mad to escape from difficulty or achieve a certain aim. These days, many people employ the tactic, sometimes in a way that is not entirely conscious; giving the people around you the impression that you are mentally unstable and will react viciously and disproportionately to being slighted makes you seem more imposing. The strategy is often performed by managers, directors and business leaders to subjugate subordinates and wrongfoot rivals. It can also be employed to avoid threatening situations, feigned mental incapacity often resulting in being dismissed or ignored. Again, these concepts can also be applied to the geopolitical sphere.

NIXON THE 'MADMAN'

'The madman theory', as Nixon and Kissinger called it, was a defining characteristic of Nixon's foreign policy. It was used as a means of discouraging the Soviet Union from attacking the US, out of fear that the apparently deranged Nixon's response would be unpredictable and unhinged. For the tactic to be successful, the madman must give the impression of being prepared to go to any extreme, regardless of the risks and consequences. In Nixon's case, the tactic relied on the fact that he had a massive nuclear arsenal at his disposal. He had to act erratically and disturbingly enough for other world leaders to believe he might be prepared to use it, in order to make them afraid to not let him have his way. During the 1968 presidential campaign, Nixon had promised to put an end to the Vietnam War, but a year into his presidency, the war was still going on and there was no sign of a peace agreement between North Vietnam, supported by the Soviet Union, and the South, backed by the US. Nixon decided to enact the madman strategy; he spread rumours that he was a radical and violent anti-communist who was unafraid of pressing the nuclear button. This reputation was carefully sculpted by Nixon himself and by Henry Kissinger, his National Security Advisor.

The madman theory had been discussed within Kissinger's academic circles since the mid-1950s in debates about the nuclear arms race. The strategy was born of game theory, a branch of mathematics that seeks to predict the decisions that will be made in competitive situations based on choices made in similar scenarios.

On 19 April 1972, Nixon gave Kissinger the message he wanted to convey to his counterpart in the Kremlin. According to official records, that afternoon the National Security Advisor flew to Moscow with the Soviet Ambassador to the United States. During the flight, Kissinger and Nixon staged a phone call that they knew the Russians would be listening into, in which the US President threatened to nuclear bomb North Vietnam if necessary. He wanted the Soviets to believe he would stop at nothing, with Kissinger then able to appeal to the common sense of the Soviets to help him curb the 'demented' Nixon. Harry Robbins Haldeman, Nixon's Chief of Staff, later said that the President was proud of his plan to make the North Vietnamese believe he had reached the point where he was capable of doing anything to end the war. However, the North Vietnamese were also prepared to sacrifice everything and both sides continued their costly and destructive military operations, which included the Christmas bombing of 1972, in which the US discharged at least 20,000 tonnes of explosives in North Vietnam between 18 and 29 December, excluding Christmas Day. The official figures included 1,600 North Vietnamese deaths, but the actual figure was probably higher. On 8 January the following year, both parties finally came to the negotiating table for peace talks.

Is trump applying the madman strategy ... ?

On 7 April 2017 the US attacked the Shayrat airbase in Syria, launching fifty-nine Tomahawk cruise missiles from two destroyers, in response to chemical weapons attacks allegedly committed by al-Assad's Syrian regime on its own people the day before. This represented a complete about-turn by Donald Trump, who had previously claimed that he was opposed to military intervention in Syria and, more generally, to US involvement in military ventures that did not directly affect US national security.

Trump suddenly changed his mind, taking the world by surprise and launching a hasty attack against a sovereign country without waiting for any independent investigation of the facts and without consulting his own allies or the UN. Although there were geopolitical interests at play (rivalry with Russia, Iranian expansion in the region and the threat to Israel of strengthening Shia groups) and domestic political considerations (discussions of his relationship with Putin during the presidential election campaign and pressure from his own Republican Party and other lobby groups), President Trump might well have been employing the madman strategy. If so, the act could be seen as a strategic demonstration of his unpredictability, in order to keep potential adversaries in a permanent state of anxiety about how he might act towards them.

Just as it is too early to say whether Trump's antics are instinctive or strategic, it is too early to say whether he will keep his promise of leading America towards a form of isolationism or if he will do the reverse and begin a phase of decisive interventionism.

... AND IS NORTH KOREA PLAYING THE SAME GAME?

North Korea is a prime example of a state that is currently using the madman strategy. Kim Jong-un boastfully publicises his nuclear tests and missile launches to warn his adversaries of what he might be capable of if confronted.[57] But what would happen if the other side called his bluff – would the madman retreat? What if he really is mad and follows through on his threats? The situation could degenerate into a clash of opposing madman strategies, with Kim Jong-un on one side and Trump on the other. By constantly raising the stakes, convinced the other will blink first, they could end up in open confrontation.

*

Frightening your adversaries into respecting your interests or doing what you want them to do is an ancient strategy that remains effective today. In geopolitics it has become particularly pertinent in the nuclear era, due to the imminent danger presented by the atomic bomb. The madman strategy can be profitable in the short term, but adversaries gradually learn to anticipate the likely consequences, and sometimes also make their own provocative feints. Opponents can also take the same strategy even further, particularly if they represent groups or countries that need not answer to a parliament or public opinion.

Ultimately this type of strategy can be considered a failure of diplomacy and negotiation, and can lead to self-destruction for whoever puts it into practice. As a deterrent, madman antics can end up being counterproductive if the much-trailed volatile, unprecedented and even suicidal response proves to be anything less than that. In the long run, the madman strategy generates more antagonism than proximity does. Traditional allies, and countries that generally prefer to stay in the shadows, can never be sure where they stand and can't tell whether the madman will one day turn against them.

Rule 21

THE TOWER OF CHAMPAGNE GLASSES

How to rule so everyone benefits

'If you organise a party, make sure your servers get some benefits'

— CARDINAL MAZARIN

Picture a glamorous party with a tower of champagne glasses arranged in a pyramid. The champagne is poured into the glass at the top and trickles down to those at the bottom. If every guest gets a full glass, there are no complaints. A similar process occurs in politics and international relations: it consists of sharing power, ideas, culture and resources, or at least making other states think you are sharing them. As long as enough of these rewards reach the lower rungs, there will be no protest or revolution. The imaginary champagne tower will only remain standing if those at the bottom get their fair share.

The superpowers, forever fearful that one or more of their 'vassal' states will stab them in the back at the first sign of weakness, make sure to pass on the dregs of their own riches to the rulers of other countries. Duly satisfied, these rulers will snuff out any anti-imperialist sentiments emerging among their people, guaranteeing stability.

BREAD AND CIRCUSES

The 'bread and circuses strategy' dates back to ancient Greece, where inequality between the classes was only tolerated because of the festivals and banquets the rich threw for everyone. Later, political rights were conceded to those citizens who could ensure the survival of the community through acts of 'evergetism', a term of Greek origin describing a willingness to do good for the city as a whole.

The application of the strategy was different in ancient Rome, where society did not depend on the wealth of rich individuals but the bounty of conquests to survive. Kaplan concluded that it was the Roman Empire's liberal treatment of its subjects that stopped the people from revolting. The term bread and circuses (*'panem et circenses'*) was conceived of by the Roman poet Juvenal, who used it to describe the way emperors entertained the masses to alleviate discontent. That the empire retained its prestige among the plebeians came to depend on the emperor, and the circus was a way for him to meet and connect with his subjects. One way to control people is to make them feel like they are participating in something bigger; sharing in tastes, spectacles, riches and triumphs. If this is achieved successfully, inequality between the classes, the waging of wars and issues of domestic policy are rarely questioned. The great works of infrastructure that supplied grain to Rome combined with chariot races, music and theatre performances and public executions to form a system of gesture politics that kept people in check.

The modern world has many examples of bread and circuses. Some authors compare the Roman Empire to the USA, with its diet of fast food, daily violence and the idolising of soldiers that ensures most Americans do not query the rationality of military interventions or lethal drone strikes, as if questioning them might somehow weaken their society.

LIQUID GOLD

The metaphor of the champagne tower brings to mind the liquid gold of our time: oil. The leaders, whether political or royal, of countries with vast oil reserves live very comfortably. Some seek to share the benefits with their people, though populations may not be afforded the same freedoms and basic rights enjoyed in other countries.

In 2005, Saudi Arabia set up a programme whereby 200,000 Saudis could study abroad every year, with all their expenses paid for by oil. This programme has been operating for over a dozen years, though it faces problems due to the falling oil price. Kuwait gave 3,500 dollars to every citizen in 2011, further illustrating the wealth disparity between people from the rich Gulf countries and the rest of the Middle East. There are legitimate questions around whether initiatives such as these represent a sharing of the nation's riches or are just a means of buying government support. Every Kuwaiti citizen has the right to a house from the government or a loan to buy one once they are married, but the waiting list currently stands at hundreds of thousands. Falling oil prices have made it harder for Kuwait and Saudi Arabia to offer these sweeteners in recent years. When the champagne stops trickling down to the glasses at the bottom, people can develop a desire to topple the pyramid.

SHARE OUT THE CORRUPTION

Nepotism, embezzlement and political cronyism are institutionalised in corrupt governments. The 'champagne tower strategy' tries to force those at the bottom of the pyramid to perform small acts of corruption, to make everyone complicit in the dishonesty; if those on the lower rungs of society lack the moral authority to call to account those higher up, the political, judicial and economic elites can continue to enrich themselves from the public purse. By the same token, the ruling party remains in power by winning the votes of people who are fully aware of its corruption, but do not care as long as the champagne keeps trickling down to them.

Rule 22

THE MULE AND THE SADDLEBAGS

How to rally people for war

'If more soldiers thought, there wouldn't
be a single one left in the ranks'

– FREDERICK I OF PRUSSIA

Some mules will kick out, bite and rear up so that saddlebags cannot be put on their backs. The animal's owners might try the 'stick and carrot' approach, but will eventually give up when faced with the animal's stubbornness. Having convinced everyone it is unsuited to work, the mule will be left in peace, perhaps allowed to graze at leisure. However, there is also a chance that it will be put down, now that it serves no purpose to its owner.

Other mules are easily persuaded to wear the saddlebags. Some are tricked with promises of a better stable and higher quality food and more freedom, while others are won round through caresses and flattery. The poor animal will be condemned to bear heavy loads for the rest of its life, and if one day, exhausted, pained or aged, it tries to shake off the heavy bags, its owner will malign it as a traitor and a disgrace. If it does not carry the bags it will end up in the abattoir.

The point is that the mule that allows saddlebags to be put on its back can never take them off again. They become part of its body and if it does protest it will become hated, with no gratitude shown for its many years of service.

The ideal mule tends not to protest much and seems quite content with the life it leads. The same can be said of military personnel. There are those who see themselves as being on some kind of sacred mission, for which they would sacrifice their life if necessary. The military was described as 'a religion of honourable men' by Pedro Calderón de la Barca, a seventeenth-century Spanish dramatist. While the soldiers may be honourable, those who give the orders are often motivated by less than honourable interests. Military personnel tend not to consider the geopolitical and economic interests that are behind the reasons for them going into battle; they are expected to make the ultimate sacrifice, no matter what the aim.

All armies have found ways to convince troops that they must be prepared to give their all for the cause. For the regular rank and file, armies seek soldiers with just enough intelligence to perform their functions.

When a country engages in a military venture not because of its own needs and interests, but to please the great power that has sought its collaboration, it is essentially putting on geopolitical saddlebags. Such countries end up with a heavy burden, often in the shape of new enemies, and are dragged into faraway conflicts that can result in terrorist attacks at home.

There are countless peacekeeping or low-intensity combat operations underway all over the world in which the countries involved have not considered the purpose of the mission they agreed to participate in; their only consideration is a desire to gain favour with the powerful country in charge.

In his autobiographical novel *Fear* (1930), the French writer Gabriel Chevallier describes the hardships he and his comrades experienced fighting in the First World War. They clung to life in pitiful trenches, fear eating away at them as they awaited the order to attack, which would almost certainly lead to their deaths. Meanwhile, those who had been able to avoid being sent to the front benefited to some degree from the war, while exalting warrior values and rallying the troops to carry on. Chevallier writes in the introduction:

> When I was young we were taught – when we were at the front – that war was edifying, purifying and redemptive. We have all seen the repercussions of such twaddle: profiteers, arms dealers, the black market, denunciations, betrayals, firing squads, torture; not to mention famine, tuberculosis, typhus, terror, sadism. And heroism, I agree. But the small, exceptional amount of heroism does not make up for the immensity of evil. Besides, few people are cut out for true heroism.

Chevallier gives an example of the 'saddlebags strategy' when he bitterly says through the mouth of his character, Jean Dartemont:

> Men are stupid and ignorant. That is why they suffer. Instead of thinking, they believe all that they are told, all that they are taught.

They choose their lords and masters without judging them, with a fatal taste for slavery. Men are sheep. This fact makes armies and wars possible. They die the victims of their own stupid docility.

War is a con

In an article entitled 'The Real Enemy is Within', US journalist Chris Hedges, a veteran war correspondent and winner of the Pulitzer Prize, wrote:

> Militarists and war profiteers are our greatest enemy. They use fear, bolstered by racism, as a tool in their efforts to abolish civil liberties, crush dissent and ultimately extinguish democracy. To produce weapons and finance military expansion, they ruin the domestic economy by diverting resources, scientific and technical expertise and a disproportionate share of government funds. They use the military to carry out futile, decades-long wars to enrich corporations such as Lockheed Martin, General Dynamics, Raytheon and Northrop Grumman. War is a business. And when the generals retire, guess where they go to work? Profits swell. War never stops. Whole sections of the earth live in terror … Military muscle exists to permit global corporations to expand markets and plunder oil, minerals and other natural resources while keeping subjugated populations impoverished by corrupt and brutal puppet regimes.[58]

That someone who is considered to be progressive and a pacifist expressed himself in this way is hardly surprising, but what is much more remarkable is that almost identical sentiments were expressed by an American general many years earlier. Major General Smedley Darlington Butler was a member of the US Marine Corps, the youngest ever captain, the most decorated military man in American history and one of only two marines to have been twice awarded the highest decoration in the country, the Medal of Honor, for outstanding heroism in combat.

In 1935, having retired from active service, Butler gave a speech that later became a short book, entitled *War Is a Racket*, criticising the American use of armed forces to benefit Wall Street.[59] He provided details of how Washington had intervened in Latin America only to satisfy the interests of leading American companies, and how businessmen had taken advantage of the army to send soldiers into bloody battles. Major General Butler's speech began:

> War is a racket. It always has been.
>
> It is possibly the oldest, easily the most profitable, surely the most vicious. It is the only one international in scope. It is the only one in which the profits are reckoned in dollars and the losses in lives.
>
> A racket is best described, I believe, as something that is not what it seems to the majority of the people. Only a small 'inside' group knows what it is about. It is conducted for the benefit of the very few, at the expense of the very many. Out of war a few people make huge fortunes.
>
> In the World War [I] a mere handful garnered the profits of the conflict. At least 21,000 new millionaires and billionaires were made in the United States during the World War. That many admitted their huge blood gains in their income tax returns. How many other war millionaires falsified their tax returns no one knows.
>
> How many of these war millionaires shouldered a rifle? How many of them dug a trench? How many of them knew what it meant to go hungry in a rat-infested dug-out? How many of them spent sleepless, frightened nights, ducking shells and shrapnel and machine gun bullets? How many of them parried a bayonet thrust of an enemy? How many of them were wounded or killed in battle?
>
> Out of war nations acquire additional territory, if they are victorious. They just take it. This newly acquired territory promptly is exploited by the few – the selfsame few who wrung dollars out of blood in the war. The general public shoulders the bill.

Elsewhere in the book, Butler broadens his topic to summarise his military life:

> I spent thirty-three years and four months in active military service as a member of this country's most agile military force, the Marine Corps. I served in all commissioned ranks from second lieutenant to major-general. And during that period, I spent most of my time being a high class muscle-man for Big Business, for Wall Street and for the Bankers. In short, I was a racketeer, a gangster for capitalism. I suspected I was just part of a racket at the time. Now I am sure of it. Like all the members of the military profession, I never had a thought of my

own until I left the service. My mental faculties remained in suspended animation while I obeyed the orders of higher-ups. This is typical with everyone in the military service. I helped make Mexico, especially Tampico, safe for American oil interests in 1914. I helped make Haiti and Cuba a decent place for the National City Bank boys to collect revenues in. I helped in the raping of half a dozen Central American republics for the benefits of Wall Street. The record of racketeering is long. I helped purify Nicaragua for the international banking house of Brown Brothers in 1909–12. I brought light to the Dominican Republic for American sugar interests in 1916. In China I helped to see to it that Standard Oil went its way unmolested. During those years, I had, as the boys in the back room would say, a swell racket. Looking back on it, I feel that I could have given Al Capone a few hints. The best he could do was to operate his racket in three districts. I operated on three continents. The trouble with America is that when the dollar only earns 6 per cent over here, then it gets restless and goes overseas to get 100 per cent. Then the flag follows the dollar and the soldiers follow the flag.

These are the bitter words of a hero frustrated at having been manipulated to fight for aims that had nothing to do with the notions of honour he had been taught and had instilled in his troops. It is the testimony of a man who remained just as brave in peace as he had been in war. General Butler is a unique example, for very few military men have the courage to express themselves in this manner, even if they have realised exactly why wars are fought.

It requires great strength of personality, self-awareness, wisdom and a degree of material freedom to avoid having saddlebags put on you. Circumstances and social pressures might make it impossible to reject them. But there are also those who voluntarily choose to wear them and live happily under their load.

PART FOUR

Understanding Human Weakness

The historian Victor Davis Hanson maintains that, while technology changes in war, 'themes, emotions and rhetoric remain constant over the centuries'. Arrogance, miscalculation, greed, honour and other emotional factors have led many generals to go to war when common sense would have advised against it.

As with war, geopolitics is often governed by human passions and frailties more than by rationality. Decisions are ultimately made by people who, no matter how level-headed, impartial, intelligent and thoughtful, cannot help but be hampered by bias, ignorance and lack of understanding. Hanson points out that the ancient Greeks viewed war to be irrational and a consequence more of powerful emotions than material needs. Barbara W. Tuchman also suggests that in matters of war reason is 'more often than not overpowered by non-rational human frailties – ambition, anxiety, status-seeking, face-saving, illusions, self-delusions, fixed prejudices'. She adds that 'although the structure of human thought is based on logical procedure from premise to conclusion, it is not proof against the frailties and the passions'.

Another very human weakness is a failure to learn from the past. The following geopolitical stones have been tripped over many times.

THE SIGNIFICANCE OF AN IDIOSYNCRASY

Understanding the idiosyncrasies of a people is crucial when planning any operation that will involve coming into contact with other cultures, traditions, religions, philosophies and lifestyles. It is foolhardy – though alarmingly common – to go to war with a people without knowing their wartime characteristics: what value they place on human life; what their military history is; what yearnings they have for revenge; whether they have a deep-rooted hatred of being invaded; how severe, tenacious or proud they can be; whether they typically solve conflicts through violence, and so on.

There remains a lack of interest in properly getting to know and comprehend the mentality, concerns and aspirations of 'the other'. Ignorance, mixed with a disdain for others and excessive doses of pride, is especially typical of cultures that assume themselves to be the most advanced in the world, something of which the West might presently be accused. Barbara W. Tuchman, meanwhile, argues that, though humans have common traits, their needs and aspirations vary according to circumstances. In reference to Vietnam, she says that 'the assumption that humanity at large shared the democratic Western idea of freedom was an American delusion'. The same thing happened with the 'Arab Spring' when Western media leapt to the conclusion that the majority of people in these countries wanted democracy installed, while in reality what they really wanted was to bring down the autocrats and impose political Islam. New governments led by Islamists subsequently took control in Egypt and Libya, and the same could happen in Syria.

Michael Howard suggests that combatants should ideally try to see things from their adversary's point of view, without necessarily sympathising with them; 'showing indifferent empathy' means understanding someone else's position without needing to defend, share or adhere to it. It is easier said than done, for humans are not generally good at putting themselves in another person's shoes.

MISUNDERSTANDINGS ABOUND

Despite multiple lessons offered by history, outside powers have made the same mistakes time and again in places such as Afghanistan, Pakistan, Iraq and Yemen. These are all places where systematic bombing and drone strikes have proliferated in recent times, in conflicts that have rumbled on for decades.

In Western countries there is an ignorance of Asia generally and of Muslim countries especially. Pedro Herranz, in his 1953 treatise *Status Belli*, speaks of how peoples elsewhere approach situations from a different angle to Westerners. Speaking specifically about the Chinese, Zbigniew Brzezinski expresses the opinion that they have developed a deep sense of cultural humiliation as a consequence of suffering exploitation at the hands of foreign powers, from the Opium Wars with Great Britain to Japan's invasion a decade later.

Understanding the people you aim to conquer is so important that Machiavelli made the following warning in *The Prince*: 'however strong your armies, you'll always need local support to occupy a new territory.' He gave the example of France's King Louis XII, who lost Milan as quickly as he had conquered it, because the same people who had opened the gates to him turned against him when they sensed they'd been tricked into believing in a brighter future. As Xenophon said, men will rise up against nobody more than those they suspect of conspiring to rule over them.

AFGHANISTAN – OR, NOT GETTING INSIDE SOMEONE ELSE'S HEAD

The Soviets neither learned from the lessons of history nor sufficiently considered the idiosyncrasies of the Afghan people, oversights which cost them the lives of at least 15,000 soldiers during the Soviet–Afghan War (1979–89), which became known as the 'USSR's Vietnam'. Despite never having been beaten in a great battle before, the Soviets were defeated by militias who were badly equipped and disorganised, no matter how much financial and material aid they received from abroad.

If anything, Washington's lack of foresight in intervening in Afghanistan, as a response to the terrorist attacks in September 2001, was even more glaring than the Soviet Union's.

The Pashtun, a stateless group of over 40 million people (13.8 million in Afghanistan and 26.6 million in Pakistan), have often been misunderstood by foreign powers in the region. They were divided between two countries in 1893, when the British established the Durand Line. Following the creation of British India in 1858, the British government sought to put as much space as possible between it and the expanding nation of Russia. Britain decided that the best solution was to create a 'buffer state' that would serve as a strategic safeguard, which they could do by establishing an official

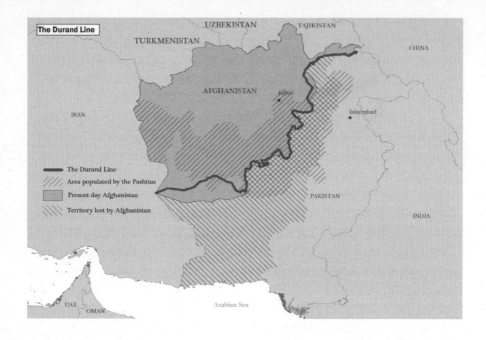

border between the British Raj and Afghanistan. The task was assigned to Henry Mortimer Durand, British India's Foreign Secretary.

On 11 November 1893, an accord was signed between Durand and the Afghan Amir Abdur Rahman Khan, guaranteeing that British India would protect the Amir and his kingdom in the event of aggression from an external enemy. A day later, on 12 November, the Durand Line agreement was signed, though it immediately became a source of conflict, and remains one today. Afghanistan lost more than 50 per cent of its territory (the entire eastern part, which today is the western half of Pakistan) as well as its sea access, becoming a landlocked nation.

The agreement triggered a humanitarian crisis: the artificial border divided cultures and tribes, in particular the Pashtun in the centre and east of the country and the Baluchs in the south. The border was initially so porous that it was impossible to control, and people living on either side ignored it, but over time it became a huge problem, and those most affected remain angry to this day that they have been arbitrarily subjected to disruption by foreigners.

The outcome was extremely positive for Britain, which achieved its geopolitical objective of keeping the Russians away from India, the jewel in the British crown. The major losers in the battle for control of Central Asia between London and Moscow were Afghanistan and its people. The Afghans were immediately suspicious of the accord, which was just one page long. It was written in English, despite the fact that the person signing it on behalf of Afghanistan, Amir Abdur Rahman Khan, couldn't understand the language; copies of the treaty had been drafted in Pashto and Dari, the two most widely spoken languages in Afghanistan, but Durand insisted that the English copy be the definitive version. Some Afghans claim the content of the translations differed slightly to the English version, specifically in that the local language versions stipulated that the agreement would stand for 100 years, after which land taken from Afghanistan would be returned to the country. The Pashto and Dari copies have long since been lost, making such claims impossible to verify, but in any case, such a notion would be unthinkable nowadays to Pakistan.

Subsequent Afghan governments confirmed the legitimacy of the Durand Line in later treaties, but this chapter of history remains open. It would be no surprise if the area saw further violence and humanitarian disaster.

A large number of ethnicities continue to co-exist in Afghanistan, including Pashtun, Tajik, Hazara, Uzbek and Turkmen, and among the Pashtun alone there are over sixty known tribes that consider themselves distinct from others, in addition to another 400 subtribes that also see themselves as unique. With a political structure that answers only to family or clan, the Pashtun have always been proud of their independence and have never accepted the authority of the government in Kabul, no matter who has led it.

The Pashtun draw on over five centuries of history, and some would argue that the Greek historian Herodotus recorded their presence about 2,500 years ago. They follow their own non-written code, the *pashtunwali*, which gathers together the principles that form the pillars of Pashtun society: *melmastia*, the duty to provide hospitality and protection to guests; *nanawatai*, providing asylum and sanctuary to fugitives; and *badal*, the avenging of any offence, theft, injury or death caused to you or a member of your immediate family. This latter concept remains little understood by most Westerners.

When a male Pashtun considers himself to be the victim of a grievance, especially if this is the death of someone close, he is obliged to gain vengeance, no matter how long it takes. Whenever a Pashtun group is attacked, their relatives feel morally obliged to take revenge on the perpetrator of the attack or on their country. The British writer Aldous Huxley said: 'Wars do not end war; in most cases they result in an unjust peace that makes inevitable the outbreak of a war of revenge.' This is true of nowhere more than Afghanistan.

A close reading of history would have warned the Soviets and the Americans against seeking to dominate these tribes. Winston Churchill, after a trip to Afghanistan in 1897, described his impressions of the Pashtuns thus:

> Except at harvest time, when self-preservation enjoins a temporary truce, the Pathan tribes are always engaged in private or public war. Every man is a warrior, a politician, and a theologian. Every large house is a real fortress. ... Every village has its defence. Every family cultivates its vendetta; every clan, its feud. The numerous tribes and combinations of tribes all have their accounts to settle with one another. Nothing is ever forgotten and very few debts are left unpaid.

General David Petraeus landed in Iraq in 2003 as commander of the US 101 Airborne Division. A graduate of West Point Military Academy, he had earned masters and doctorate degrees at Princeton University, where his final dissertation was titled 'The American Military and the Lessons of Vietnam'. He seemed not to be fazed by the fact that Iraq was embroiled in deadly violence and chaos when he arrived: he knew that Mosul presented an ideal opportunity for him to put into practice everything he had learned about irregular warfare. His source of inspiration was *Counterinsurgency Warfare: Theory and Practice*, the 1964 book by the French lieutenant colonel David Galula. After spending ten years studying subversive tactics used in China, Greece and Indochina, Galula was sent to Algeria where he tried out the tactics he would later outline in his book. The US Counterinsurgency Field Manual, produced by General Petraeus in December 2006, was based to a large extent on Galula's work.

When Petraeus took charge of the transition in June 2004, Iraq was in a terrible mess but, by following Galula's guidelines, Petraeus brought about a major reduction in violence and volatility. As he noted in the foreword to a French re-release of Galula's book in 2008, military interventions in foreign countries had until very recently been discussed in terms of obliterating the insurgency and withdrawing, but Galula preached that nothing could be achieved without gaining the support of a majority of the local population, and without there being a government in place which that majority considered to be legitimate and honourable.

Petraeus was later presented with an almost impossible challenge that would either crown him as the greatest general of the twenty-first century or force him to admit that his success in Iraq had been the result of a unique set of circumstances. Afghanistan, muddled with poverty and religious fanaticism, seemed to repel Petraeus's ambitions. Having fended off invasions since the time of Alexander the Great, the Afghans prepared to do to Petraeus what they'd done to British soldiers a century and a half ago and Soviet ones more recently.

When Petraeus took the helm at the United States Central Command headquarters in Stuttgart in October 2008, Afghanistan was witnessing an increased guerrilla offensive, with terrorist groups sheltered in the mountainous border with Pakistan and the Taliban routing a minimal force of international troops. One of Petraeus's objectives was to win the hearts and minds of the Afghan people, which was what he'd done in Iraq, in order to allow Afghans to take charge of their own security and gradually discharge the multinational forces carrying out this onerous task.

For this to happen the needs of local populations would have to be satisfied and there would have to be a palpable improvement in their quality of life. It was a complex problem given that the values of democracy, liberalism and human rights that Petraeus believed he was bringing to the country were alien concepts to most Afghans. Petraeus was aware that, compared to Iraq, Afghanistan was unruly; in Iraq he had worked with a relatively educated population, in an environment with many elements of modernity, and in a society that had experienced a solid state and feelings of nationhood, as well as the prosperity brought by oil. In Afghanistan, large numbers of people were living an existence that was relatively unchanged since the Middle Ages, they felt more loyalty to clan and tribe than to a nation they did not recognise, and refused to entertain the idea of international borders.

The task was titanic given that Afghan territory is 50 per cent larger than that of Iraq, considerably harsher and less hospitable, and home to a population that – though similar in number – is dispersed and fragmented. Petraeus knew all of this by the time President Obama appointed him Commander in Chief of the International Security Assistance Force (ISAF) and of the United States forces in Afghanistan in July 2010. It was a post he held for just one year, leaving the role having proved himself unable to repeat what he'd achieved in Iraq, with the country even deeper in chaos.

Not understanding the idiosyncrasies of peoples leads to irreparable mistakes being made. The formulas that were successful in one place will not necessarily work in others.

DISREGARD FOR THE ARAB WORLD

T.E. Lawrence, a British military officer and writer who took part in the Arab revolt during the First World War, reflected upon the mutual lack of understanding between the Western and Arab worlds in his 1926 book *Seven Pillars of Wisdom*. Lawrence says of the Arabs: 'They were a dogmatic people, despising doubt, our modern crown of thorns. They did not understand our metaphysical difficulties, our introspective questionings.' He levelled a similar charge at his fellow British citizens, and at Westerners in general, in *Revolt in the Desert*, written a year later: 'Arab minds moved logically as our own, with nothing radically incomprehensible or different, except the premises: there was no excuse or reason, except our laziness and ignorance, whereby we could call them inscrutable or Oriental, or leave them misunderstood.'

In the Arab world, there is a tradition of obedience towards a strong ruler, whether a tribal chief, family patriarch, spiritual leader, powerful businessman or member of the ruling classes. This person is afforded the maximum respect, unless he falls into disgrace or is surpassed in his greatness, in which case he loses all prestige. This is similar to what happens with the Salafist jihadi group leaders who are followed loyally by their supporters for as long as they remain dominant. If their status diminishes, their disciples are quick to change allegiance.

While in the West people are rarely prepared to fight for principles or prestige, the Arab world revolves around a culture of honour – it is central to Arab lives and must be maintained at all costs; lying, fighting and cheating can all be valid if employed in order to defend your own or your family's honour. If a man is unable to protect his honour, the shame may lead him to seek revenge on whoever offended him, employing violence if necessary.

The Arab world is difficult to understand for those from less close-knit societies, in which few things are afforded value, social principles have been watered down and traditions have often become banal or been lost. People from Western society in which every stance is allowed and tolerated are always going to struggle to understand a society based on the opposite principles.

THE GENERAL WHO WON WITH SCHOOLS AND HOSPITALS

The French general Hubert Lyautey began his military career in Indochina in 1894, where he devised an innovative way for European armies to behave in their colonies. Lyautey's strategy, which combined a reduction of military operations with political and social initiatives, was applied with some success in North Africa, where he began by departing from the traditional method of subjugating colonised populations entirely through force, and instead advocated prioritising social and economic development and using less force to back it up. This would be applied by more mobile units that would have more contact with local people; in this way, he argued, the colonised would be more likely to accept their condition and less inclined to support opposition movements.

The culmination of this approach came when Lyautey, by now a brigadier-general, was sent to Oran in Algeria to suppress a revolt.

Once he had persuaded his superiors to give him total military and political freedom to manage the situation, he decided not to engage troops against the rebels but to employ only a minimal use of force. Instead, he set out to win the support of tribes by offering them protection and promising them hospitals, schools and other tools for social development. After this he was sent to Morocco, where he allowed local customs to continue and sought to boost the local economy and create jobs, reserving the use of military force only to guarantee security and serve as a deterrent in extreme situations.

DISDAIN FOR THE VIETNAMESE PEOPLE

Another lesson that the Americans learned the hard way came in Vietnam, where their unsuccessful war strategy did not consider that an entire people might prefer to die than be subjugated. It wasn't as if they hadn't been warned; in 1963, when the US expanded its engagement there, the Soviet premier, Nikita Khrushchev, told a high-level American official: 'Go ahead and fight in the jungles of Vietnam if you want to. The French fought there for seven years and had to give up in the end. Perhaps the Americans will be able to stick it out for a little longer, but eventually they will have to give up too.'

Perhaps the best summary of the situation comes from Võ Nguyên Giáp, the general in command of the North Vietnamese army during the conflict:

> In a thousand years of rule we were never assimilated. The Vietnamese people have an unbending patriotic spirit. The French said that we couldn't win at Dien Bien Phu, but we won. When the Americans came, many people said we couldn't win. In short, it was the human factor that determined victory.

In writing about the war, Barbara W. Tuchman was critical of Washington's underestimation of North Vietnamese commitment. Astonishingly, the White House overlooked all the evidence of nationalist fervour and longing for independence in North Vietnam. Tuchman also highlighted Washington's lack of understanding of Asian stoicism and fatalism. In short, the Americans did not do their homework and were ignorant of Vietnam's history, traditions and national character. A glance at any textbook on the region would have revealed a long history of resistance to foreign regimes.

When Washington sought to negotiate with Hanoi it found, in the words of Kissinger, 'dedicated Leninists who saw themselves as the inexorable spokesmen of an inevitable future, absolute truth and superior moral insight'. The White House didn't know how to handle people who were unprepared to accept anything other than the USA's immediate and full withdrawal.

YOUR BIGGEST STRENGTH IS YOUR BIGGEST WEAKNESS

The Chinese strategist Sun Bin believed it was possible to defeat an enemy ten times bigger than yourself, provided you took them by surprise when they were unprepared. Two lessons can be taken from this. The first is that power and might are meaningless if you don't know how to use them intelligently. The second is that the weaker party will try to make the most of its scarce resources and catch its more powerful opponent unawares; Machiavelli identified ability and perseverance as the weapons of the weak.

Displaying your power can show your weaknesses. In the legend of David and Goliath, the seemingly invincible giant towers over his opponent, but Goliath's height and his heavy armour make him clumsy and slow. The slight David is able to use his skill to fight the battle in a way that favours him, going close enough for his sling-shot to be deadly, but staying out of Goliath's reach. Showing your muscles can be enough to warn away most potential adversaries, but opponents who feel compelled to fight will seek to defeat their more powerful adversary in less obvious ways; immense military power can be a double-edged sword and advertising the fact that you feel invincible could work against you.

The Chinese colonels Liang and Xiangsui point out that the dominant power tends to have the most enemies and face the most threats, which in recent history has certainly been the case with the United States. According to Marenches, the raw might of the US and its allies, who are often characterised by secularism and a lack of respect for traditional values, are challenged by 'political soldiers', be that the Viet Cong or the mujahideen, who are motivated by faith, philosophy or belief, with values for which they are prepared to make the ultimate sacrifice.

ASYMMETRIC WARFARE: A BRIEF HISTORY

In Aesop's 'The Gnat and the Lion', a gnat goes up to a lion and says 'I do not in the least bit fear you, nor are you stronger than I am. For in what does your strength consist? You can scratch with your claws and bite with your teeth, but I am altogether more powerful than you; and if you doubt it, let us fight.' The gnat buzzes into the lion's face and stings it on the snout, causing the lion to scratch itself with its claws until it dies.

This Greek fable from the sixth century BC teaches us much about the aim of terrorism: to provoke a disproportionate reaction that does more harm than the original attack.

Anyone entering a confrontation from a position of inferiority must find an element of superiority, no matter how limited in scope. The adversary's strong points must be avoided and their weak points targeted. Rules will have to be disrespected and disregard shown for potential losses of life. The confrontation should be drawn out for as long as possible, the better to wear the opponent down materially and psychologically.

There is always asymmetry in combat, and the weaker side must find a way to make an impact. Colonel Capaz Montes defines irregular warfare, which today is usually called asymmetric warfare, as a confrontation in which one side employs markedly different means of combat, tactics and weaponry to those of its adversary. This sort of conflict has been the norm throughout history, and large-scale clashes between two major blocks such as the two world wars have been the exception rather than the rule.

During the twenty-seven years of the Peloponnesian War (431–404 BC) only two major land battles took place: in Mantinea (418 BC) and Delos (424 BC). As Thucydides relates in his treatise on the war, given the asymmetry between the naval power of Athens and Sparta's almighty infantry, most of the fighting came through surprise attacks, harassing fire, terrorist actions (as we would call them today), sieges, sabotage and well poisoning.

Alexander the Great is renowned for his success in several major battles against the Persians, but less known is the fact that he spent most of his time combating insurgencies in the Balkans, the Hindu Kush and Bactriana, suffering significant losses in the process. In what is now Afghanistan, he confronted bands of warriors led by feudal lords who were passionately committed to their independence. Protected by a terrain that was hostile to the invader, these guerrillas adopted a strategy of harassment, sending smaller or larger groups of horsemen to attack isolated units of Alexander's army, before fleeing to the steppe or the desert and reappearing somewhere else a few hours or days later.

Perhaps one of the most emblematic examples of unequal struggle in which the theoretically weaker side emerged victorious is the Spanish War of Independence (1808–14), in which the Spanish people took up arms against their French occupiers. Around 200 guerrilla groups killed an average of forty French soldiers per day, using irregular tactics that ranged from shooting stragglers to ambushing small escorts. With patience and perseverance, and without ever engaging in battle, the guerrillas inflicted thousands of deaths each year upon Napoleon's troops, which amounted to over half a million deaths over the course of the seven-year war, more than were killed on the battlefield in the same period.

In his writings on guerrilla warfare, T.E. Lawrence offers a number of suggestions about how the weak should act against the strong, based on his experiences of the Arab Revolt against the Turks in the First World War:

1. Be superior in one aspect that may be decisive.
2. Never enter into contact with the enemy.
3. Never give an enemy soldier a target.
4. Draw on faultless intelligence.
5. Make ample use of propaganda.
6. Create a dynamic and well-equipped unit that is as small as possible.
7. Seek out the adversary's weakest link and focus solely on that.
8. Initiate moral battles, not physical ones.

9. Hit and run, do not pressurise but strike.
10. Use powerful explosives.
11. Impose the maximum irregularity in formation.
12. Have an untouchable base at your disposal.
13. Ensure a friendly population.
14. Enjoy total mobility.

The Maoist campaign in the Chinese Civil War is an example of the successful application of Lawrence's advice. The Red Army was small and weak, badly armed and faced immense logistical difficulties, but through prolonged warfare in which it made ample use of its guerrilla units – skilfully commanded by Mao Zedong – and concentrated its energies and efforts, it was able to defeat the Kuomintang, the Chinese Nationalist Party, even though they fought in a conventional manner, had help from a number of major countries, were well supplied in terms of weapons and materials, and had the numerical advantage.

In the recent conflicts in Afghanistan and Iraq, rebel fighters sought to prolong the conflict, cause as many losses as possible, create a sense of permanent insecurity, undermine national cohesion through fear, break the unity of international alliances, force democratic governments to violate their own principles and prompt the populations of those countries to clamour for decisions that favoured their cause. These fighters have a free hand to focus on winning the battle of minds against an enemy that would crush them militarily, because they don't have to consider public opinion or answer to parliament.

In the modern world, it seems like the weak have a better chance of defeating the strong than previously – the strong, out of respect for democratic principles and public opinion, rarely feel able to use their full might. And while not winning is defeat for the powerful, simply not losing is victory for the weak.

Terrorism

Terrorism is the asymmetrical strategy par excellence, and an extremely efficient means of inflicting pain and suffering on the societies it targets. Armed groups influenced by extremist political and religious ideologies, irrespective of the aims they are pursuing, whether insurgency, revolution, separatism, expelling an invader or sectarian struggles, tend to carry out terrorist acts as part of a wider course of action.

Terrorists seek to overcome an adversary they judge to be much greater than them, while at the same time publicising and justifying their cause in order to attract extra funds, supporters and fighters. Aware that terrorism is a spectacle, these organisations equip themselves with their own, often highly professional, communication agencies, which they use to divulge messages that are carefully staged to gain the maximum amount of media attention, with the aim of intimidating people and influencing domestic and international public opinion.

Extremist groups that commit terrorist acts are aware that in the modern world the image is king, and also that modern conflicts can be decided by public opinion: it is not enough for them to cause damage and suffering – they must show the world that they constitute an omnipresent and formidable threat. For terrorists, communication is as important as action: the true measure of the success of an attack is the audience's response. Publicity, as Margaret Thatcher said, is the oxygen on which terrorists depend.

This oxygen is often obtained from the Internet; cyberspace can be turned into a place of confrontation at minimal cost, providing terrorists with immediacy, universality and a degree of protection, for it is very difficult to control. If the objective of such groups is to terrorise the general public and attract funds and acolytes through the widespread divulgence of their message, is the Western media not contributing to their success by broadcasting their communications? Where does the duty of the press to inform begin, and the public's right to be informed end?

EMPLOYING SUICIDE

The motives for suicide attacks are as varied as the places where they are carried out. In most cases there is a strong nationalist component, focused on hatred of the foreign invader, the occupier or the enemy of local religion and culture. The aim is usually to pressure an occupying force to withdraw, to recover or preserve sovereignty or lost rights. Other motivations include sectarian struggles or demands for equality and justice.

The first well-documented examples of suicide attacks were those of Jewish Zealots in the first century AD, and were performed as part of their struggle against Roman rule. The most aggressive members of this community, known as *Sicarii* – literally, the violent men – did not hesitate to commit suicide in pursuit of their aims or to avoid falling into enemy hands.

Another widely known example is that of the Ismaili Assassins, also known as the *Hashshāshīn*. In the eleventh and twelfth centuries, in what is now Iran, the Shia Muslim Ismaili confronted the Sunni majority, which they had determined to destroy and expel. Their actions were designed to generate the maximum impact through terror. They had no qualms about carrying out attacks in public places and did not care whether they were detected, caught or killed.

In the Vietnam War, the Viet Cong employed over 20,000 people on suicide missions, in some cases using entire units. Indeed, it came to be considered a regular combat tactic in the context of confronting such an overwhelmingly superior enemy. More recently, suicide bombing has been a hallmark of several terrorist campaigns, in particular those affiliated to the Salafist jihadi movement.

KNOW YOUR ENEMY

Politicians who launch reckless ventures for nefarious reasons like to blame the intelligence services or the general staff of the armed forces for inadequately informing them, but in most cases rulers read only what pleases them and only hear what they want to hear. Anyone who warns them of the dangers of their scheme, or points out obstacles, is simply ignored.

On the other hand, having access to more information does not necessarily make victory more likely. Indeed, an excess of information can slow down the decision-making process or paralyse it with too many options. Too much information can also result in excessive confidence and a false sense of security, or block out alternative ways of thinking, all of which means that overloading the enemy with information can be a powerful weapon.

Being convinced that you are stronger than you really are in war is a common mistake. It is human nature to see yourself as superior to others, but it is nevertheless inexcusable for a well-resourced military force not to be self-aware, particularly because this tendency can lead manifestly superior forces to sacrifice their advantage by going into battle underprepared and overconfident. Weaker combatants are inevitably more conscious of their limitations – they will seek to manoeuvre the confrontation towards whatever battleground best suits them, while an arrogant opponent will allow this to happen and will also tend to generate conflicts or let themselves get sucked into them at the slightest provocation, convinced of an easy and speedy victory.

NOT BEING PREPARED FOR THE UNEXPECTED

As we have seen, being bigger and stronger than an opponent is not always an advantage. A heavyweight boxer would not necessarily defeat a judo expert: the bigger man may fail to land a punch on his more agile opponent and fall to a fatal trip. The same thing happens in geopolitics, and once a war starts, the outcome is always uncertain. Major powers may feel the need to flex their economic or military muscles, but they should not feel obliged to react to every provocation. Moderation is key, in terms of both the force used and the regularity with which it is applied. Being convinced of your own strength when you don't actually have much of it is another thing entirely, and generally leads to a great deal of trouble and suffering.

Every major strategist who has ever written about conflict has emphasised that it is unpredictable; Liddell Hart called it the 'realm of the unexpected', while Napoleon referred to the importance of the art of surprise. The same is true of geopolitics, but in both fields being surprised often stems from being insufficiently aware of how events might unfold; subjective perceptions of situations can be a consequence of cultural and even moral factors that distort reality. Winston Churchill believed everything was constantly moving and that only those who were aware of this and able to adapt would survive.

Because predicting the future is impossible, the unexpected must be expected. This is known as 'black swan theory': black swan events are those that force everything that preceded them to be reconsidered. In our globalised and fast-moving world they are more common than ever, with established concepts forever being challenged and overturned. In the nineteenth century, Bismarck warned that future events should be predicted no more than four to five years ahead; the time frame would now be considerably shorter.

A classic tactic of military strategy advises manoeuvring according to the most likely scenario, but putting a safeguard in place for the most dangerous one. In other words, carry out your plans without taking excessive precautions that will slow you down or limit your progress, but avoid being reckless.

There is no guarantee the current state of affairs will hold; a bad situation can get worse and past solutions will not necessarily work in the future. Defeat must be planned for, as well as victory. Emotional intelligence is a key tool in all this; you are less likely to be surprised if you can put yourself in another person's place, listen empathetically and accept the ideas of others.

In short, success will come to those who know how to respond when no one else does. As Machiavelli writes in *The Prince*, 'He who successfully adapts his actions according to the nature of the times will be successful, while he whose actions clash with the times will not be.' Reacting to the unexpected requires a prepared, open and flexible mind. This is not the same thing as being laissez-faire or letting fate run its course: it means having a plan, but also being aware that it will probably not be carried out in full.

War is a process of constant adaptation, in which mental flexibility is essential. According to Liang and Xiangsui:

> War needs support from technology, but technology cannot be a substitute for morale and stratagem; there is no formula for war, no one has ever been able to use one method to win all wars; it needs mathematical precision, but precision can sometimes render it mechanical and rigid, so it needs artistic inspiration to adapt to constant changes on the battlefield.

There are two main philosophical camps in this area: those who follow Carl von Clausewitz's classic theories of warfare and those who subscribe to the teachings of the Swiss general Antoine-Henri de Jomini. Jomini believed war could be studied analytically and that the application of the appropriate procedures, based on mathematical and scientific principles, could guarantee victory. By contrast, Carl von Clausewitz was vigorously opposed to the notion that action could be calculated in this way; he was adamant that the effects of war, the morale and character of the combatants and the likelihood of developments all defied mathematics. He explained that no plan is capable of withstanding the 'friction' of the first contact with the enemy, which sends developments spinning out in all directions.

No amount of technology can remove the possibility of being taken by surprise. As Machiavelli said, 'there is nothing so capable of success as that which the enemy believes you cannot attempt'. Liddell Hart said much the same thing in advocating an 'indirect approach': always choosing the least expected course of action.

UNCERTAINTY IN THE MODERN WORLD

No matter how enlightened a society is, momentous historical events can take people by surprise. The fall of the Berlin Wall, the collapse of the Soviet Union, the 9/11 terrorist attacks and the 2008 financial crisis suggested that global unpredictability might be increasing. The acronym VUCA (volatility, uncertainty, complexity and ambiguity) was developed by the US Army War College in Pennsylvania after the Cold War in the 1990s and is used to define the present world and the foreseeable future. At the time, the world had gone from being dangerous but stable to being deeply unstable, making it extremely difficult to plan ahead, manage risks, foster change and solve problems.

To the four terms in VUCA, three more might now be added: immediacy, acceleration and simultaneous disparities. Immediacy because events occur and are reported on a rolling basis, largely as a result of advances in telecommunications technology, with analysts and leaders expected to comment on them and make decisions long before they have run their course, when consequences cannot be known or learned from.

From the first century AD up until the beginning of the twentieth, people lived much as their ancestors did, or major changes to lifestyles and customs could at least be mapped out century by century. But in modern times this has accelerated beyond recognition: everything evolves at staggering speed, and new forms of social media mean that ideas can be divulged and manipulated as never before. It is practically impossible to predict which ideologies or habits will prevail even just a few years from now.

The modern era also features simultaneous disparities. Despite globalisation, there are huge differences and inequalities between countries and people. One source is demographic: while more developed countries see their populations diminish, the populations of less advanced countries are growing exponentially. This is connected to the huge increase in urban populations, to the detriment of rural ones, and the growing middle classes, which demand ever greater consumption of resources. Globalisation also results in a strange co-habiting of world views that are often incompatible: people adhering to one way of life may consider another to be patently inferior, a belief that can lead them to try to export their own system to places that do not want or suit them.

The keys to surviving our current volatile world are agility to react and flexibility to adapt to change. It is not the strongest and most intelligent who will survive, but those who adapt best and fastest to new circumstances.

THE FALLACY OF THE QUICK WIN WITHOUT LOSS

Armies are usually sent into battle believing they will win quickly and without suffering major setbacks. Their leaders also tend to think war will be brief and easy, maximum return for minimum risk. Excessive confidence leads to ill-judged fights being picked, enemies being underestimated and states going into battle underprepared.

Sparta entered the Peloponnesian War convinced it would achieve an easy victory over Athens that would boost its power and prestige at minimal cost. In the American Civil War, the south was convinced it would triumph through military superiority, for most US Army officers were southerners. Hitler thought his Blitzkrieg would bring a quick and profitable victory, and Washington thought the same when entering the Vietnam War. In the Middle East in 2003, US neoconservatives insisted that 'liberating' Iraq would be a military walk in the park – Defense Secretary Donald Rumsfeld famously predicted the war would last six days.

In *Why Nations Go to War,* John G. Stoessinger concludes that a declaration of war is usually the result of four misperceptions: the leader's image of themselves; the leader's image of the adversary; the leader's reading of the adversary's intentions; and the leader's understanding of the adversary's capacity and power. This makes the leader primarily responsible for a country going to war, but we shouldn't only blame leaders; sometimes it is the citizens who become overly emotional about war, thinking it a mere foreign excursion with the promise of medals and honour. The outbreak of the First World War was largely met with enthusiasm among people who had forgotten the horrors of war, with peace having held since the Franco-Prussian War of 1870.

THE MISMATCHED SECOND BOER WAR

When Great Britain went to war with the South African Boers in October 1899, London was convinced it would win an easy victory: the previous year they had inflicted a terrible defeat on the Dervishes at Omdurman, in Sudan. The discipline of a regular army had made a difference, but the determining factor had been Britain's technological superiority: the Dervishes had been armed with spears and muzzle-loading guns, while the British forces had automatic rifles, machine guns and artillery.

In South Africa, a British army of almost half a million men would be taking on fewer than 50,000 Boers. A quick victory over an enemy with inferior weaponry and organisational structures seemed assured, but the Afrikaners knew how to adapt to the circumstances and, instead of taking their opponents on in open battle, they used guerrilla tactics; this led to the British committing extreme acts of violence against the sections of the civilian population that supported the guerrillas and interning them in the first concentration camps in history. The British Empire did eventually triumph, but victory came at a high cost: it took three years of fighting, in which 50,000 soldiers lost their lives and hundreds of millions of pounds were spent.

SAUDI ARABIA GETS ITS FORECASTS WRONG

On 25 March 2015, Saudi Arabia began an air campaign known as Operation Decisive Storm against the Houthi people in Yemen out of fear that the city of Aden would fall into rebel hands and allow Iran to gain undue influence in the country. The young Saudi Defence Minister, Mohammad bin Salman Al Saud, said it would be a fast and straightforward war. He assembled a coalition force of Bahrain, Egypt, the United Arab Emirates, Jordan, Kuwait, Morocco, Qatar and Sudan, countries with huge fortunes or armies, with the US and the UK providing logistical support; it seemed impossible that Operation Decisive Storm would not be an immediate and emphatic success.

However, despite being well supplied with weaponry, thousands of mercenaries from Sudan and Latin America and the implementation of a rigid naval blockade, victory proved elusive and Saudi Arabia remains embroiled in a chaotic war; the prospect of installing a government capable of ensuring any kind of peace is distant.

Mohammad bin Salman Al Saud – the youngest Defence Minister in the world and heir to the Saudi throne since June 2017 – might have found it useful to read a history of the civil war in North Yemen before starting the offensive. In this conflict, fought between 1962 and 1970, Egypt, supported by the Soviet Union, joined the Yemeni republican forces, which had enacted a *coup d'état* to depose the monarchist leader, Imam Muhammad al-Badr. The Egyptian President Gamal Abdel Nasser sent 70,000 troops to support the republic, but they encountered a hostile environment and highly motivated, battle-hardened fighters. Faced with the impossibility of victory, Nasser ended up withdrawing, but the damage was done: 'Egypt's Vietnam' left physical and mental scars and hindered Cairo in the Six-Day War with Israel.

LACK OF RESPECT FOR RELIGIOUS CULTURE

Skilled leaders not only take great care not to offend religions, but also emphasise that they respect them. The Persian Emperor Cyrus the Great had the intelligence to respect the nationalist and religious sentiments of all the peoples he conquered in the Middle East; one of his most celebrated gestures was the liberation, in 539 BC, of some 40,000 descendants of Jews who had been held captive in Babylonia by Nebuchadnezzar II half a century earlier. Cyrus authorised them to return home to Palestine, decreeing that all religions would be tolerated. His successor, Darius the Great, governed the Achaemenid Empire via a system of 'satraps', regional provinces that were characterised by, among other things, a freedom to practise whichever religion had prevailed before the region was annexed. During the occupation of Egypt, Alexander the Great understood the political importance of ingratiating himself with the Egyptian clergy, visiting temples and offering sacrifices to the gods in every city he passed through.

THE INDIAN REBELLION

In 1857, a mutiny began among Indian soldiers employed by the British Empire. The reasons for it were complex, but there can be no doubt that a lack of cultural and religious understanding played a significant role. One factor was that the close relationship between British East India Company officers and local troops, which had enabled the British to get a feel for local culture, had been lost. The arrival in India of the families of the British command fostered an environment whereby British officers and functionaries were privileged, distancing them from local languages and traditions.

Another factor was the introduction of modern British technology, which was seen by the Indians as a threat to their way of life and socioeconomic structure. Innovations such as the railway deepened their concern about the gradual introduction of European customs and the creeping process of Christianisation, feelings that were further provoked by the outlawing of certain ancestral practices, such as child marriage. The justice system imposed by the British was also seen to be manifestly disadvantageous to the locals.

Although it was not the determining factor, the main argument the organisers of the insurrection used to justify the revolt was that the paper cartridges in the army's newly introduced rifles had been greased in animal fat. The Indian troops were reluctant to tear them using their teeth, as was customary – if the fat came from pigs it was offensive to the Muslims, while if it came from cows it was offensive to the Hindus. The British did everything they could to convince the troops the fat did not come from animals, and proposed that the Indian soldiers either prepare a covering they deemed more suitable or else break the cartridges using their hands instead of their teeth, but the damage had already been done – the Hindus and Muslims (of whom there were almost 200,000 in the British army) were convinced that it was all part of a deliberate strategy by the British to undermine their socioreligious values and impose European ones. Their fears were not necessarily unfounded: Britain was interfering in Indian culture in ways that suggested a plan to Christianise the country.

Back in Britain, embellished accounts of outrages committed by the Indian rebels against European men and, in particular, women portrayed the uprising as a terrible affront: Britain had generously sought to extend Christian civilisation to India and its efforts had been met with not just rejection, but violence. The rebellion made a strong impression on Queen Victoria; she was witness, among an audience of 25,000 people at Crystal Palace, to the incendiary proclamations of the Baptist preacher Charles Spurgeon, who said 'the religion of the Hindoos is neither more nor less than a mass of the rankest filth that ever imagination could have conceived. The Gods they worship are not entitled to the least atom of respect … the sword must be taken out of its sheath, to cut off our fellow-subjects by the thousands.'

The preacher's words had all the characteristics of a call to holy war. Indeed, his words were taken literally in places such as Cawnpore, where the British Brigadier-General James Neill forced rebel prisoners to lick the blood of their European victims from the floor before executing them, and Peshawar, where forty rebels were tied to the end of a cannon which was then fired. An editorial in *The Times* demanded that 'every tree and gable-end in the place should have its burden in the shape of a mutineer's carcass'. For zealots, the rebellion was not a consequence of alien customs being imposed, but of modernisation not being imposed quickly enough.

Nevertheless, it was understood by some that a lack of cultural awareness had played its part, and the British East India Company was dissolved a year later. London reorganised its army and re-formed its system of governance in India, which came to be known as the British Raj, under the direct rule of the crown.

MISTAKES MADE IN THE MUSLIM WORLD

American political scientist Samuel P. Huntington believes that the West's attempts to impose its own values and institutions and maintain military and economic superiority, while persistently inter-fering in conflicts in the Islamic world, have generated a deep sense of animosity among Muslims.

Another crass error has been interference for spurious rea-sons in electoral processes in Muslim countries. An example of this occurred in Algeria in the 1990s, when the Islamic Salvation Front (FIS), the first Islamist party in Africa, was expelled from power. The FIS had been founded in 1989 and won municipal elections the following June, gaining a 54 per cent share of the vote, enough to encourage it to develop a programme to transform the country into an Islamic state. But after it obtained 47 per cent of the vote in the first round of the general election in December 1991, the army sus-pended the electoral process and outlawed the FIS, putting 10,000 supposed Islamists in prison camps and prompting a civil war that would last until 1997. The lesson this taught the Muslim world was that embracing the democratic process and winning elections was no guarantee of securing power; local elites backed by Western countries would never allow an Islamist regime to take hold in a country with foreign interests. The only way to access power was, therefore, to seize it by violent means.

A similar intervention was made in Egypt in 2012, when the Muslim Brotherhood was expelled from power despite having legi-timately won democratic elections.

By 2012, 11 years of involvement in Afghanistan had failed to bring peace or root out terrorism, but it ought to have provided enough time to learn the basics of local culture. However, in February of that year, the US military ordered the removal of all copies of the Koran and other Islamic texts from the library at the Parwan Detention Facility on the outskirts of Bagram, the most important US base in Afghanistan, because of a fear that the books were being used to spread extremist messages.

In the early hours of 21 February, a truck escorted by a military vehicle pulled up beside the barracks' rubbish dump, before two US soldiers began to unload bags of books and throw them into the incinerator. The task was performed routinely, with no attempt to hide the bags' contents. Eyewitnesses were shocked to discover that the bags were full of copies of the Koran. Emotional and enraged, they demanded that the soldiers stop what they were doing; the Koran was a holy book and must not be burned.

Startled by this unexpected reaction, the soldiers left; two bags of books already in the incinerator were starting to burn. The Afghans tried to extinguish the flames and retrieve the books, but a dozen copies were totally burned or partially destroyed. Carrying the singed copies they'd managed to salvage, the workers rushed to inform the other Afghans at the base. The news spread like wildfire, and within a few hours, thousands of people had gathered outside the gates of the base to protest angrily at this grave offence against the faith of most Afghan people. As news of the affront spread, demonstrations sprang up all over the country, and there were violent attacks on properties owned by foreigners, especially Americans.

This anger was not confined to the man in the street: a member of the Afghan police force working at the Interior Ministry in Kabul, shot a US commander and a US lieutenant colonel dead. With Afghanistan in the grip of unrest, foreign personnel were withdrawn from ministries and other administration buildings, leading to the total suspension of all bureaucratic activities, an indication of just how dependent the country had become on international assistance as well as economic aid. Around fifty people died in the protests and 200 were injured. Protests also spread into neighbouring Pakistan, where tens of thousands of people, already resentful at suffering regular drone attacks, demonstrated against the USA.

The Taliban encouraged the demonstrations, rallying the Afghan people to demand the immediate withdrawal of foreign troops, whom they accused, not without reason, of showing a lack of respect for religion and culture. They also called for Afghan military personnel and policemen to turn against NATO's troops. At the end of August 2012, following a lengthy investigation, the US Army announced that it had punished six soldiers with administrative sanctions for burning the holy books, while reiterating that no malice or disrespect towards Islam had been intended. It had been a huge failure of 'cultural intelligence' to not understand that the Koran is a most holy and important object for any Muslim, whether moderate or extreme.

Epilogue

A new world war currently appears unlikely. That said, we live in a time of extreme uncertainty and tremendous change, which, aided by technology, makes for a complex geopolitical environment. The rapid escalation of a minor dispute into a high-intensity clash between major powers cannot be ruled out, but the new norm is a permanent state of low-level tension. For the most part, battles are fought through economics, disinformation, terrorism, subversion and criminal activities. Economic warfare merits particular attention, undertaken for financial interests and fought using financial tools – such confrontations are growing and all countries are participant, whether or not they choose to be. Geoeconomical and geopolitical wars, be they regional or global, are intimately related. They are increasingly being fought in cyberspace, through the fraudulent obtaining of data, the corruption of systems and servers, the leaking of information and technology theft.

A number of other factors also contribute to heightened instability, particularly mass migratory movements, climate change and natural disasters. Then there are demographic imbalances, changing power dynamics, socioeconomic inequalities, health risks, terrorism and a general state of unrest in many parts of the planet. Much of this tension would disappear if each country, or each group within a country, was able to develop in accordance with its own political-ideological system and existing characteristics (its history, culture, religion, traditions and degree of development, etc.) and without others seeking to impose anything on them. In a world of perfect harmony, there would be no need for alliances. Peaceful cohabitation does not require the full integration of all groups, much less their assimilation to a majority way of life. It is enough that everyone be incorporated into society, of which they feel a part and share in its rights and duties, with tolerance for difference balanced by respect for communal laws. Resources would be shared fairly within and between states, nullifying the sense of instability that leads to violence. Reality, alas, is rather different.

From everything I've said in this book, it ought to be clear that what's 'good' and what's 'bad' is highly subjective, dependent on what side of the argument you're on. All nations pursue their objectives by whatever means they have available. Everyone is out for themselves, pursuing their own interests, with differing degrees of transparency and legitimacy. Intelligence services and armies have basically the same role everywhere: to defend their country's interests.

A significant cause for alarm is that we appear to be edging ever closer to the society George Orwell described in *Nineteen Eighty-Four*, in which information manipulation is standard, people are subjected to constant vigilance and individual freedoms disappear. It's an environment in which people are free to think but afraid to do so. If we continue down this path, we will end up with the perfect dictator, who appears to be democratic but isn't. In *Brave New World*, Aldous Huxley describes a wall-less prison that inmates are evidently content to be confined in due to consumerism and entertainment.

In writing this book I want to make people more aware of how much they are manipulated; to encourage them to come together and make collective decisions that might change society for the better. My ultimate aim is to create a world that strives for and prioritises human security over national security in its geopolitical decision-making. I know this is a utopian vision, but it is one to which it is surely worth aspiring. We'll have to work together to achieve it. I merely hope to have made a modest contribution by awakening a few sensibilities.

Notes

1   The limited definition of the 'Western world' encompasses Europe, the United States of America, Canada, Australia and New Zealand. A broader version includes developed countries in Latin America, along with Israel and South Africa.

Part Two

1   Many years later, Muammar Gaddafi, Saddam Hussein, Hugo Chávez and other leaders who attempted to change prevailing economic models and circumvent the supremacy of the dollar would pay a heavy price for their daring.
2   This is precisely what is happening now. Iranian expansion has reached Syrian, Iraqi, Lebanese and Yemeni territories and plans to reach Afghanistan. For this reason, the Trump administration is seeking to reset the balance by confronting Iran.
3   Hoff, Brad, 'New Hillary emails reveal propaganda, executions, coveting Libyan oil and gold', *Levant Report* (4 January 2016). Available at https://levantreport.com/2016/01/04/new-hillary-emails-reveal-propaganda-executions-coveting-libyan-oil-and-gold.
4   For more information, *see* http://www.publico.es/internacional/francia-asegura-35-del-petroleo.html and http://www.liberation.fr/planete/2011/09/01/petrole-l-accord-secret-entre-le-cnt-et-la-france_758320.
5   The CFA franc (African Financial Community franc) is the common currency in fourteen African countries, almost all of them former French colonies.

6   http://umoya.org/2017/02/02/escandalo-segun-un-periodico-aleman-africa-desembolsa-400–000-millones-de-euros-cada-ano-a-francia.

7   As many people have cynically noted, international loans are not supposed to be paid back, quite the opposite: they are a means of ensuring the dependency and submission of the debtor country.

8   Available at http://circulaire.legifrance.gouv.fr/pdf/2011/09/cir_33781.pdf.

9   The Paris School of Economic Warfare, set up in 1997, is a world reference in economic intelligence.

10   The Armenian genocide can be considered the first of the twentieth century. From 1915 to 1923, between a million and a half and two million Armenian civilians were deported or exterminated by the Young Turks government of the Ottoman Empire. In 1975, sixty years after the massacre, two groups emerged in Armenia with a thirst for revenge: the Armenian Secret Army for the Liberation of Armenia and the Justice Commandos of the Armenian Genocide. Although they held rival ideologies, both organisations agreed that Turkey had to assume responsibility for the genocide and economically compensate survivors and their descendants. Between 1975 and 1985, the two groups took the lives of over forty Turkish diplomats and their family members.

11   Ironically, the following phrase is attributed to Adolf Hitler: 'Perhaps the biggest and greatest lesson from history is that nobody learns the lessons of history.'

12   Relations with Saddam Hussein were so positive at this time that in 1980 the Iraqi leader received the keys to the city of Detroit in recognition of the donations he had made to local churches there.

13   The failed European Defence Community (EDC) is an example of France's ambiguous contribution to the construction of the European Union. The EDC was proposed in 1950 by the French Prime Minister, René Pleven, to furnish the newly emerging Europe with a unified armed forces. This would ensure that, except in exceptional circumstances, individual states would not have the military capacity to start wars with other European countries. The initiative was supported by the United States, which saw it as a way of bolstering NATO against the threat of the Soviet Union. The EDC treaty was signed on 27 May 1952 by Belgium, France, Italy, Luxembourg, the Netherlands and West Germany. However, the French National Assembly unexpectedly voted down its ratification in August 1954,

aborting a genuinely European defence force at birth. At the time, rejection of the treaty was blamed on Gaullist concerns about loss of sovereignty.

This would not be the last time France paralysed the European project. On 29 October 2004, the heads of state and government of the twenty-five countries that then comprised the European Union signed the Treaty of Rome that would establish a constitution for Europe, also known as the European Constitution. Before ratifying the treaty, some European parliaments chose to subject the treaty to a referendum. France again featured among the countries that opposed it, with 54.87 per cent voting against.

14 Something similar might have happened many decades later if the European Union and Russia had aligned. Such an occurrence would have notably disadvantaged the United States, which would perhaps have felt obliged to take measures to prevent it or, if need be, destroy it.

PART THREE

1 A French expression applied to restrictions on the movement of people to prevent the spread of contagious diseases. It is used metaphorically to refer to measures aimed at preventing the spread of supposedly dangerous ideologies.

2 It is calculated that a further 6,000 warheads have been withdrawn ready to be dismantled, an especially laborious and costly process. Of those that remain operative, some 4,000 warheads are ready to be used and 1,800 are kept in a state of high alert ready for rapid deployment. Many weapons have been dismantled not for humanitarian reasons, but economic ones: keeping them in an operative state is very expensive. In any case, it is impossible to know exactly how many nuclear weapons are truly operative for this remains the sort of closely guarded state secret that no country wishes to reveal.

3 Some experts put this figure as high as sixty, but without providing conclusive proof.

4 The figures offered by different experts and specialist centres vary between fifty and 300 kilotonnes, but they are based exclusively on vibrations in the ground caused by the explosion. The consensus is that it was below 100 kilotonnes and very probably around the sixty kilotonne mark as cited. Nor is there any certainty that a thermonuclear bomb (hydrogen) was deployed, though this is what Pyongyang officially announced it to be.

5   At the height of the city's wealth, most Athenians earned a public salary for making various contributions to the community.

6   The Muslim Brotherhood originated in Egypt, where it was formed by Hassan al-Banna in 1928. It still has a strong presence in Egypt despite being expelled from power there (a power legitimately achieved through the ballot box) by a *coup d'état* in July 2013. It is also increasingly influential in Turkey.

7   As can be gathered by the graphic, based on the 'Military Balance 2017' report published by the International Institute for Strategic Studies (IISS), the USA assigned 604,452 million dollars to military spending in 2016, while China spent only 145,039 million dollars. While the difference in absolute terms is huge, China hasn't provided the UN with official data since 2014, so the figures are estimates based on Chinese government claims.

8   The SCO is an intergovernmental entity dedicated to cooperation in matters of security, economics and culture, formed by China, Russia, Kazakhstan, Kyrgyzstan, Tajikistan, Uzbekistan, India and Pakistan.

9   The Chinese President's comparison of his country to a big cat awakening could be an allusion to a quote attributed to Napoleon Bonaparte: 'China is a sleeping lion. Let her sleep. For when she wakes, she will shake the world.'

10   The Sykes–Picot accord, signed on 16 May 1916, was a secret pact between the United Kingdom and France, with Russia's consent, intended to define their respective spheres of influence and control in the Middle East, in anticipation of the defeat of the Ottoman Empire. Paris would control Lebanon, Syria and northern Iraq, while London would rule over Transjordania and southern Iraq. Palestine would remain under international rule and not be included among the Arab regions afforded independence. Russia, to which Palestine was originally to have been allocated, exited the accord following the 1917 revolution. This accord was ratified after the war by the League of Nations.

11   Hoff, 'New Hillary emails', *Levant Report*.

12   Ritzer, George, *The McDonaldization of Society* (Pine Forge Press, Thousand Oaks, 1993), available (in Spanish) at https://socialesenpdf.files. wordpress.com/2013/08/ritzer-george-la-mcdonalizacion-de-la-sociedad.pdf.

13   Entitled: 'Documents expose how Hollywood promotes war on behalf of the Pentagon, CIA and NSA'. Available at https://medium. com/insurge-intelligence/exclusive-documents-expose-direct-us-

military-intelligence-influence-on-1–800-movies-and-tv-shows-36433107c307.

14 *See* https://www.janes.com, with 2016 figures published and available at https://news.ihsmarkit.com/press-release/aerospace-defense-security/global-defence-exports-expected-decline-first-time-ever-jan.

15 Fleurart, A., Wezeman, P., Wezeman, S., Kuimova. A. and Tian, N., 'Trends in international arms transfers 2017' (March 2018). Available at https://www.sipri.org.

16 The DCLinks website has since been taken down.

17 Obama, meanwhile, declared his support for Macron. The European media passed on news of an encouraging phone call made by the former US President to the French candidate.

18 Carlson, John and Yeomans, Neville, 'Whither goeth law – humanity or barbarity?', in Smith, Margaret and Crossley, David John (eds), *The Way Out: Radical Alternatives in Australia* (Lansdowne Press, Melbourne, 1975); Dunlap, Charles J., Jr, 'Law and military interventions: preserving humanitarian values in 21st century conflicts', Carr Center, Harvard University, Washington (2001).

19 'Vida y muerte de las "intervenciones humanitarias" de Occidente en el resto del mundo', *El Diario* (10 June 2017). Available at https://www.eldiario.es/theguardian/Vida-muerte-intervenciones-humanitarias-Occidente_0_651285631.html.

20 *See* http://www.globalr2p.org.

21 On 22 February 2017, a South African court declared the decision to leave the ICC unconstitutional because the government had not consulted parliament. On 8 March, South Africa withdrew its request to leave.

22 In June 2017, a research team from the Organization for the Prohibition of Chemical Weapons released a report confirming the use of sarin gas against civilians on 4 April 2017 in the area of Khan Shaykhun, in the province of Idlib, Syria. The report did not specify who used it.

23 The full Resolution 2249 can be found here: https://www.security-councilreport.org/atf/cf/%7B65BFCF9B-6D27-4E9C-8CD3-CF6E-4FF96FF9%7D/s_res_2249.pdf.

24 The Special Air Service (SAS) as well as the Special Boat Service (SBS), the Special Reconnaissance Regiment (SRR) and the Special Forces Support Group (SFSG) form Britain's special operations forces, famous for their battlefield interventions and also for having been deployed in numerous covert operations, including counterterrorism.

25 Hedges, Chris, 'The real enemy is within', *Truthdig* (September 2015). Available at https://www.truthdig.com/report/item/the_real_enemy_is_within_20150906.

26 Marozzi, Justin, 'Gaddafi has chemical weapons and he's ready to use them', *Daily Mail* (2 March 2011). Available at http://www. dailymail. co.uk/news/article-1362022/Libya-Muammar-Gaddafi-chemical-weapons-hes-ready-use-them.html.

27 Hoff, 'New Hillary emails', *Levant Report*.

28 Habitually attributed to Goebbels, these are paraphrases rather than quotes.

29 The origin of the word, in the pejorative sense of spreading and fostering particular ideas, comes from the Sacra Congregatio de Propaganda Fide ('Sacred Congregation for the Propagation of the Faith'), an office set up by the Vatican in 1622 with the purpose of spreading Catholicism during the Counter-Reformation, in answer to the Protestant reforms of Martin Luther.

30 Chomsky, Noam, *Media Control*, Seven Stories Press, New York, 2002. Extract available at https://chomsky.info/mediacontrol01/.

31 Full letter available at https://founders.archives.gov/documents/Jefferson/99–01-02–5737.

32 Timsit, Sylvain, 'Stratégies de manipulation' (undated), http://www. syti.net/Manipulations.html.

33 *See* Parry, Robert, 'How the US flooded the World with Psyops', *Consortium News* (25 March 2017). Available at https://consortiumnews. com/2017/03/25/how-us-flooded-the-world-with-psyops.

34 Chen, Adrian, 'The Agency', *New York Times Magazine*, 2 June 2015. Available at https://www.nytimes.com/2015/06/07/magazine/the-agency.html?_r=0.

35 Livingston, Steven and Eachus, Todd, 'Humanitarian crises and US foreign policy: Somalia and the CNN effect reconsidered', *Political Communication* 12: 4 (1995). Available at http://www.tandfonline.com/doi/abs/10.1080/10584609.1995.9963087.

36 Gilbert, an intelligence officer and captain in the US Army, spoke German and was the prison psychologist where Göring, founder of the Gestapo and Chief Commander of the Luftwaffe, was held. The conversation took place on 18 April 1946 in Göring's cell, with no witnesses, rather than during the trial itself. Gilbert jotted down the conversation in his diary, where he recorded observations of the trials and conversations with the prisoners that he later presented in *Nuremberg Diary* (1947), published in New York.

37 This argument became a recurring strategy of US foreign policy, applied in a multitude of scenarios whenever the national interests of the US were at stake. It is linked to the geostrategy of lawfare.

38 These include Carl Bernstein, Darrell Garwood, David Pope, Deborah Davis, Fred J. Cook, James DiEugenio, John D. Marks, Lisa Pease, Richard Helms, Servando Gonzalez, Russ Baker and Victor Marchetti.

39 For more information see, for example, https://www.cia.gov/library/readingroom/collection/family-jewels.

40 *See* Carl Bernstein, 'The CIA and the media', *Rolling Stone* (20 October 1977). Available at http://www.rollingstone.com/music/pictures/rolling-stones-biggest-scoops-exposes-and-controversies-2-aa-624/journalists-exposed-as-secret-cia-operatives-81185346 and http://www.informationclearinghouse.info/article28610.htm.

41 Dittus, Rubén, 'La opinión pública y los imaginarios sociales: hacia una redefinición de la espiral del silencio' [Public opinion and social imagination: towards a redefinition of the spiral of silence], *Athenea Digital* 7 (2005): 61–76. Available at http://www.raco.cat/index.php/Athenea/article/viewFile/34168/34007.

42 Lévy, Jacques, 'Geopolitics after geopolitics: a French experience', *Geopolitics* 5:3 (2007): 99–113. Available at http://www.tandfonline.com/doi/abs/10.1080/14650040008407693.

43 Begun on 5 December 2013 and finished on 31 October 2016, with the objective of preventing killings between Muslim and Christian militias in the country.

44 *See* https://thesentry.org and specifically the report https://cdn.thesentry.org/wp-content/uploads/2017/05/MakingAFortune_May2017_Sentry_Final.pdf.

45 Remarks to the National Foreign Policy Conference for Leaders of Non-Governmental Organizations, Loy Henderson Conference Room, US Department of State, Washington, DC, 26 October 2001. Available at https://2001–2009.state.gov/secretary/former/powell/remarks/2001/5762.htm.

46 Declassified 27 May 2008, with the code CIA-RDP88B00443R001404090133-0. Available at https://es.scribd.com/document/344768700/CIA-Syria-Pipelines#from_embed.

47 This 800km-long pipeline was built by the Soviets in April 1952. It begins in the Kirkuk oil fields in Iraq and emerges at Baniyas, on the Syrian coast. It was one of the first targets of US bombing in the 2003 invasion of Iraq, to deprive Saddam of an important source of revenue.

48 Partially declassified and edited, this was revealed 8 December 2011, with the code CIA-RDP86T01017R000100770001-5. Available at https://www.cia.gov/library/readingroom/docs/CIA-RDP86T0 1017R000100770001-5.pdf.

49 This was available at https://www.wikileaks.org/plus/cables/06DAM ASCVS5399_a.html but has since been removed.

50 In his book *A Desordem Mundial* ('Global Disorder'), published in 2016, as well as in interviews given to several different media, such as those available at http://www.amersur.org/politica-internacional/ moniz-bandeira-estados-unidos and http://old.operamundi.com. br/dialogosdosul/moniz-bandeira-o-estado-brasileiro-parece-desintegrar-se/12112016.

51 Entitled 'Disinformation: A Primer in Russian Active Measures and Influence Campaigns', it can be consulted at https://www.intelli-gence.senate.gov/sites/default/files/documents/os-trid-033017. pdf. Another report was presented on the same date and before the same committee: 'Russian Active Measures and Influence Campaigns' by Eugene B. Rumer, Director of the Russia and Eurasia Program of the Carnegie Endowment for International Peace. Rumer reached similar conclusions to Rid. Rumer's report is available at http:// carnegieendowment.org/2017/03/30/russian-active-measu-res-and-influence-campaigns-pub-68438.

52 Initially denominated the Middle East Treaty Organization (METO).

53 According to some historians, in the 1960s and 1970s, the USA, UK and France also supported and financed the Muslim Brotherhood in order to have it confront left-wing Arab parties backed by the Soviet Union, and urged it to make an attempt on the life of the President of Egypt, Gamal Abdel Nasser.

54 Called Agro Pontino in Italian, the marshes are located in the Lazio region, to the south-east of Rome. The Roman Via Appia crosses this area of ancient marshland.

55 For more information *see* http://www.amersur.org/politica-inter nacional/moniz-bandeira-estados-unidos and http://old.operamundi. com.br/dialogosdosul/moniz-bandeira-o-estado-brasileiro-parece-desintegrar-se/12112016.

56 For more information *see* https://www.thebureauinvestigates. com/stories/2015–04-01/monthly-drone-report-march-015-us-drone-strikes-drop-50-as-chaos-envelops-yemen and http://www. theatlantic.com/international/archive/2014/12/the-us-stopped-torturing-terror-suspectsand-started-droning-them/383590.

57   Neither the US (which has facilities on the Korean peninsula and on boats nearby), South Korea or Japan have ever felt the need to employ their antimissile capacities – Terminal High Altitude Area Defense (THAAD), Aegis system and Patriot missiles – against North Korea's missile tests. This is probably a strategic decision to conceal from North Korea, but also from China and Russia, the capacity of the systems to destroy ballistic missiles in flight. The systems will likely remain unused unless there is a genuine threat of one of North Korea's missiles making a direct hit on any of the territories. Beijing and Moscow would undoubtedly like to know how Washington would react to a nuclear attack; how it would use its weapons in a preventive way and how it would carry out conventional and cybernetic actions against an adversary with a nuclear capacity in order to neutralise those weapons and prevent them from being used; and how the US people and the rest of the world would react to a new use of a nuclear weapon. Launching missiles and nuclear tests gives Pyongyang a trump card with which to negotiate and request economic aid, as it has done in the past.

58   Hedges, 'The real enemy is within', *Truthdig*.

59   The full version is available at https://archive.org/stream/WarIsARacket/WarIsARacket_djvu.txt and https://www.ratical.org/ratville/CAH/warisaracket.html.

Bibliography

Andelman, David A. and Marenches, Alexandre de, *The Fourth World War* (Morrow, New York, 1992)

Bernays, Edward Louis, *Propaganda* (Horace Liveright, New York, 1928)

Bernier, François, *Viaje al Gran Mogol, Indostán y Cachemira* (Espasa-Calpe, Madrid, 1999)

Bin, Sun, *The Art of War* (EDAF, Madrid, 2007)

Bouthoul, Gaston, *Tratado de polemología* (Ediciones Ejército, Madrid, 1984)

Brzezinski, Zbigniew, *The Grand Chessboard* (Basic Books, New York, 1997)

Bullitt, William C., *The Great Globe Itself* (Charles Scribner's Sons, New York, 1946)

Bülow, Bernard von, *Memoirs of Prince von Bülow* (Espasa-Calpe, Madrid, 1931)

Butler, Smedley Darlington, *War Is a Racket* (Feral House, Los Angeles, 2003)

Capaz Montes, Fernando Oswaldo, *Modalidades de la guerra de montaña en Marruecos. Asuntos indígenas* (Alta Comisaría de la República Española en Marruecos. Inspección de Intervención y Fuerzas Jalifianas, Ceuta, 1931)

Célérier, Pierre, *Geopolítica e Geostratégia* (Pleamar, Buenos Aires, 1979)

Chang, Ha-Joon, *Kicking Away the Ladder: Development Strategy in Historical Perspective* (Anthem, London, 2002)

Chevallier, Gabriel, *Fear* (Serpent's Tail, London, 2011)

Chomsky, Noam, *Media Control* (Seven Stories Press, New York, 2002)

Chomsky, Noam and Herman, Edward S., *Manufacturing Consent* (Pantheon Books, New York, 1988)

Clarke, Richard A., *Against All Enemies* (Free Press, New York, 2004)

Clausewitz, Carl von, *De la Guerra* (La Esfera de los Libros, Madrid, 2005)

Coffey, Michael, *Days Of Infamy* (Hyperion, Boston, 1999)

Bibliography

Daoren, Huanchu, *Back to Beginnings: Reflections on the Tao* (Shambhala, Boulder, 1990)

Einstein, Albert and Freud, Sigmund, 'Why War?', *The Complete Psychological Works of Sigmund Freud*, Volume XXII (Vintage, London, 2001)

Eltchaninoff, Michel, *Inside the Mind of Vladimir Putin* (C. Hurst & Co., London, 2018)

Entraygues, Olivier, *La pensée politique de J.F.C. Fuller* (Le Polémarque, Nancy, 2015)

Esparza, José Javier, *Historia de la yihad* (La Esfera de los Libros, Madrid, 2015)

Fraga Iribarne, Manuel, *Guerra y conflicto social* (Instituto de Estudios Políticos, Madrid, 1962)

Frattini, Eric, *Manipulando la historia* (Temas de Hoy, Barcelona, 2017)

Friedman, George, *The Next Decade* (Doubleday, New York, 2010)

Fukuyama, Francis, *The End of History & The Last Man* (Free Press, New York, 1992)

Fuller, J.F.C., *The Conduct of War* (Rutgers University Press, New Brunswick, 1961)

Gallois, Pierre M., *Geopolítica. Los caminos del poder* (Ediciones Ejército, Madrid, 1992)

Görlitz, Walter, *La compra del poder* (Dopesa, Barcelona, 1976)

Greene, Robert, *The 48 Laws of Power* (Viking, New York, 1998)

— *The 33 Strategies of War* (Viking, New York, 2006)

Guangqian, Peng and Youzhi, Yao (eds), *The Science of Military Strategy* (Military Science Publishing House, Academy of Military Science of the Chinese People's Liberation Army, Beijing, 2005)

Haldeman, H.R. and Dimona, Joseph, *The Ends of Power* (W.H. Allen & Co. Ltd, London, 1978)

Hanson, Victor Davis, *The Father of Us All* (Bloomsbury, New York, 2010)

Hastings, Max, *The Secret War* (William Collins, London, 2015)

Herranz, Pedro, *Status Belli* (Las Antorchas, Madrid, 1953)

Heuser, Beatrice, *The Evolution of Strategy* (Cambridge University Press, Cambridge, 2010)

Howard, Michael, *The Causes of Wars* (Temple Smith, London, 1982)

Huntington, Samuel P., *The Clash of Civilizations* (Simon & Schuster, New York, 1997)

Kaplan, Robert D., *The Revenge of Geography* (Random House, New York, 2012)

— *Warrior Politics* (Random House, New York, 2002)

Kennedy, Paul, *The Rise and Fall of the Great Powers* (Random House, New York, 1987)

Kissinger, Henry, *Diplomacy* (Simon & Schuster, New York, 1994)

— *On China* (Penguin, New York, 2011)

— *World Order* (Penguin, New York, 2014)

Labévière, Richard and Thual, François, *La bataille du grand Nord a commencé* (Perrin, Paris, 2008)

Lang, Anthony F., *Agency and Ethics* (State University of New York Press, Albany, 2002)

Launay, Jacques de, *La diplomacia secreta durante las dos guerras mundiales* (Belacqva, Barcelona, 2005)

Lawrence, T.E., *Guerrilla* (Acuarela & A. Machado, Madrid, 2008; originally appeared as 'Guerrilla Warfare' in *Encyclopedia Britannica*, fourteenth edition, 1926)

— *Revolt in the Desert* (Jonathan Cape, London, 1927)

— *Seven Pillars of Wisdom* (Wordsworth Editions, Ware, 1997)

Lenin, V.I., *La guerra de guerrillas* (Editorial Progreso, Moscow, 1973)

Liang, Qiao and Xiangsui, Wang, *La guerre hors limites* (Rivages, Paris, 1999)

Liddell Hart, B.H., *The Other Side of the Hill* (Cassell, London, 1948)

— *Strategy* (Faber and Faber, London, 1954)

Lorot, Pascal and Thual, François, *La géopolitique* (2nd edn, Montchrestien, Paris, 2002)

Maalouf, Amin, *Disordered World* (Bloomsbury, New York, 2011)

— *In the Name of Identity* (Arcade Publishing, New York, 2000)

Macías Fernández, Daniel, *El islam y los islamismos* (Fundación Investigación en Seguridad y Policía, Madrid, 2015)

Marenches, Alexandre de and Ockrent, Christine, *Dans le secret des princes* (Stock, Paris, 1986)

Milne, Seumas, *The Revenge of History* (Verso, London, 2012)

Moniz Bandeira, Luiz Alberto, *A desordem mundial* (Civilização Brasileira, Grupo Record, Rio de Janeiro, 2016)

Noelle-Neumann, Elisabeth, *The Spiral of Silence* (University of Chicago Press, Chicago, 1984)

Nye, Joseph S., Jr, *Soft Power* (PublicAffairs, New York, 2004)

Olier, Eduardo, *Los ejes del poder económico* (Pearson, Madrid, 2016)

Renouvin, Pierre, *Historia de las relaciones internacionales* (Ediciones Akal, Madrid, 1990)

Ritzer, George, *The McDonaldization of Society* (Pine Forge Press, Thousand Oaks, 1993)

Rogan, Eugene, *The Fall of the Ottomans* (Penguin, London, 2015)

Sánchez Ferlosio, Rafael, *Sobre la guerra* (Ediciones Destino, Barcelona, 2008)

Bibliography

Servent, Pierre, *Les guerres modernes* (Buchet Chastel, Paris, 2009)

Shaw, Martin, 'Risk-transfer militarism, small massacres and the historic legitimacy of war', *International Relations* 16: 3 (2002): 343–59

Sorel, George, *Reflexiones sobre la violencia* (Alianza, Madrid, 1976)

Stoessinger, John G., *Why Nations Go to War* (St Martin's Press, New York, 1982)

Thual, François, *Contrôler et contrer* (Ellipses, Paris, 2000)

— *Géopolitique des Caucases* (Ellipses, Paris, 2004)

— *La planète émiettée* (Arléa, Paris, 2002)

Tuchman, Barbara W., *The March of Folly* (Knopf, New York, 1984)

Tzu, Sun, *El arte de la guerra* (Altorrey, Buenos Aires, 1996)

Ulfkotte, Udo, *Gekaufte Journalisten* (Kopp, Rottenburg, 2014)

Verstrynge, Jorge, *Frente al imperio* (Foca, Madrid, 2007)

Vicens Vives, J., *Geopolítica* (Universidad de Barcelona, Barcelona, 1950)

Weinberger, Eliot, *What I Heard about Iraq* (Verso, London, 2005)

Zakaria, Fareed, *The Post-American World* (Norton, New York 2008)

Zedong (Tse-tung), Mao, *La guerra de guerrillas* (Editorial Huemul, Buenos Aires, 1963)

Zimbardo, Philip, *The Lucifer Effect* (Random House, New York, 2007)

Acknowledgements

My first words of thanks must go to Francisco Martínez Soria at Editorial Ariel for having proposed that I write the book in the first place and for showing the confidence that I could pull it off. Without his advice and constant support, I certainly wouldn't have been able to.

The same goes for my family. My children provided constant encouragement, sometimes stubbornly so. At several points, when I became overwhelmed with other commitments, they talked me out of throwing in the towel. Furthermore, my daughter Irene, born journalist that she is, proved relentless in revising my writing, while my wife put up with many moments of stress with typical stoicism. Without all their support, I would never have finished the book.

I am likewise very fortunate to have been able to count on the support of many good friends, some of them former students who immediately offered to help when I told them about the project. They did so by suggesting ideas, correcting drafts or acting as researchers and consulting documents.

The project was also embraced enthusiastically by Ángel Gómez de Ágreda, Air Force colonel, General Staff graduate and one of the most capable and best prepared military men I know, and by Delfín Mariño Espiñeira, Lieutenant Colonel at the Engineers Corp Polytechnic, former technical advisor to the Ministry of the Presidency, and blessed with the sort of clear-sightedness that spots an error a mile off. Luis Antonio González Francisco, member of the Military Police and a brilliant researcher and analyst, never stopped advising and orientating me. Daniel Martín Menjón, military history and strategy enthusiast, provided invaluable help

Acknowledgements

by forever steering me in the right direction. Mario Sánchez Grasa, activist for social causes, provided a moral compass. Clara Palacios Fernández showed a remarkable readiness, initiative and capacity for getting stuck in. Nuria Hernández García was an outstanding collaborator and key to the book's development.

And last but not least, my most effusive thanks go to you, dear reader, for taking the trouble to pick up this book. I only hope it has proved to be a useful and enjoyable read.